Wednesbury, Ancient And Modern: Being Mainly Its Manorial And Municipal History

Frederick William Hackwood

WEDNESBURY
ANCIENT AND MODERN:

BEING MAINLY ITS

MANORIAL AND MUNICIPAL HISTORY.

BY

FREDk. WM. HACKWOOD, F.R.S.L.,

Author of

" The Story of the Black Country," " Christ Lore,"

&c., &c.

———

LIMITED ISSUE.

Reprinted from " The Wednesbury Herald " of June 29th, 1901—July 5th, 1902.

———

1902

WEDNESBURY: RYDER AND SON, SPRING HEAD.

CONTENTS.

LIST OF ILLUSTRATIONS.

WEDNESBURY:

ANCIENT AND MODERN.

BY FREDK. WM. HACKWOOD, F.R.S.L.,

Author of "Religious Wednesbury" and other Topographical Works on Wednesbury, Darlaston,
West Bromwich, Tipton, Smethwick, Sedgley, and the Black Country
of South Staffordshire generally.

1.—A GENERAL DESCRIPTION: LOCATION AND COMMUNICATIONS.

Wednesbury, geographically, is situated in the basin of the Upper Tame, which occupies that portion of South Staffordshire in the dip between the Sedgley ridge on the west, and the heights of Barr on the east. The former hills constitute a watershed, which parts this basin from that of the Stour and other streams finding their way to the Bristol Channel on the south-west; while all the waters flowing through Wednesbury find their way to the German Ocean on the north-east. The Tame rises in two main heads. one north and one south, which come together at Wednesbury, and then flow eastward in one main stream. The first head rises near Bloxwich, and comes southward through Bentley and James Bridge; the second takes its rise at Warley, and flows northwards through Oldbury and Great Bridge.

After the union of these two head-waters at Wednesbury, the Tame flows eastward to Aston, which, as its name signifies, was the "East-town" in its relative position to ancient Wednesbury. Here the Tame is joined by the Rea from Birmingham, and then sweeps northwards to join the Trent at Tamworth.

Wednesbury is not only at the confluence of these two sources, but is in the very centre of the upper Tame Valley. As a natural boundary, the northern affluent parts Wednesbury from Walsall between James Bridge and Bescot. Another feeder stream running in the very opposite direction to Bescot, divides the Delves portion of the parish from Walsall. The southern affluent parts Wednesbury from West Bromwich between Lea Brook and Bescot, and on again along the southern side of the Delves; but the latter portion of the parish has no natural dividing line between its eastern side and the two parishes of Walsall and Great Barr. The Lea Brook is a tiny watercourse rising in Willingsworth, and forming a natural boundary between Wednesbury and Tipton.

On its western side where it touches Darlaston and Bilston, Wednesbury has no natural boundary line.

Wednesbury, vulgo Wedgbury—a statutory grant of the year 1699 is careful to describe it as "Wednesbury als Wedgbury —is an ancient market town situated in the southern division of the Hundred of Offlow, in South Staffordshire.

It is nearly in the centre of England, and 118 miles from London. It is also mid-way between four important towns; Birmingham lying eight miles towards the south, Wolverhampton five miles towards the north, Walsall three miles towards the east, and Dudley four miles towards the west. (These points of the compass are by no means exact; they are only given to indicate a general sense of direction. And be it also observed, Walsall is the only one of the four whose boundaries actually touch those of Wednesbury).

Since 1867 Wednesbury has been a Parliamentary Borough; it originally included the parishes of Wednesbury, West Bromwich, Tipton, and Darlaston. In 1885 West Bromwich became an independent Parliamentary borough, so that Wednesbury constituency now includes only the three parishes. At the same redistribution of seats (1885) Wednesbury, which had been in the Eastern Parliamentary Division of Staffordshire as regards its "forty-shilling freeholders"—previous to being given the borough franchise in 1867, it had been an integral part of the South Staffordshire Parliamentary Division—was placed in what is known as the Handsworth Division, one of the most populous one-member constituencies in the United Kingdom.

Wednesbury became a Municipal Borough in 1886. In 1890, Wednesbury, having a population of only 26,000, was not large enough to become a county borough, as its neighbours on all four sides of it did ; namely, West Bromwich, Dudley, Wolverhampton, and Walsall. While these boroughs became independent of the Staffordshire County Council, and obtained full and direct control of those financial " aids " which are made from the National Exchequer towards certain expenses of local government, the status of Wednesbury was not advanced ; it remained a non-county borough, and elected two representatives to the County Council of Stafford, the four wards of the municipal borough constituting two county divisions, one called the Central Division (Market and Town Hall Wards) and the other the Suburban Division (Kings Hill and Wood Green Wards). The standard of population set up for a county borough was 50,000 ; and it was suggested that Wednesbury might be united to Tipton and Darlaston to form one " Black Country County Borough," but the suggestion was allowed to fall through, local jealousies being too pronounced to permit even the acceptance of public financial advantages.

Ecclesiastically, Wednesbury has since 1894 constituted a Rural Deanery, embracing the same three parishes which make up the Parliamentary borough ; namely, Wednesbury, Tipton, and Darlaston. It is in the Archdeaconry of Stafford, and in the diocese of Lichfield, Province of Canterbury.

Strangely enough, the afore-mentioned three parishes are all in different Poor Law Unions ; Wednesbury being included in West Bromwich Union, Tipton in Dudley Union, and Darlaston in Walsall Union.

Wednesbury is in the very heart and centre of the Black Country. Its postal area overruns the parochial boundaries, and extends into several of the adjacent parishes ; its head Post Office, by virtue of its central urban position, offering facilities for a quick delivery of all postal communications.

Its railway communications are also very good. There is a passenger station at Wednesbury on that branch of the Great Western Railway which runs (since 1854) between London and Birkenhead ; a small wayside station also serves the outlying district of Moxley. The London and North-Western system has another passenger station at Wednesbury, on that section which runs between Dudley and Walsall, and originally known as the South Staffordshire Railway (1846). The famous old Grand Junction Line of the same system touches the fringe of the parish, and in the early days of railways (1837) gave direct communication with London from Wood Green Station. Bescot Station was opened half-a-mile south-east at the junction of a short branch into Walsall. The Darlaston branch of this system, cut from Wednesbury Station in 1863, has been closed to passenger traffic since 1887, when it failed to compete successfully with the tramways. Another branch runs out of Wednesbury Station, between the Darlaston and Dudley lines, through Ocker Hill and Princes End, to join the Stour Valley line at Tipton. Between the Great Western and the

London and North-Western systems, an extensive transfer of goods and mineral traffic is effected at Wednesbury, on the Lea Brook Sidings. The Midland Railway Company possess running powers into Wednesbury, for goods and minerals only, over the London and North-Western line. There is a total length of 4½ miles of railway lines, within the parish boundaries.

This town is the centre of the South Staffordshire Tramway System, and contains its offices and engine sheds. The lines radiate to all four points of the compass ; northwards to Darlaston, and southwards to Handsworth ; eastwards to Walsall, and westwards to Dudley. When first opened in 1880 all the lines were worked by steam traction. In 1892 the Walsall line was newly equipped with the overhead electric traction. Owing to the excessive cost of its promotion the Company was too much over-capitalised at the outset to make it a paying concern. Yet it is well patronised, particularly on the lines with most frequent service of cars. The Walsall service, from White Horse Inn, Bridge Street, runs every twenty minutes, the first penny stage being Wood Green Church. From the same point there is a half-hourly service to Darlaston for one penny, and, also, in the opposite direction, the first penny stage out of Wednesbury being Hawkes Lane, Hill Top. From the Dartmouth Arms Hotel, Holyhead Road, or the Great Western Railway Station, the Dudley service is every forty minutes, and the first penny stage is Ocker Hill. At the start the Darlaston section continued to Moxley, where it met the horse trams from Wolverhampton ; but this section was speedily abandoned as too unprofitable. From Darlaston there is a line through James Bridge to Walsall, also electrically equipped. The tramways within the parish measure 4 miles, 4 furlongs, 149 yards in length.

Although the local canals were made in the first instance for the express purpose of connecting the busy factory hearths of Birmingham with the prolific collieries at Wednesbury (1768), it is strange that there is such a small length of canal (1728 yards) within the parish boundaries, and that mainly on the outskirts, along the Moxley border. The reason for this is that the ancient " coal works " of the town lay in Wednesbury Old Fields—that part of the parish cut off between the Great Western Railway and Lea Brook—and the Bradley side of Moxley. There is a short length of the Tame Valley Canal at the Delves ; but in the centre of the town, where so many of the ironworks are located, there is no canal communication. This has been found such a deprivation to the manufacturing interests that a proposal was once made to canalise the Tame, and so provide wharfage accommodation along its banks for Mesty Croft and Wood Green. The levels, however, would not permit of an easy junction with the existing artificial waterways.

The area of Wednesbury is comparatively small, extending to little more than a total of

2,000 acres. In shape it is not unlike a figure 8, with the narrow connecting neck at Bescot. The urban portion is the larger, embracing 1,530 acres; the rural portion, known as the Delves, contains 600 acres. The two portions were anciently connected by a road; the outlying portion is now cut off from the town, and the Delves can only be reached from Wednesbury by a series of awkward railway crossing steps. Within living memory the two portions of the parish were connected by a farmers' accommo-dation road; the making of the Grand Junction Railway reduced this to a field path and level crossings. The consequence will be, that whenever the Delves developes into a residen-tial district, it will be as a suburb of Walsall, rather than a part of Wednesbury.

The boundaries of the parish of Wednesbury are all co-terminous with those of the muni-cipal borough, and of the School Board district of Wednesbury.

II.—PRIMEVAL WEDNESBURY.

FOREST AND FEN.

The prehistoric Stone Age had three epochs. The first was the Glacial period, in which this country, and Europe generally, were covered with ice, which descended from the North Pole and mountain heights into the plains, leaving only the plateaux as a refuge for man and beast. When at last the ice-fields shrank back to their original limits many species of animals had become extinct through the severity of the cold.

Now, what relics of the Ice Age are there to be found in and around Wednesbury? It has been asserted that there were formerly to be found within the parish boundaries several boulder stones, fragments of rock unlike any-thing in the immediate vicinity, carried by the action of glacial ice, and dropped into their respective positions as the ice melted and re-laxed its grip. There was one, many years ago, on the footpath at the bottom of Earps Lane, where it was used as a horse-block by the women who rode pillion-wise to Wednes-bury market. A much larger one, with a flat, table-like top, stood in a recess of the High Bullen footpath, immediately below the King's Arms Inn; this was for centuries used as a seat by the loungers and idlers of the town to gossip around. Both these have long since disappeared, and it is therefore impossible to say if they were boulders or not. But what is believed to be a similar rock at the corner of Trotter's Lane, Hill Top, is certainly not an erratic or boulder stone, but a piece of basalt from the adjacent sand-beds at Holloway Bank; several pieces like it may be seen built into the foundations of the cottages close by.

Wednesbury, however, is geologically built on glacial drift, Church Hill being a drift mound, as are also Holloway Bank, and the sand-beds at Moxley and at Hall Green Mr. W. Jerome Harrison, F.G.S., is of opinion that these sinuous ridges and whale-back mounds of sand, gravel, clay, etc., mark the drainage lines of the glaciers; or may indicate the points at which the glaciers finally melted. In Britain this mantle of drift, which is continu-ous from Cape Wrath, dies away in ordinary sands and gravels in the Midlands, and dis-appears altogether north of the Thames valley.

Man eventually made his appearance in this locality, which we now call Wednesbury. The earliest settlers here were Celts. These and their immediate Teutonic successors have left us certain place-names, the examination of which may be interesting and not altogether unprofitable. Although the configuration of the whole district may have been altogether different in these prehistoric times, it might perhaps be possible, with the aid of the nomen-clature first applied by man to its various localities to recall to the mind's eye the aspect of the surface around primeval Wednesbury. Standing on Wednesbury hill and gazing out-wards, the scene which met the eye of its earliest human inhabitant would be very dif-ferent from that which is now presented to the Wednesbury man's view.

To the north, and curving round to the east-ward, a dense forest dominated the whole landscape, and stretched away farther than the eye of man could reach. The more distant recesses of this vast sylvan region were scarcely ever penetrated by the light of day, so dense were the heavy growths; but at the eastern foot of the slope, and in the immediate fore-ground, its woody fringe opened out towards the stream into a spacious glade of greensward —the "Wood Green." At that time a squirrel might have leaped from tree to tree, and never set foot upon the solid soil, all the way from Wednesbury to the Peak; unbroken woods stretched from Old Park, through Bloxwich Wood, Cannock Chase, and Needwood Forest right into Derbyshire. These immense forests condensed the rain, induced a damp and chilly atmosphere even in summer-time, and ob-scured the sky with constant rain clouds dur-ing the other seasons.

To the south, and, occasionally, wherever breaks in the skirting woodlands permitted, glimpses might be caught of the winding stream. As it appeared then, in many parts of its course unconfined within any containing embankments, it formed quite a succession of broad and shallow lakes, which were chained together by the deeper and narrower courses of the flowing current. As a dry season al-ternated after a wet season, it then presented the ordinary appearance of a narrow stream-let; but when the storms of winter prevailed, or even after ordinary rainfalls, so readily did the shallows broaden out into pools of water, that the earliest riparian inhabitants were almost constrained to designate it "The Flood Water"—for so the name-word "Tame" signifies.

Looking southward, the view was open and fairly clear of timber down to the banks of the stream. So also was it bald of trees where it rose suddenly in a "Bald Hill" ("Ball's Hill"). On this nearer side, however, a "ridding" ("Ridding Lane") had been artificially accomplished by the hands of man; while on the farther side the higher banks rolled away into sandy wastes of broom, heather (on "Brom"-wich "Heath"), and lyng (at the "Lyng"). Immediately beyond, the whole of Warwickshire was then practically occupied by the Forest of Arden.

Turning to the right, and gazing out to the west, the whole of the low-lying depression stretching between the Wednesbury hill and the heights of Dudley was one undrained morass. In the deepest portion of this watery fenland was a broad mere ("Broadwaters"), beyond which was an extensive sedgy lea ("Sedgley"), and to the north of which was a treacherous marsh ("Hoo Marsh")—a piece of bog-land which, less than two centuries ago, John Wesley described as a quagmire.

The heavier rainfalls, the streams choked by falling timber, and swollen out into broads, the occurrence of marsh and morass on all the lower levels, and the consequent frequency of fogs, would make hills such as that which uplifted itself at Wednesbury a site not wisely to be neglected by the uncivilised Celt, who first sought settlement in this vicinity.

III.—CELTIC AND ROMAN VESTIGES EXAMINED.

Was Wednesbury occupied by the Ancient Britons? There is no direct evidence that it was. Yet it has been said that both Wednesbury hill and Walsall hill were ancient Celtic fortifications, and that a British trackway ran from one to the other, through the Wallows. Primitive man always utilised the tracks by which animals descended from the higher ground to their watering-places.

A British camp was always on a hill, and generally on an inaccessible one. This qualification was scarcely possessed by Wednesbury hill; but the midland district, inhabited by the Cornavii tribe, like many other of the flatter and less rugged portions of the land, had to be defended as well as might be by artificial means.

A British camp was made of no particular shape, but followed the contour and other irregularities of the surface, of which advantage was taken in many ways, as to steepen, to bank up, and to surround by a ditch. Perhaps a breastwork of stockades, with interlacing wickerwork, would add to the height of an earthwork.

The only entrance to the camp was defended by fallen trees. At that time the great forest which covered the whole of central England, of which Cannock Chase, Sutton Coldfield, and the Forest of Arden were late survivals, practically encompassed Wednesbury hill.

From the single outlet of the British camp on Wednesbury hill there would appear to have diverged two roads, both of easy descent, and well suited to the war-chariots used by the Britons. One road was that already mentioned as a trackway, now called Vicarage Road, and the other led towards the stream, and is now known as Church Street.

Another essential to a British encampment was an adequate water supply. Wednesbury

hill possessed two excellent wells, which served as part of the public supply down to the middle of the nineteenth century. One, known as the Vinegar Well (originally called the Vineyard Well, because it adjoined the vineyard of the Manor House), was situated in Hall End, and within living memory was embowered in the hedge-row trees of a wayside recess. A public footpath is said to have led across the churchyard to this well. The other was the Boniface Well, situated on the Little Hill, from which water was sold to about 1840. The Vinegar Well was always a free well. No doubt it was annually decorated with flowers at the usual yearly festival, and may have had a wayside crucifix above it in pre-Reformation times.

Had we entered the forest-land which environed British Wednesbury, and endeavoured to thread our way along one of its very few paths, we might have found a clearing such as that of the "Ridding," which was probably made there because it was along the brook-side that the Briton could best cultivate his little patches of flax and wheat in times of peace. In our passage we might have come upon herds of goats, flocks of horned sheep, and troops of horses and small-sized oxen; we may have even stumbled upon a solitary swineherd tending his hogs in their search for roots or fallen acorns and beech mast. The wild denizens of the forest then included the bear, the wolf, and the fox, from which the flocks had to be defended by large dogs; the game which helped the food supplies of the ancient Briton included the roe, the stag, the wild boar, the hare, and, perhaps, the elk. Among the arts of peace then practised were spinning and weaving linen, dressing skins—some not improbably supplied by the beavers which made their home in the Tame waters—making pottery, boats and oracles; ornaments, implements, and weapons of wood, stone and metal, were produced.

The indirect evidence of a Celtic occupation of Wednesbury Hill may now be examined. There were two Celtic peoples who are known to have occupied the district of South Staffordshire. They both spoke a language of the same stock, with dialectic differences. The first recorded inhabitants were the Ordovices, a Gaelic branch. But when Ptolemy the geographer wrote his Survey of Britain at the beginning of the second century, this tribe had been replaced by the Cornavii, whose capital was at Wroxeter, and who are known to have fortified Wall, near Lichfield. Now the ancient road just mentioned as running from

oaks, some estimated at 2,000 years old, and one with a girth of 9½ yards.

Nightingale's "Staffordshire," p. 1054, records that the remains of large oaks have been dug up in Wednesbury Road, at Rotten Meadow, near Wednesbury.

The name Mesty Croft is believed to have been originally Mansty Croft. If so, Mansty is a Celtic word meaning "the little path."

Moxley is a name said to contain in its first syllable the Celtic Moc, signifyng "pig"; this is extremely doubtful. Similarly in the name Crankhall Lane, the "Crank" is said to be a Celtic word for "hill," often used in field names.

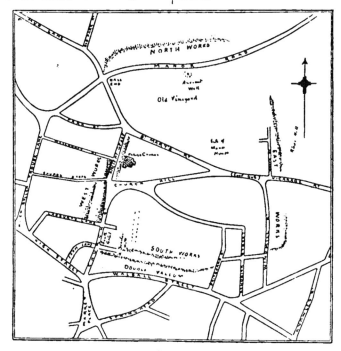

PLAN

Shewing Traces of Supposed ANCIENT EARTHWORKS AT WEDNESBURY.

Wednesbury to Walsall, by way of Caldmore, was continued on to Wall.

The district through which this road ran was an important one in the hierarchy of the Ancient Britons. It was the centre and very core of Britain, where Druidism, with its exclusive mysticism, had fixed its ultimate high court and chief temple. The high lands of Barr, Aldridge, and Cannock Chase are usually identified as the strongholds of the Druids, where they performed their highest rites and most solemn ceremonies. The name Barr is Gaelic, and signifies "an eminence"; the name Cannock was Cnock, equivalent to the Irish name Knock, and means "a hill." On Cannock Chase are still to be found the remains of giant

Monway is generally derived from Mon, separate; which makes the whole word signify the "separate way." Mr. W. H. Duignan, however, ranks the name alongside that of Monmore, giving the derivation of the common syllable Mon from the Irish moin, "a bog"; hence they signify respectively the "Bog-way" and "the Big bog." Monway was certainly near the Broadwaters quagmire and the Hoo Marshes, and it is highly probable the name is of Celtic origin.

Trouse Lane, on the face of it, seems to have derived its appellation from some personal name; but no family of the name of Trouse is known to Wednesbury history. This drives the etymologist to other possible sources of derivation. This lane or road may perhaps have been called by the Celts the Tros, meaning the road running high and dry "above" the level of the marshy land which stretched for some miles to the westward of it.

Another corrupted place-name which seems to be a memorial of the Celtic occupation of Wednesbury is Rose Hill, which till recently was applied to the slope of the Church Hill towards North Street. Undoubtedly, Rose Hill is but a corruption of Rhos Hill. Rhos signifies "moorland," and is a cognate word with "rush," the plant characteristic of moorland swamps; and which may yet be found in the depressions of colliery wastes lying round Hobs Hole and Vicarage. Rhos, in some form or combination, might have been the original Celtic name for Wednesbury, before it acquired its present characteristically Teutonic appellation.

After all, the most significant etymological relic pointing to a Celtic occupation of Wednesbury is found in the terminal "bury." The fact that the Saxon invaders made and called it a "burh" indicates clearly enough the presence of dispossessed Celts. Or why the necessity to fortify the place at that early period? Against whom but Britons was a stronghold necessary?

Traces of earthwork fortifications round Wednesbury Hill still remain. The graaf at the west end of the churchyard is accepted by the county historians as part of Ethelfleda's fortifications. But faint traces of a square camp may be made out by a careful examination; and this would be earlier than the Saxon circumvallation. (See "Religious Wednesbury," p. 7).

Roman camps were always rectangular. Did the Romans, in succession to the Britons,

utilise the natural advantages of Wednesbury Hill as a place of strength? The Cornavii tribe are known to have become friendly with their Roman conquerors; and, further, to have made Wall into a permanent station, which they named Etocetum. It is, therefore, just within the range of possibility that the Romans also temporarily occupied both Walsall and Wednesbury Hills when occasion required. The only objection to the theory is that Etocetum was only fourteen miles away; a proximity which would make a castra exploratoria, that is, a temporary camp pitched in the enemy's country, or a castra æstiva, that is, a summer camp used as a base of operations, quite unnecessary. The other evidences of the presence of the Romans in Wednesbury are equally inconclusive.

The street-name Portway, is often accepted as a memorial of the Roman occupation of the town in which it occurs But it is just as probable in the case of the name Portway Road in Wednesbury that it is of Anglo-Saxon origin. (See "Olden Wednesbury," p. 4). Or if it really dates back to the Roman period, it may have been a "salt-way" from Droitwich, through Oldbury and Wednesbury, to join the Chester Road beyond Bloxwich. (See "Religious Wednesbury," pp 7 and 13).

No Roman pottery, or other trace of domiciliary occupation, has ever been found in Wednesbury; a fragment of Roman glass, however, has been found in Monway Field.

Reeves' History of Westbromwich, p. 88, recorded the discovery, at Wednesbury, in 1817, of Roman coins of the reigns of Nero, Vespasian, and Trajan, all of the first century. A coin of Carausius, who reigned in Britain from 287 to 293, was found at Wood Green when the railway was being cut, seventy years ago.

IV.—THE SAXON SETTLEMENT.

While the occupation of Wednesbury by either Briton or Roman is a matter of doubt, of the town's existence in early Saxon times there can be no question whatever. Its development at that period seems to have been from the settlement of a Saxon family, to the choosing of the place as the site for a Saxon temple, and the subsequent extension of a fortified residence into a "burh" or fortified town. Who was the first Teutonic settler to take up his abode in Wednesbury is not known. It is not improbable he named the settlement after himself, as did the original possessors of Handsworth (the "worth" or property of Honde), Bilston (the "town" of Bill's folk), Darlaston (the "town" of Deorlav), Dudley (the "ley" or pasture of Dudda), Willenhall (the "hall" of Willan), Birmingham (the "home" of the Berm family), and of thousands of other places. Mr. W. H. Duignan formerly held the belief—since abandoned as untenable —that the founder of Wednesbury was some chief, whose personal name was Woden, and

that he called the place Woden's Burh, after himself. ("Religious Wednesbury," p. 2).

The term Burh does seem to have been at first applied to the fortified house of a strong man. The pioneer settler among these invading hordes of Saxons was one whose dominating force of character best fitted him to become a petty chief among his free-born fellows. His log-built dwelling was the first to rise in the place he determined upon as best suited to his own fancy and requirements, whether it were a clearing to be made in the wood, or, as may have been the case at Wednesbury, a position taken from the over-awed Briton.

The surrounding forest provided the pioneer with every requisite for building, as well as shafts and handles for his tools. The settler, having erected his house, tilled his scanty fields, and gradually enlarged his borders; he attracted, in course of time, a number of other men, less enterprising than himself, and willing to take up their residence under his protection. So the clearing gradually grew, in consequence of the felling of timber for the village use. Thus a community was formed, which in the earlier Saxon times was called a Manor, or a lordship, and which, in after times, with the advent of Christianity, and the erection of a church, often became co-terminous with a parish. With the Manor came the peace-pledge; Wednesbury Court Leet and its view of frank-pledge remain with us to this day.

The Folk-mote was a meeting at which the affairs of the village were arranged; a sort of Saxon Village Council. It was originally held under some sacred tree; the place-name, Wednesbury Oak, still indicates the location of this ancient meeting-place. Here officials were appointed, public lands re-distributed, and other business transacted.

This form of aggregation and growth seems, however, to have been of later date to that period in which Wednesbury was founded as a Saxon settlement. The manorial form, with the lordship of one man over his fellows, came somewhat later. On their first arrival in Britain, the only tie between the Saxon settlers was that of blood, or kinship. In its earlier phases, it was a settlement of clans or families. Reminders of this clanship among the early settlers of the vicinity are to be found in the occurrence of "ing," signifying "descendants" or "sons of," in the various place-names around Wednesbury. Thus we have Tipton, or Tibbington, the ton, tun, or town—really a village community—founded by the family of Tibba, or Tibbe; Willingsworth, the Worth, or estate founded by the clan of Willan; and Fallings Heath, where continued to dwell the heathen descendants of Farl, outside the later fortified and Christianised Wednesbury.

These new colonists, dwelling among the subjugated Britons, whom they had deprived of their lands, had to combine for mutual support and protection. They arranged themselves into Hundreds of warriors; doubtless we have in the afore-mentioned names, Tib, Willan, and Farl, the identity of three of these picked champions or heads of families who represented the "Hundred" at their public meetings. It is not improbable that the Hundred Court was held at Sedgley; historical inference points in that direction. The Hundred was called Offlow, after the name of the leading chief, Offa, if not, indeed, after that famous King of Mercia who built the earthwork from the Dee to the Wye, which is known as Offa's Dyke.

The Hundred Mote was also an open-air assembly, held under the shade of some large tree. Here took place the important ceremony of pledging fealty to their leader; every warrior touching with the tip of his uplifted spear that of Offa, or whatever the name of the chosen chieftain might have been. The Hundred was divided into ten parts of ten families each; and the court of such "tything" or township, in after generations, ultimately resolved itself into the Parish Vestry. Thus the Tibbings dominated one tything, which in due time formed the parish of Tibbington or Tipton; the estate of Hondes became the parish of Handsworth; and so on.

The strength of Wednesbury, whether natural or artificial, was apparently sufficient to constitute it a Saxon "burh" or fort. If the first pioneer settler had called it after his own personal name, as was the custom among these Teutonic leaders, it is evident that the re-naming of the place was effected shortly after. The hill, for its military strength, or for some other reason sufficiently weighty, was made the centre of Woden worship, and as such became known as Woden's burh. This, in the course of time, was modified into Wednesbury, just as Woden's dæg became Wednesday.

Several considerations will point to the importance of the Wednesbury settlement as a place of somewhat greater military strength than was possessed by the others immediately surrounding it. The altitude of its hill gave it a natural advantage over them. It is one of the two positions lying mid-way between the heights of Barr and Sedgley, Walsall hill being the other. It had not improbably been fortified before.

One relic of the old Saxon fortification is found in the place-name Moat-field or Mott-piece, by which was known the sites of Pritchard Street and Kendrick Street, before they were cut up into building land some thirty years ago. This field lay under the line of the southern earthworks, and seems to have contained the last remnant of the ancient moat. There can be little doubt that in "Moat-field" we have preserved to us a name relic of the "Mota," or "Motte," which was the broad and deep circumscribing ditch of the ancient Saxon fortification. For though the mounds of the Anglo-Saxon were usually artificial, they were not always so. At Wednesbury it seems to have been a partly natural platform scarped artificially—the remains of the escarpment being still plainly discernable at Ethelfleda Terrace.

V.—THE NAME OF WEDNESBURY.

The origin of the name of this town has given rise to some amount of controversy; as also has its identity with other names of great similarity mentioned by ancient chroniclers.

The common opinion is that the name "Wednesbury" was derived from that of "Woden," or Odin, the Saxon god of war; the terminal "bury" being the Anglo-Saxon "burh" or "byrig," signifying an earthwork, and hence a fortified town.

This derivation is sometimes disputed; and sometimes other places bearing similar names are put forward as the historic originals, which claim to be identical with the places mentioned in the old chronicles. An examination of these names will at least disclose the fact that none of them have retained their original shape with greater consistency than that of "Wednesbury," if the parallel name of "Wednesday" be accepted as a fair standard of comparison.

Taylor, in his "Words and Places," says:—"But of the prevalence of the worship of Woden and Thunor we have wide-spread evidence. Wednesbury in Staffordshire, Wisborough Hill in Essex, Wanborough in Surrey, Wanborough in Wilts, two Warnboroughs in Hampshire, Woodnesborough in Kent and Wilts, and Wenbury in Devon, are all corruptions of the Anglo-Saxon word 'Wodnesbeorh,' a name which indicates the existence of a mound or other similar erection dedicated to Woden." A reference is also given to Kemble's "Saxons," vol. 1, p. 344, and mention made of Godesberg, near Bonn, the German form of which was anciently Wodnesberg.

But the word "beorh," from which all these other English place-names are derived, signifies a hill—not a fortified hill. Its signification is certainly rather wide; for its means a hill, a mountain, a heap, an earthwork, and a barrow or burrow. A burrow is a burial tumulus; but it is not a burgh, a borough, or a fortress.

Professor Toller, of Manchester, gives the following opinion:—"Possibly 'bury' in Wednesbury is not 'burh'—a town, but 'beorh,' a hill. Grimm, in his 'Mythology' (cap. 7), notes a number of 'Woden's hills,' and the name of the town of Wednesbury may have a similar origin."

An authority to be quoted is Charnock, who, in his "Local Etymology," says:—"Wednesbury, in co. Stafford, from 'Woden's-beorg,' from 'Woden,' the Saxon god of war; 'beorg' a hill, or 'burg' a fortified place. We find in Domesday that this town, previously to the Norman Conquest, had belonged to the Saxon kings."

The next authority worthy of quoting is Flavel Edmunds, who says, in his "Names of Places"—"Wednes., English, from 'Woden.' Examples, Wednesbury and Wednesfield (Staffordshire), Woden's fortification, and Woden's field."

Professor Arber has been referred to, in consequence of a Walsall archæologist (some years since deceased) formulating the opinion that the name was not derived from "Woden," but from "Wode" or "Wood"; Wednesbury having been almost entirely within the bounds of Cannock Chase, and the letter n being merely intrusive.

The learned Professor of English, in reply, said:—"In the reprint of the "A. S. Chronicle" by B. Thorpe (Record Office Publications), the name

Woddesbeorge
Wodnesbeorge

is, by Mr. Thorpe, taken to be that of Wansborough, and not of Wednesbury. The Anglo-Saxon 'beorge' is equivalent to 'burh,' a fortified town. The 'Wednes' is clearly from Woden, like our 'Wednesday.'"

The theory of a derivation from Wode has never found favour elsewhere. The propounder, however, honestly believed that Wednesbury signified "the strong place in the wood"; the strong place being Wednesbury Hill, always conspicuous in the surrounding landscape.

But this heresy of substituting "Wode" for "Woden" is easily set aside. The fact is, the name of Woden entered into the composition of so many place-names simply because this god was specially invested with the protection of ways and boundaries.

Woden being the god charged with this duty of safe-guarding places against witchcraft, disposes also of the next heretical opinion—that Woden was a man.

Mr. W. H. Duignan is no mean authority on place-names in general; on those of Staffordshire he is undoubtedly the chief authority. For a number of years Mr. Duignan has held the opinion that Wednesbury was derived from a personal name, Woden, and not from the name of the god. However, he is at last converted to the more generally accepted theory. He has read up all the great authorities, not the least of whom is Jacob Grimm; and those entitled to give a reliable opinion are all decided that Wednesbury was named after the god Woden. It was not the custom of the Anglo-Saxons to name their children after their gods; it would have been regarded as impious. Therefore, Wednesbury could not have been called after any person named Woden; as Handsworth, for instance, was named after Honde, or Birmingham after the chief Berm. It was undoubtedly named from its Temple of Woden; as several places in Germany have similarly derived their names.

The glossary to Mallet's "Northern Antiquities" (a most reliable authority), says, p. 561: "Several places still retain the name of Odin, as Odensberg in Sweden, Odenwald in Germany, Wednesbury in Staffordshire," etc.

Professor Windle, of Birmingham University, has no doubt whatever on this point. In his "Early Britain," p. 184, writing of the religious beliefs of the Saxons, he says: "The names of some of their principal deities still remain in daily use, as the names of the days of the week. Woden, or Odin, whose name is found in our Wednesday, has given it also to many other objects in England, such as the Wansdyke, and to places, such as Wednesbury, near Birmingham, or Wodens-beorh, where the hill on which stands the Church of St. Bartholomew is said to have previously possessed a temple dedicated to the worship of Odin."

In fact, this derivation of Wednesbury is now so universally adopted, that it appears in the school history books, and is taught throughout England.

Clearly the original name was Anglo-Saxon. The different ways of spelling "Wednesbury," particularly in its Latinised forms, during the Middle Ages, will be both interesting and instructive. Here are a few examples:—

Wadnesberrie.—"Doomsday," 1085.
Weadesbyrig.—"Wednesbury Papers," p. 79 (and "Students' Atlas").
Weddesbury.—"Weston Church," 1552.
Weddesbyrie.—"Leland," 1538.
Wednesbury.—"Inquis. post mortem," 4 Hen., IV., No. 36.
Wedgebury.—[Common.]
Wednesbiri.—"Staffordshire Assize Roll," 12 H. III.
Wednesbr'.—"Testa de Nevill," 1171-2.
Wednesbure.—"Deed," 1620.
Wednesburie.—"Deed," 1594.
Wednesbury.—[Early Spelling.] "Inquis p.m." 4, Hen. IV., No. 17.
Wedonesbury.—"Inquis, p.m." 2 H. VI., No. 36.
Wodenesburi.—"Pleas of the Forest," 1286.
Wodensbeorg.—"Saxon."
Wodnesbyri.—"Staffs. Assize Roll," 56 H. III.
Wodnesberi.—"Mag. Rot. Pip.," 29 Hen. II.
Wodnesberia.—"Mag. Rot. Pip.," 16 Hen. II.
Wodnesb'ia.—"Mag. Rot. Pip.," 1169-70.
Wodnesburi.—"Testa de Nevill," 1171-2.
Wodnesburia.—"Mag. Rot. Pip.," 11 Hen. II.
Wodnesbury.—"Pleas of Forest," 1300.
Wodnesbyri.—"Pleas of Forest," 1271.
Wothensbeorg.—715 A.D. [Battle.]

Among the "Staffordshire Pipe Rolls," Hen II., 1186-7, Wednesbury appears
Wodnesberia

Also among the "Plea Rolls," January, 1226, is one in which Philip de Heronville sued William de Heronville for the Manor of
Wotnesburi.
in Co. of Stafford. The case was not decided, but a future day for hearing was granted, and consequently it re-appears among the "Rolls," November, 1227 (nearly two years after), with the spelling altered to
Wednesbiri.

On a tablet in Weston Church is "John, son and heir of John Mytton, of Weston, Esq., who married Eustance, daughter of Sir Richard Beaumont, of

Weddesbury, in County of Stafford, departed this life February 16th, 1552."

Shaw, in his "History of Staffordshire," says the name is certainly Saxon, and called in Camden
Weadesburg
But more properly it is
Wodensborough.

Continuing his history, we read that Simon de Heronville held the Manor of
Wonnesbury
of the heir of Henry de Oylli.

In Bagnall's "History of Wednesbury" we find the following:—
Wednesbeorg.
Wothnesbeorg.
Wadnesberrie.
Wodnesbury.

A strange form of the name is "Wendenesbir," which occurs in "Testa de Nevill," a "Book of Fees of the Exchequer," which appears to have been compiled near the reign of Edward II., partly from inquests taken on the presentment of jurors of hundreds before the justices itinerant; and partly from Inquisitions, upon writs awarded to the Sheriffs for collecting scutages, aids, etc.

The "Students' Atlas" (Collins and Sons, London), on map 37, "Britain Under the Saxons," gives the name spelt "Weadesbyrig," followed by the modern name of "Wednesbury" in brackets, so that there is no mistake as to the identity of the place meant.

A number of Escheats have been searched for the spelling of this name. In 4 Henry IV. it was spelt
Wedenesbury.

In 2 Henry VI. its form was
Wedonesbury.

But even then it may be noticed that in 4 Henry IV., 7 Henry IV., and 12 Edward IV., its present form obtained, viz.,
Wednesbury.

Other variations in spelling may be noted with interest as this history proceeds. Then there is the matter of pronunciation, which has exercised some critical minds.

The spelling of a proper name is by no means a guide to its pronunciation. The names Derby and Abergavenny, when used as the territorial titles of nobility, become Darby and Abergenny. But as applied directly to the places themselves, the spelling of the name Uttoxeter, and of Alnwick, give no clue to their pronunciations as Utchetter, and as Anick. In the same way it is doubtful whether the spelling of Wednesbury gives any clue to its proper pronunciation. In many books of the seventeenth and eighteenth centuries, the name is often given as Wedgbury; and more frequently, when the writer desires to be explicit, two names are given, and the reader is allowed his choice of Wednesbury, or of its alternative, Wedgbury. The old phrase

"Wedgbury Cocking," becomes absolutely insipid when pronounced "Wednesbury Cocking." A local expert's opinion is that the proper pronunciation of the town should be Wedgbury. It has the true ring about it, and it certainly has antiquity on its side, to say nothing of the popular prejudice in its favour. In a certain great case tried in one of the superior law courts of London, the most eminent barrister of the day repeatedly employed this form of pronunciation.

VI.—WODEN (OR ODIN) AND WODEN-WORSHIP.

Woden is but another form of the name Odin, which the Middle Germans called Odan, the Old Saxons called Wodan, and the Anglo-Saxons pronounced Woden.

Around the personality of Odin much confusion has grown up. That such a person did exist seems tolerably certain; according to one authority he lived about 70 B.C.; while another authority places him thirty years later (40 B.C.). The historical monuments of Northern Europe go no farther back than the arrival there of Odin, an epoch which was just anterior to that of Christ.

It was apparently about the time that Rome had reached the zenith of her power, and Cæsar was about invading Britain, that a certain barbarian chieftain named Sigge held sway in the forests of Scythia. When Mithridates fled into these Scythian wilds, in order to draw Pompey after him, he hoped to rouse his barbarian neighbours in Pontus to a resistance of that aggression which threatened them all alike. But the military genius of Pompey proved too much for both the King of Pontus and his new ally, the Teutonic chieftain Sigge.

Sigge, then forced to fly from Roman vengeance, changed his name to Odin, which seems to have been that of the supreme deity among the Teutonic nations. There was nothing new or strange in the assumption of such name, as many nations gave their pontiffs the name of the god they worshipped; and Sigge, being full of ambitious projects, took care to avail himself of a title which would procure him most respect among the peoples he meant to subdue to his own will. He, at first, merely presided over the worship paid to the deity, and passed among his followers for a man inspired by the gods. It is little wonder that soon after his death, the man Odin (as he must now be called) was confused with the deity whose name he had appropriated.

Odin had commanded the Æsir, whose country lay between the Caspian and the Black Sea, and whose principal city was Asgard, famous throughout all the circumjacent countries for the worship there paid to the supreme god. Having drawn under his banner all the youth of the neighbouring nations, Odin set forth on a march of conquest towards the north and west of Europe, directing his course to Scandinavia.

Holstein and Jutland fell into his hands. Funen next submitted, and there he built the city which bears his name, Odensee. Denmark was conquered, and on its throne was placed his son Skjold (Shield), whose descendants were called Skjoldungians. Passing on to Sweden, the reigning prince there, named Gylä, dazzled by the brilliant conquests of Odin, paid him divine honours. The Swedes came in crowds to do him homage, and he quickly acquired supreme authority over them. The regal title was bestowed upon his son Yngvi, and his posterity after him; hence arose the dynasty known as the Ynglingians, of which the Swedish nation was afterwards so proud.

Gylfi being dead or forgotten, Odin ruled supreme over all the petty kings around him. He founded Sigtuna (Sigge's town), a city no longer existing, but which was situated in the same province as Stockholm, now the capital of Sweden.

Before setting forth upon the conquest of Norway, the throne of which he ultimately gave to his son Sœming, he consolidated the worship of the gods at Sigtuna. The new worship, with its many magical secrets, was committed to the care of a supreme council of twelve pontiffs, who not only guarded the new religion, but administered justice, and watched over the public weal generally. Odin was now recognised, not only as a supreme sovereign, but as a god.

After all these glorious achievements, Odin retired to Sweden, where, perceiving that his end was drawing near, he resolved not to wait for dissolution by lingering disease. So, assembling his companions in arms, and his supporters in council, he gave himself nine wounds in the form of a circle with the point of his spear, and as many other cuts with his sword. As he lay dying, Odin declared he was going back to Asgard to take his seat among the gods at an eternal banquet, at which he would afterwards gladly welcome, and receive with all honours, those warriors who bore themselves bravely in battle, and died sword in hand.

Odin came to be regarded as the supreme deity of the Scandinavians, the king of gods and men. As God of War he was supposed to hold his court at Valhalla, surrounded by warriors who had fallen in battle; every brave Anglo-Saxon who fell fighting was believed to go straight to Valhalla, there to feast evermore with Odin, and drink their wine from the skulls of their enemies.

As presiding god, Odin always had two ravens, one to sit on each of his shoulders, and bring him tidings of all that passed in the world. (From this belief has originated the nursery saying, "A little bird told me that").

Odin's wife was Frigga, and one of his mythical sons was Balder the Beautiful, the tale of whose untimely slaughter, through the guile of the evil god Loki, is finely told in Norse mythology.

From the Edda, a religious code containing the ancient Scandinavian mythology, we learn that—"Odin is named Alfadir (the "Allfather") because he is the father of all the gods, and also Valfadir (the "Choosing Father") because he chooses for his sons all those who fall in combat. For their abode he has prepared Valhalla," etc., etc.

Immediately upon his death, Odin's remains were carried to Sigtuna, where, conformably to a custom he had introduced into the north, the body was burnt with much pomp and magnificence. Such was the closing scene in the career of this extraordinary man, whose ruling principle is supposed by some learned authorities to have been guided solely by a desire for revenge upon the Romans, those enemies of universal liberty, who had driven him from his native wilds.

Pretending only to be the priest or prophet of Odin, the ignorance of succeeding ages easily confounded the priest with the deity itself; and hence has arisen that medley of fact and fiction which has always clustered around the remarkable history of the deeds of a hero, with the attributes of a deity—of the Teutonic conqueror, Sigge, commonly known to us as Odin.

Icelandic chronicles paint Odin as a man extremely eloquent, and most miraculously persuasive. The force of his harangues, intensified by the extempore verse of a fiery and poetic fancy, no listener could long resist. He sang tender and melodious airs, which made the very plains and mountains open and expand with delight, and drew the ghosts from their infernal caverns to stand motionless and spell-bound before him. So said the chroniclers.

Besides teaching the Scandinavians the art of poesy, he was also the inventor of the Runic characters which prevailed so long among that people.

He was a seer who could foretell events. He was an enchanter who could transform himself into any shape, raise the dead to life, or strike the living with instant death. Certainly as a warrior, who had always sought the thickest of the carnage, it had always seemed that he was invulnerable, and the bearer of a charmed existence.

Many sovereign families of the north have claimed descent from this great semi-historical personage. The name Odin signified nothing more than the supreme god of the Teutonic nations; but flattering poets and historians never failed to honour the warrior whose praises they were singing, with a pedigree that was always traced back to the national god of war. Thus were the descendants of Odin constantly multiplied; consequently, when Hengist and Horsa led the Anglo-Saxon invasion of this country, it is not surprising to learn that they counted Odin, or Woden, in the number of their ancestors Queen Victoria's pedigree has been carried back to Odin. Indeed, the supposed founders of many northern dynasties are manifestly no other than the deities worshipped by the ancient Scandinavians, anthropomorphised to flatter the vanity of their earliest rulers.

Snorri, the ancient historian of Norway, is responsible for very much of what we know respecting Odin, the great god and hero of the north. The legend of Odin is founded on the Ynglinga Saga, which forms the first book of Snorri's Chronicles of the Kings of Norway. Some critics have contended that the whole story of the so-called historical Odin was the invention of Snorri himself. All of which is ably discussed in Mallet's "Northern Antiquities" (Bohn's Antiquarian Library, published by George Bell and Sons, London).

Odin, the god, is often represented holding a sword in his hand. The festival of Odin was celebrated at the beginning of spring, in order to give welcome to that pleasant season, and especially to obtain of the god of battles happy success in any projected expedition against a foe.

Human sacrifices were part of the worship of Odin. Thus, in the history of Norway, it may be read that Earl Hakon offered his son as a sacrifice to Odin to obtain the victory over the Jomsburg pirates; and Aun, King of Sweden, devoted to Odin the blood of his nine sons, to prevail on that god to prolong his life. The ancient history of the north abounds with similar examples.

This worship having once been practised on Wednesbury hill, some account of its dread ceremonial may not be out of place.

In the midst of the Temple of Woden stood an altar, on which the sacred fire was always kept burning. Surrounding this place of sacrifice were many kinds of iron and brazen vessels, used in the various ceremonies; among them was one of superior size, which was used to receive the blood of the victims.

When animals were offered up, they were slaughtered at the foot of the altar; the carcase was opened, and an augury was drawn from the entrails, as among the Romans. The flesh was sometimes dressed, and served up in a feast prepared for the assembly, horse-flesh not being rejected in this connection.

When a human sacrifice was offered, the victim was laid upon a great stone, and instantly strangled or clubbed on the head. A Woden Stone of this nature is said to have been set up first in a grove at Wednesfield, and afterwards removed to the Temple of Woden at Wednesbury.

In whatever manner the immolation of a human victim was made, the priest, in slaying, always took care to consecrate the victim by pronouncing the formula, "I devote thee to Odin," or "I send thee to Odin." Part of the blood was sprinkled on the worshippers, and part on the sacred grove; while all altars, images, and temple walls, both inside and out, were also besprinkled. The bodies were either burnt, or suspended in the sacred grove in which the temple was built; so that Odin's grove was always full of the bodies of men and animals who had been sacrified to that dread god.

The sacrificial ceremony concluded with feastings of much barbaric splendour, at which the celebrants drank immoderately. The kings or chief nobles drank first, healths in honour of the gods; everyone drank afterwards, making some vow or prayer to the god whom they named. When Christianity supplanted Woden-worship, the early Christians of these northern regions actually drank healths to the Saviour, the Apostles, and the Saints, a pagan custom which the Church had no option but to tolerate for some time.

This great German god, Woden, is always identified with the Roman god, Mercury. The other Teutonic gods, Thor, Tuesco, Frigga, and Sœter may perhaps correspond severally with the Roman deities Jupiter, Mars, Minerva, and Saturn.

The names of the days of the week were derived from these Anglo-Saxon deities. Thus Sunday was dedicated to the worship of the Sun; Monday to the worship of the Moon (Diana); Tuesday to Tuesco (Mars); Wednesday to Woden (Mercury); Thursday to Thor (Jupiter); Friday to Frigga (Venus?); and Saturday to Sœter (Saturn).

It is known that the Saxons displayed a remarkable skill in goldsmith's work; and among the remains of their art are still to be found ornaments bearing the image of the great deity Woden.

At Wednesbury Town Hall the heathen deity is depicted in stained glass as a bold character in a martial attitude, and clad in nondescript armour, with a broad sword uplifted in the right hand; evidently copied from Pinnock's "History of England."

The portrayal of Woden has been made the subject of a most careful study by the late Sir E. Burne-Jones, R.A. Great attention has been paid to the accessories in the picture. The seated figure has the two ravens on one shoulder. This treatment regards them as Hugin and Munin; that is, "mind" and "memory." At the feet of the god are his hounds; black, long-tongued, and fire-eyed. His spear is a great reed, which, after being thrown at beast of the chase, or at an enemy, returns again to his hand.

The old superstition of the Wednesbury colliers relating to Gabriel's Hounds (recorded on p. 135 of Bagnall's "History of Wednesbury"), was the last remnant of the old Norse mythology which lingered in Wednesbury. Gabriel's Hounds of the 17th century were but Woden's Hounds of the 7th century.

Woden is really the prototype of the legendary, "Spectre Huntsman."

This dread god, according to ancient belief, indulges at times in a weird hunt, riding a dappled grey horse. His hounds take part in the infernal hunt, and the ravens also accompany the chase. But the fierce ride of the huntsman never takes place except amidst the howl and din of a raging tempest; indeed, the wind is always blowing a gale wherever the phantom horse but grazes at large.

Swedish folklore contains another variant— "Oden's hundar"—of the same superstition. There is extant much lore of the "Spectre Huntsman" and the "Seven Whistlers." See "English Traditional Lore" (Gentleman's Magazine Series), p. 55.

VII.—FROM WODEN WORSHIP TO CHRISTIANITY.

The great Teutonic invasion of this country commenced in 449, when Hengist and Horsa founded the kingdom of Kent. The latest comers were a body of Anglians, who, under a chief named Crida, founded the kingdom of Mercia, or the March-land bordering on Wales, about the year 600. Mercia was entirely inland, centrally situated between Northumbria and the Thames, and stretching from East Anglia to Wales.

For nearly a thousand years after this the designation applied to Staffordshire men was Angli. Or sometimes men of Staffordshire were known as Mediterranei. These appellations, which appear in many ancient deeds, documents, and records (see Manley's "Interpreter," published in 1684), seem to indicate both the descent and the location of the early inhabitants of this county.

In the 8th century Mercia held the highest place amongst the kingdoms of the Saxon Heptarchy. But it was as a Pagan State. During the period of this supremacy the Woden-worshipping town of Wednesbury enjoyed its highest renown. And it was this ascendancy of the ancient Norse faith which directly brought about the downfall of Mercia.

The county historians assume an earlier Christianity during the Roman occupation, and tell us that about A.D. 586 "Crida, a Saxon, the eleventh from Woden, the first king of Mercia, conquered the Britons, and destroyed all the Christian Churches within the counties of Stafford, Warwick," etc., etc., etc. A further assumption is that all the Christians from this Midland area were driven into Wales; and that the whole country was plunged once more into the darkness of heathenism.

After the arrival of St. Augustine and his missioner monks in 597, the Christian faith made steady headway in all the Saxon states except one. In Mercia the Middle English still clung tenaciously to the old northern gods of their ancestors.

Mercia, under King Penda, remained obstinately pagan. Penda was grandson of Crida

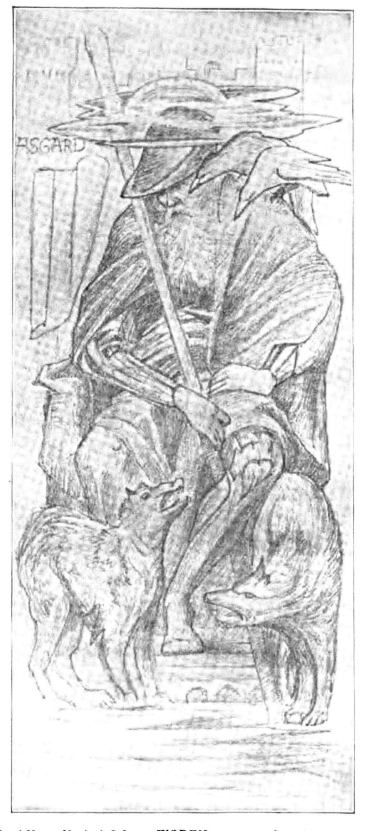

ASGARD

WODEN.   [*449, Oxford Street, London, W.*

of Mercia. and twelfth in nominal descent from Woden.

All the children of Penda embraced Christianity; and one son, Peada, introduced missionaries from the north. Penda tolerated the new religion only when it suited his policy. He subjugated Wessex, and compelled the West Saxons to renounce Christianity. In 655, when nearly 80 years of age, he fiercely resolved to war against Northumbria, chiefly on account of religion. Although thirty English and British chiefs followed him to battle, after a long and furious encounter he was overthrown and slain. The Mercian nobles took his youngest son Wolfere (Guelph is the modern form of the same name), and placed him on the throne. Mercia then quickly became Christian. The temple of Woden in Wednesbury was adapted, converted to, and consecrated for Christian worship, and dedicated to St. Bartholomew.

By the special orders of Pope Gregory the Great, who sent Augustine to England, all the idol temples of the Saxons, if well built, were to be retained and converted into churches. This instruction was, no doubt, carried out in Wednesbury, where the temple of Woden would be of more than ordinary merit in architectural construction.

Where the praises of Woden had hitherto been sung in high revelry, the praises of the Holy Trinity were now rendered in a manner quite as irreverent. The sprinkling of a little holy water on the fabric could not possibly alter the character of the worshippers. War songs mingled with hymns for some considerable time.

It was this adaptation of heathen temples to Christian worship which was no doubt responsible for the retention of so many pagan customs, ceremonies, and seasons in the festivals of the church.

The location of Saxon churches may be very generally restricted to two kinds of sites. The one was the ancient burial mound. If the missioner-priest who brought Christianity among the pagan Saxons found a "low," or other burial site, to which the population attached the least sanctity, the priestly diplomat was clever enough to locate his little wooden church there. He welded his new Christianity on to their ancient religion, and utilised their old prejudices to his own purposes. If the

Saxons interred their dead in burial mounds during their paganism, they certainly buried in consecrated ground after their conversion. But in not a few cases the consecrated churchyard had once been a pagan place of burial. The other kind of site selected by the early Christian missionaries was a tower or stronghold. The wooden church was not infrequently attached to a stone tower; this may be accepted as one of the causes of churches having towers.

This selection of the sites of ancient parish churches is a subject of much interest. Wednesbury parish church seems to owe its location to the two main causes of selection—strength of position, and an association of sanctity with the chosen spot.

Wednesbury Oak and Gospel Oak are closely contiguous, if not practically identical places. At the former was anciently performed the Saxon ceremony of swearing fealty; at the latter it became the practice to read the Scriptures on Rogation Days. This affords another instance of the conversion of a chosen site from one purpose to another, as the march of events demanded.

The destruction of the temple of Woden at Wednesbury is the subject of an illustrated article in Ryder's "Annual" for 1897. Chapter II. of "Religious Wednesbury" tells the story "How Christianity came haltingly to Wednesbury."

Wolfhad, son of Wolfere, an apostate king of Mercia, accidentally finding the cell of St. Chad, at Stowe (near Stafford), was converted by the Saint to the true faith. He then brought his brother Rufin to the man of God, and he also was baptized. Both these brothers were shortly afterwards murdered at the cell of St. Chad by a pagan relative, about 658. They were both honoured as martyred Saints, their death being commemorated on July 24th. They were buried at Stowe, not at Stone, as often erroneously stated.

Wolverhampton was named after this King Wolfere, the place being called Wolfere's High Town (Anglo-Saxon hean for "high"), as he erected a church here between 657 and 675.

(See Dr. Oliver's "History of Wolverhampton," pp. 6-7. The derivation of the name from Wulfruna is, however, now the one generally adopted.)

[The illustration on p. 15 was designed by the late Sir Edward Burne-Jones, Bart., for Messrs. Morris & Company, for a production in stained glass. Reproduced by permission specially for this work by Murray B. Bladon, Esq. For description see p. 14.]

VIII.—THE TWO BATTLES OF WEDNESBURY. A.D. 592 AND 715.

Wednesbury was in Mercia, the last formed, but by no means the least important, of the seven kingdoms of the Heptarchy. Mercia means "the March," or the "boundary land," and was so called because it was on the boundary of Wales; thus the town of Wednesbury was situated in frontier land of the Heptarchy, the debatable land where the conquering Saxon, or to speak more correctly, the conquering Angle—for the "marches" were conquered by Anglian chiefs who were for some time subject to the kings of Northumbria—had to contest its ownership with the defeated, but long unsubjugated, Briton. Around the west midland locality took place the final struggle between the invading Teutons and the patriotic Celts; between the dominant invaders and the retreating natives—and these Anglo-Saxon conquerors, with a characteristic assumption of superior right (and to them the right of might was pre-eminently in advance of that of original possession or of all other claims), styled their beaten foes the Welch or "foreigners."

During the internecine struggle of the Heptarchy two battles were fought at Wednesbury. Local legend has named Wigmore and King's Hill as the sites of ancient battle-fields, but no historic fact has been adduced in support of this.

The recorded facts of the first battle are but few. The Anglo-Saxon Chronicle says, under the year 592: "In this year there was a great slaughter in Britain at"—here the name is differently spelt in four ancient copies extant. "Woddesbeorge," "Woddesbeorge," "Woddesbeorge," and "Wodnesbeorge"—"and Ceawlin was driven out."

Monkish orthography varies very much, because the monks were in the habit of dictating to each other; consequently the proper names of localities of which both reader and writer were ignorant suffered most in the spelling. The Bodleian MS of the A.S. Chronicle has it "Wodnesbeorge," which an A.S. scholar would certainly translate into Wednesbury. The termination "beorge" (which has come to be pronounced "bury," and sometimes "borough") signifies a hill. Wednesbury stands on a hill, so that the termination "beorge" is as favourable to it as to any other place.

Every commentator, down to Professor A. J. Church, who has recently published a work entitled "Early Britain" (Fisher Unwin's "Story of the Nations" series), interprets the place of this battle as Wanborough, in Wilts. No authority, no good or sufficient reason, is ever adduced in support of such interpretation. Mr. W. H. Duignan has investigated this matter, and gives excellent reasons in favour of the place of this battle (and that of the year 712 also) being Wednesbury. He says:—"A strong argument against Wanborough is that it does not, and never did, bear any name which could be twisted, even by Canon Taylor or Dr. Charnock, into Woddesborough, or Wodnesbury. Wanborough was granted by Ethelwulf, or Adulf, King of the West Saxons, to Winchester Cathedral, in 854, and in the grant (No. 477, Cartularium Saxonicum) is several times spelt 'Wenbeorge.' In Domesday it is 'Wemberge.' I take it therefore to be absolutely certain that Wanborough is not the 'Woddesbeorge, or Wodnesbeorge,' of the A.S. Chronicle, and that the locality must be sought elsewhere.

"That the right name of the place is 'Wodnesbeorge' is further evidenced by 'Ethelwerd's Chronicle,' written in the tenth century. Ethelwerd, and the A.S. Chronicle, both introduce Ceawlin to us, in 556, as a Saxon chief fighting against the Britons at Beranburh (Banbury), and, in 560, as succeeding to the kingdom of Wessex. In 577, they tell us, Cuthwin and Ceawlin (who were brothers) fought against the Britons, and slew their kings, and took three of their most distinguished cities, Gloucester, Cirencester, and Bath. In 584 Ceawlin and Cutha fought the Britons again, at 'Fethanleage' (supposed to be in Gloucestershire), and Cutha fell, but Ceawlin 'reduced a multitude of cities, and took immense spoils.' Then Ethelwerd writes:—'An: 592. There was a great slaughter on both sides at a place called Wodnesbyrg, so that Ceawlin was put to flight, and died at the end of one more year.' Florence, of Worcester, who wrote in the latter part of the eleventh century, says, under the year 562:— 'A battle was fought at a place called Wodnesbeorh, that is 'Woden's Mount,' in which there was a great slaughter, and Ceawlin was driven from his kingdom.'"

This sanguinary incident of 592 is also recorded by William, of Malmesbury, who, however, was not born till 1065. The Ceawlin mentioned was King of Wessex, and second Bretwalda—that is, "Britain-wielder," or Overlord of all Britain.

The battle was fought in the early Pagan era of the Saxons; and the name of the place at which Ceawlin was finally overthrown two years later, by a combined force of Saxons and Britons, is given as Wodendic; "after which," says William of Malmesbury, "he forthwith died."

It is not known where this "Woden's Dyke" was; but its existence illustrates the frequency with which "Woden" entered into the Saxon names of places. In Staffordshire we have a Wednesfield, which was, as its name implies, the "field," or place where the trees of Cannock Forest had been "felled"—in all probability, for the worship of Woden.

Mr. Duignan contends that "Wednesbury is a more likely locality than Wanborough to have been the scene of a battle between Saxons and Britons in 592, for the following reasons: The Saxons clearly drove the Britons before them west and north. In 552 Cynric fought and routed the Britons at Salisbury (about 30 miles east of Wanborough). Four years later Cynric and Ceawlin defeated them at Banbury, far north of Wanborough. In 571 Cutha, or Cuthulf, brother of Ceawlin, fought them at Bedford, and took from them Leighton (Buzzard), Aylesbury, Bensington, and Eynsham (near Oxford); and, in 577, Ceawlin again fought them, and captured Gloucester, Cirencester, and Bath. By this time the power of the Britons must have been completely broken in Wilts, if they were not entirely driven out of it, and yet, if we accepted Wanborough, they must have been in great force there. It is much more likely that, having beaten them before him up to Banbury and Oxford, he was raiding north, and carving out of their country the subsequent kingdom of Mercia." Thus much for the battle of 592.

The second historic battle of the same name (Wodnesbeorg) took place in the year 715.

Mercia had now become supreme among the Saxon kingdoms. Wulfere of Mercia, forced the King of Sussex ultimately to accept Christianity, and then bestowed the Isle of Wight upon him. This indicates the power of Mercia. But under his successors this power began to decline Ceolred King of Mercia, had to contend with Wessex for the supremacy.

Writing of these rivals, Professor Church, in the work already quoted, says (p. 14):—"The two met in battle at Wednesbury, in Shropshire. Both sides claimed the victory, which, however, inclined to the West Saxons. This was in 715. The next year Ceolred was smitten with sudden madness as he was feasting with his thanes, and very soon after died."

The phrase "in Shropshire" is a trifling error on the part of the learned professor. Wednesbury is some nine or ten miles outside the limits of Shropshire. But the historian evidently means Wednesbury in Staffordshire, as there is no place in county Salop bearing a name approaching that of Wednesbury.

All previous writers and commentators, without citing any authority, and apparently by mere guess, also interpret this place into "Wansborough," adding, in their ignorance of the locality, an "s" to the "n," which Wanborough never had. The A.S. Chronicle says: "An.: 715. In this year Ine and Ceolred fought at"—here three ancient copies say, "Woddesbeorge," and two "Wodnesbeorge." Ethelwerd's Chronicle says:—"An.: 715. After a year Ina and Ceolred fought against those who opposed them in arms at Wothnesbeorge." The "th" is a mistake of the scribe easily accounted for. In A.S. "th" and "d" are so much alike that they are frequently used one for the other in ancient MSS.

Florence of Worcester, writes:—"A.D. 715. Ina, king of the West Saxons, and Ceolrid, king of the Mercians, fought a battle at a place called Wodnesbeorg." Henry of Huntingdon, who wrote his chronicle about 1135, says:—"A.D. 715. There was a battle between Ina, in the twenty-sixth year of his reign, and Ceolrid king of Mercia, the son of Ethelred, near Wonebirih, where the slaughter was so great on both sides that it is difficult to say who sustained the severest loss. The year following Ceolrid departed this life, and was

buried at Lichfield." "Wonebirih" is certainly more like "Wenbeorg" than "Wodnesbeorg," and Henry's evidence may be said to favour Wanborough; but the evidence of the other chronicles in favour of "Wodnesbeorg" would appear to be overwhelming.

Ina was the king of the West Saxons who first acknowledged the Welshman as a man and a citizen free to hold land. Ceolred was king of the Mercians. The battle between these rivals might have been fought in either kingdom; but, as Ceolred was beaten (and, dying soon afterwards, was buried at Lichfield), it would seem that Ina was the stronger, and more likely to be the invader of Mercia, in which Wednesbury was situate.

Mr. W. H. Duignan has further discussed the question whether there was any other "Wodnesbeorg" which might have been the scene of either or both battles. He says:—"There was a place of that name within the manor of Alton, Hampshire, as appears by the will of Ceolwin in 905, printed in Thorpe's Diplomatarium Anglicum, 492. It is mentioned as a mere boundary, and does not appear to have been a town, hamlet, or inhabited place. The will, describing the place bequeathed, says (translated into modern English):—'The boundaries of this land at Aweltune (Alton), are: First, from the westmost spring right up to the old highway to the west of Wodnes beorge; then to a stone at Charlcomb's head,' etc., etc. The proper translation of 'Wodnes beorge' is 'Woden's hill.' But (showing how an error, once creeping into history, is adopted by writer after writer), Thorpe, an accomplished Anglo-Saxon scholar, actually translates it into 'Wanborough, though Wanborough, the only Wanborough in England, lies in another county, and forty miles from Alton. This 'Wodnes beorge' has entirely disappeared, and no subsequent trace of it is to be found on map, or in record. Alton, in 592, was within the kingdom of the South Saxons, and it is more unlikely that the Britons then fought Ceawlin there, than even at Wanborough. It is still more unlikely to have been the scene of the battle of 715, as Ina and Ceolred could have had no object in fighting each other in another king's dominions, even if permitted; and Ceolred would have been very rash to court a battle nearly a hundred miles out of his own territory. Crida founded the kingdom of Mercia about 586, and as the Britons could only be driven slowly before the Saxons, nothing is more likely than that they (the Britons) held Wednesbury in 592; but they must, by that date, have been driven far north, and somewhat west, of Wanborough.

"Matthew of Westminster, who wrote about 1370, speaks of both battles as being fought at 'Wodnesbirch.' He wrote in Latin, and perhaps knew little of Anglo-Saxon. The mistake in the terminal is not surprising; but the 'Wodnes' is clear."

Conclusively these two battles were both fought at Wednesbury, notwithstanding that the great historians have fixed them at Wanborough, Wimbledon, and other places further south than Staffordshire.

IX.—WEDNESBURY FORTIFIED BY PRINCESS ETHELFLEDA.

The Saxon settlement of this country had no sooner been effectuated than the Danish irruption set in. It was in the year Lichfield was erected into an archbishopric by Offa, King of Mercia, that the Danes first appeared on the English coasts (A.D. 787).

Alfred's life-long struggles with the Danes are a matter of history. This great King had ascended the throne after a series of disasters to the Saxon arms. The peace of Wedmore in 878 divided the kingdom between Saxon and Dane; the dividing line ran from London to Chester, through Shrewsbury, the Danes agreeing to keep east of that boundary. As they disregarded their treaty obligations, thirty years of constant turmoil ensued, in which Wednesbury and the whole of the Staffordshire side of Mercia were often involved. (Mercia was first divided into counties during this period—"Staffordshire" therefore dates from 876).

Mercian interests were almost predominant in the newly-formed kingdom of united England. Alfred married a Mercian wife, and his sister, Elswitha, was the wife of Burhred, King of Mercia, who was eventually driven from his throne after twenty years of conflict with the Danish invaders.

The Danes had made their way into the Midlands both up the Severn and up the Trent. They had contrived to bring their flotillas up the Tame itself, at least some distance. And when they permanently settled in the heart of England, their influence on the locality became more marked.

Neighbouring places possess names of Danish origin—as Clent, which signifies "a crag." On the Delves at Wednesbury there were excavations known as Dane-shafts; they were excavations made by the Danes in their search for metals, after they had become a settled people here ("Olden Wednesbury," p.22).

Beete Jukes, in his geological survey of the South Staffordshire coalfield (1859), does not fail to notice that on "Delves Green are many old pits in the lower coal measures, from which the blue-flats ironstone had formerly been got." As to the date of the getting, this eminent authority ventures no opinion.

The Delves is an outlying heath—a remnant of that encircling boundary of free and unappropriated (or "common") land which girdled Wednesbury when it was first settled by its Saxon founders. A fanciful derivation of its name connects it with that of Delve, the servant of the god Thor. But more probably it was derived from the Saxon "delfan" to dig, a form of which is seen in "dell" and "dale."

In 901 Alfred the Great was succeeded by his eldest son, Edward the Elder, who had to combat other influences besides Danish aggressions and Welsh invasions. His cousin Ethelwulf, son of Alfred's elder brother Ethelred, allied himself with the Danes, and aspired to the English throne.

In overcoming this formidable combination Edward the Elder received the greatest assistance from his sister, Ethelfleda, whose husband was Ethelred, Earl of Mercia. Much fighting, burning, and plundering took place, in which this history is not directly concerned; but in all that concerns Mercia Ethelfleda took a prominent part. As to Ethelred, he had been rewarded by Alfred, for his previous loyal services, with the Princess Ethelfleda's hand and fortune.

Nine years Ethelred and Ethelfleda fought incessantly to rid Mercia of Danish aggression; in the course of which Ethelwulf, the pretender, was slain. In 910, says the Anglo-Saxon Chronicle, "the Angles and the Danes fought at Teottenhale (Tettenhall)," on the 5th day of August, and "the Angles gained the victory." The Danes were returning with rich spoils from a raid in the west when this defeat overtook them. To avenge the disaster the Danes came from the north in the following year (911), and on exactly the same day of the month encountered their opponents very near the previous battle ground; a fact which seems to indicate the strategic importance of the locality. This second engagement took place, according to Fabius Ethelwerd, at Wodensfield (Wednesfield), three Danish chieftains falling in the conflict. In support of this it is said that lows, or burial grounds of great warriors, have been found at Wednesfield and at Wrottesley.

Harwood's revised "Erdeswick's Staffordshire" (1820) contains the following in the Preface (p. xii):—"In 911, at Wednesfield, Edward the Elder defeated the Danes in a battle, in which two of their kings, two earls, and nine other chiefs were slain; memorials of it are to be seen at South-Low-field; in North-Low-field the barrow has been levelled."

In 912 Earl Ethelred died, but, thanks to him and his wife, Edward was now secure on the throne of England. For eight years longer Ethelfleda continued her active and vigorous support of the English cause. Although the Danes had settled in many places on this side of the Watling Street boundary, it was now as peaceable citizens, overawed by the determined policy of Ethelfleda. She became known as Lady of the Marchlands, ruling Mercia to the admiration of the English and the fear of her foes.

To secure Mercia against future molestation on the part of the Danes, and also from fear of Welsh invasions from the west, Ethelfleda erected a number of fortresses. Besides serving as fortified posts, these strongholds had a commercial use. They became the seats of market towns and trading stations, laws being made (A.D. 925) to forbid all bargaining outside their walls, where contracts could not be enforced.

Ethelfleda's chief concern was to provide a base of defence. On one side was Wales, or North Wales, as it was called to distinguish it from West Wales (now Corn-Wales). Wales at that time advanced towards Mercia as far as Monmouthshire, Herefordshire, Shropshire, Cheshire, and partly into Worcestershire and Gloucestershire. Then on the other side was the Dane-law, or country of the Danes, occupying the east of England. While King Edward built castles at Hertford and at Witham in the east, Ethelfleda erected five strongholds against their western enemy.

These five castles were Bridgnorth, Tamworth, Stafford, and Warwick, with Wednesbury in the centre of the quadrilateral formed by the other four. Bridgnorth had long been a Danish stronghold; Tamworth had been King Offa's capital, containing both a palace and a mint; Stafford and Warwick had been important enough to give their names respectively to two newly-formed shires in 876; and Wednesbury had been of some importance as a religious (Woden-worshipping) centre, and also as a "burh." Eyton's "Staffordshire Domesday," p. 20, says "Ethelfleda's castles were usually combined with burghs."

These castles of Ethelfleda were an advance on the previous Saxon fortifications, although they were not fortresses of solid stone masonry. They were built of heavy timbers on plinths, or foundations of stone; earthwork ramparts and ditches of deep water added to their defensive strength.

Nightingale's "Beauties of England and Wales," published in 1813, says of Wednesbury Church—"Around the churchyard is a large graff, in which the vestiges of the ancient fort may be distinctly traced."

Harwood's "Staffordshire," pp. 293-4, says that Wednesbury is "more properly Wodensburgh; and, like Wodensfield, or Wednesfield, derives its name from Woden, the Saxon god of battle. . . . In the time of the Mercians it had a castle, fortified by Adelfleda, the governess of the Mercian kingdom. Its vestiges are visible near the churchyard." This was written by an acknowledged authority in 1820.

Some doubt has been thrown on the existence of a castle at Wednesbury. No traces of it can at the present time be discovered in the foundations of the old church. But for the matter of that no Saxon remains can be traced in the existing ruins of Stafford Castle. The nature of their structure perfectly accounts for this. Kemble, in his "Saxons in England," Vol. II., gives an account of the towns of that period, and in enumerating those which rose to eminence at the close of the Danish wars, says that the duchess Æthelfled erected the following fortresses:—"In 910, the burh at Bremesbyrig; in 912, those at Scargate and Bridgnorth; in 913, those at Tamworth and Stafford; in 914, those at Eddisbury and Warwick; in 915, the fortresses of Cherbury, Warborough, and Runcorn; in 917 she took the fortified town of Derby; and in 918 Leicester," etc., etc.,

Wednesbury Castle is not mentioned. The Warborough (Weardbyrig) is said to be in Oxfordshire, and the only other name approximating to Wednesbury is Eddisbury (Eadesbyrig) (Chron. 914), which Kemble suggests as being Eddisbury, near Tarporley, in Cheshire. Bremesbyrig is said to be Bromsgrove.

Again, Shaw, in his "History of Staffordshire," V. 2, p. 83, says Wednesbury is recorded "as having been fortified by Ethelfleda, Lady of the Mercians, against the Danes, in the year 914," and he quotes Roger of Hoveden as an authority. Roger says, under the year 911, that Ethelfleda "founded the city which is called Eadesbyrig." Commenting on this, Mr. W. H. Duignan also claims Eadesbyrig as Eddisbury, and not as Wednesbury.

Dr. Plot's history of the county, written in 1686, says of Wednesbury that "the renowned Egelfleda, who governed the kingdom of Mercia with so good conduct, fortify'd this Town against the Danes who infested her Nation." All the county historians since that date have repeated the statement relative to the erection of a castle at Wednesbury.

Another eminent authority, to wit, Sharon Turner, says, in his "Anglo-Saxons," that "Wedesborough Castle was built to co-erce the Welch on the west." This spelling of the name approaches to Wednesbury nearer than it does to Eddisbury. Camden's spelling of Wednesbury, in 1586, is "Weadesburg." And lastly, as another argument in favour of Wednesbury being the favoured site, is the indisputable fact that the manor was "of the ancient demesne of the crown," as recorded by Domesday Book in 1086.

The career of Ethelfleda was an eventful one. When Owen, a Welsh sub-king, invaded Mercia, she drove him out, pursued him, and took the town of Brecknock by storm. He escaped, fled to the Dane-law for protection and assistance, but the vigorous Ethelfleda followed him up to Derby. She stormed Derby, although with heavy loss to the English, took it, but not Owen, who killed himself rather than fall into the hands of this determined princess.

Meanwhile King Edward was gaining successes in the east, and not only brought the Danes to subjection, but won many pagans to Christianity.

Ethelfleda, on her part, gained possession of Leicester, where the Danish garrison surrendered to her prowess. The Danes of York soon followed this example; but this was the last success of her life. She died at Tamworth on the 12th of June, 920.

The death of Ethelfleda was a serious blow to King Edward. Yet it had the effect of consolidating his kingdom, for the daughter whom Ethelfleda left did not succeed to her power, and Mercia became part of the English kingdom.

The Lady of the Mercians was a most remarkable woman. She seemed to have inherited many of the great characteristics of her august father, Alfred the Great. In both warfare and statecraft she had all the attributes of a man. When her husband died, she assumed the control of his earldom, and became a closer companion and a more intimate counsellor to her royal brother. To her was confided the education of her nephew Athelstan; and at Tamworth he learnt from her both statesmanship and the art of war. Saxon England owed much to this able princess.

X.—THE CLOSE OF THE SAXON PERIOD.

The earliest documentary allusion to Wednesbury which has never been disputed, is on the foundation deed of Burton Abbey, as confirmed by King Ethelred. The date is 1004, and the spelling is "Wodnesbyri."

The Earl of Mercia, in the reign of Ethelred the Unready, was Wulfric Spott. In 1002 he founded a Benedictine Abbey at Burton, dedicated to the Virgin, and to St. Modwen, an Irish nun and anchoress who, nearly two centuries previously, had settled on an island in the Trent, opposite to Burton. It has been said that this foundation was an act of expiation and remorse for the part Wulfric had played in the massacre of the Danes that year (1002). But it is more than probable that his deadly rival, the base Edric Streone, who ousted him from his Earldom, was the actual instigator of this treachery. Wulfric was a relative of Ethelred, and in the end was slain fighting against the Danes at Ipswich, in 1010.

For five centuries the history of Burton was the history of the Abbey, whose abbot ruled the town. The estates with which Wulfric endowed the foundation were of enormous extent, running into twenty-six townships in Staffordshire, besides lands in Derbyshire and Warwickshire. The earl's charter needed the confirmation of the King to make it valid. Anciently, a man held his land only "for a day," and at his death it again became "folcland" or common land. Gradually a right to devise grew up with the consent of the King and his Witan; "folcland" (folk-land) was converted into "bocland" (book-land) by charter. This transaction of Wulfric was witnessed in a confirmation dated 1004 by the King and his five sons, two archbishops, ten bishops, twelve abbots, three dukes, and twenty thanes. The right to devise land lapsed at the Conquest, being inconsistent with feudal law; it, however, gradually came into force again till all great landed estates became hereditary.

This ancient charter gave two hides (say 240 acres) of land in Wednesbury to the abbey of "Byrton." Other strange spellings of local proper names in this document are "Walesho" for Walsall (it is "Waleshale" in the second indorsement); "Gageleage" for Gailey; "Deorlafestun" for Darlaston (the more ancient place of this name, near to Stone); "Wilinhale" for Willenhall; and the second indorsement evidently alludes to Priestfield in Wolverhampton, in the item bequeathed as "Priests' land of Wulfrenehampton 8 hides."

We now approach the Norman Conquest, which produced that famous land register of William I., known as the Domesday Book. Wednesbury appears fully described in that ancient roll. But first must be considered the closing scenes in the history of Mercia, in which that of Wednesbury was more or less involved.

Harwood's "Survey of Staffordshire" (p. xiii) says that Ethelfleda had large possessions in this, one of the seventeen counties which comprised Mercia; and that Saxon castles existed at Wednesbury, Tamworth, Dudley, Kingston Hill, near Stafford, and in Beaudesert Park. The royal possessions of Ethelfleda, of which Wednesbury was part, seemed to have reverted to the crown, while her high office passed to Leofric, who became Earl of Mercia, and whose wife was the renowned Godiva of Coventry; afterwards to their son Algar, who was father of Earl Edwin—a Saxon prince slain by William the Conqueror, under circumstances now to be related.

Leofric, Earl of Mercia, died at Bromley, Staffs., on 31st August, 1057; his wife, the well-remembered Godiva, surviving the Norman Conquest of 1066 by a few years.

Their son, and successor in the Earldom of Mercia, Algar, had in 1055 formed a treasonable alliance with North Wales, and gained a signal success against the English. He died in seclusion about 1062, still an opponent to Harold at the court of Edward the Confessor. His two sons, Edwin and Morcar, succeeded, and the latter was promoted to the forfeited earldom of Tostig in Northumbria.

Edwin of Mercia was present at the dedication of Westminster Abbey, 28th December, 1065; he also witnessed the death of the Confessor, 5th January, 1066.

That the two brother earls were friends of Harold may be inferred from the fact that they were deputed to watch the north on his behalf against Tostig. They were defeated, however, at Fulford, five days before the battle of Stamford Bridge (1066).

When William the Norman landed in the south he did not find among his opponents any of the forces of the Mercian earls, who in January, 1067, formally tendered their submission to the Conqueror. Consequently there was as yet nothing to bring war into Staffordshire.

In the month of March following the two earls accompanied William into Normandy, but whether as honoured guests, or as captive hostages, it would be difficult to hazard a guess with any confidence.

In 1068 Edwin, being refused the hand of one of William's daughters, retired with Morcar to his province, and armed his vassals. The Conqueror thereupon commenced the erection of Warwick Castle; but he did not enter Staffordshire, and ultimately peace was made between the King and the two earls.

It was in 1069 that, according to Ordericus, the only trustworthy chronicler of the period, trouble began to overtake Staffordshire, of which the said historian was a native. In that year there was an insurrection in the county as formidable as any which characterised that fateful period. When William the Conqueror marched into Staffordshire, he found nothing but anarchy; the people, armed and unarmed, split into factions; impiety rampant, and discipline, whether civil or religious, set at nought. Such was the lamentable condition in and around Wednesbury at this period of national distraction. Stafford town was the chief centre of the disturbances. Throughout the county slaughters and evictions devastated the entire region for the next sixteen years—certainly to the time of the compilation of the Domesday Book.

In the winter of 1070 William again marched into Staffordshire, when he built the castle at Stafford, whereby to hold more firmly Edwin's escheated earldom of Mercia; for this Saxon prince seems to have been deeply concerned in these insurrections. As to Morcar, he had openly joined Hereward the Wake in the Isle of Ely.

Upon another outbreak in Staffordshire ensuing, in the course of which William's castle at Stafford was destroyed, vengeance fell heavily upon all who were implicated. Edwin was assassinated, it is believed by William's orders; and the county was laid waste. Of the earldom of Mercia—of which little more will be heard—the King kept the greater share; smaller portions were, however, given to Norman favourites. The Norman barons introduced into this district will be named in a later chapter.

It is clear that the desolation of Staffordshire had not passed away fourteen years later, for the Domesday Book details numerous "mansiones vastæ" (empty houses) and "terræ vastæ" (unoccupied estates). Depopulation of the county had been brought about by the slaughter of the inhabitants, or their emigration to other parts of the country; the cause of which may be attributed to the savagery of the Conqueror's policy, the patriotism of the Saxon inhabitants, or more probably, according to Eyton, to the internecine feuds of antagonistic races.

The Domesday Book shows the Saxon possessions of every manor or estate. From this it is evident that Wednesbury manor, if at any time it had belonged entirely to the Earls of Mercia, as apparently it did to Wulfric, had now passed into the hands of the King altogether. While the Domesday "tenant in capite" possessing Alrewas is set down as Earl Algar ("Algar Comes"), and the tenant in chief of Bromley is given as Harold (not recognised as "King," but as "Heraldus Comes"), "Wadnesberie cum appendiciis" is shown to have been in the holding of Edward the Confessor ("Rex Edwardus"), from whom it now passed to the Conqueror ("Rex Willelmus"), as had also the other two manors named. Wednesbury is shown to be of the old dominions of the crown ("vetus dominicum coronæ"), while Alrewas and King's Bromley were among the estates forfeited by those who took sides with Harold against William; these are classified under "Terræ Regis," and not with the demesne lands under "Terræ Edwardi Regis." All of them, and many other Mercian estates, became "Terræ Regis Willielmi." In all the Hundred of Offlow, only Bescot, Willenhall, Wigton in Tamworth, and Wednesbury, with its members, Bloxwich and Shelfield, are set down as formerly belonging to the Sovereign, Edward the Confessor.

XI.—NORMAN WEDNESBURY, DESCRIBED IN 1086.

From the Norman invasion in 1066, till its complete subjugation in 1070, this midland district was in a state of mild but chronic insurrection. Till 1068 no Norman had passed the Humber, and but few had penetrated so far north as this district of Mercia. In that year, however, the Norman monarch made a rapid conquest of Warwick, Leicester, and Derby, and may then have touched upon this town and its fortifications. If it were fortunate enough to have escaped on this occasion, the chances are that it was in the following year (1069) that the region around Wednesbury felt the full weight of the Conqueror's vengeance, when he defeated the Welsh Borderers under the Saxon patriot Edric the Forester, near Stafford, and followed up this victory by laying waste all the surrounding territory.

A sweeping displacement of the original landowners then took place, and Robert de Toenei, standard-bearer of Normandy, was instated as the new territorial governor of the county; he took upon himself a new name from his castle of Statford (Stafford). The total population of the county of Stafford, over which this noble was put to rule, was but 3,178, all told.

In 1086 the Conqueror ordered the compilation of Domesday Book. This was a great national land register, in which the King could see, not only the territorial extent of his new dominions, but exactly the nature of them, and the tenures under which they were held; as also the former possessors under the Saxon monarchs. William's commissioners set down every detail necessary for the purposes of a feudal system of government.

Staffordshire seems to have been in the same circuit with Warwickshire and Oxfordshire, as the same commissioners surveyed these three counties.

Staffordshire was divided into the old Saxon divisions called Hundreds, for the administration of the law. It was at this time, also parcelled out into fiefs, or feuds, or holdings, belonging to various territorial lords. Among the more important of these great feudal landowners in Staffordshire were:—The King, the Bishop of Chester; Westminster Abbey; Burton Abbey; Abbey of St. Remigius at Rheims, in France (holding Lapley and Wheaton Aston); the Collegiate Churches of Stafford and of Wolverhampton; Roger, Earl of Shrewsbury; Hugh de Montgomery, Earl of Arundel; Henry de Ferrers (Chartley); Robert de Toenei (Stafford); William fitz Ansculf (Dudley); and others. The barony of Dudley comprised 25 lordships in this vicinity. Mercia had now ceased to exist, and its very name became lost. Norman nobles now held the bulk of it.

The Bishop of Chester held very extensive territories in Staffordshire. His church had held these lands before the Conquest, and the Bishop was, in fact, the greatest forest landlord in Staffordshire, his holdings including 4,320 acres at Brewood, 11,520 at Eccleshall, and 93,740 at Lichfield. Though less concentrated, the Bishop's woods in this county were in extent more than double those of the King himself. (See "Records of Smethwick," p. 19).

At that time Cannock Forest (called "Chenet" in Domesday) was a Royal Chase of 34,560 acres, exclusive of 8,640 acres outlying at Rugeley. This manor of the King's was afterwards increased at the expense of the Bishop's Woods, but to the contraction of Offlow Hundred.

William the Conqueror's holdings (terra regis) in Staffordshire may be divided into three classes—

First, as King, he held all the old estates which had belonged to Edward the Confessor, and his other Saxon predecessors on the throne, and which were termed Vetus Dominicum Coronæ, included in which were the manors of Wednesbury, Bilston, Willenhall, Tettenhall, and others.

Secondly, as Earl, he acquired the estates escheated from Edwin, the late Earl of Mercia; included in these were part of the burgh of Stafford, the manors of Cannock, King's Bromley, and some twenty other manors.

And, thirdly, certain wastes, from which Saxon thanes had been evicted, were forfeited to the crown.

The Domesday entry relating to Wednesbury may be substantially translated as follows:—

"The King retains Wadnesberie and its appurtenances. It contains three hides. The arable land is nine carucates; one in demesne, and one servant and sixteen villeins, and eleven borderers have seven carucates. There is a Mill of two shillings rent, and one acre of Meadow; also a Wood, two miles in length, and one in breadth."

The "appurtenances" referred to are Bloxwich and Shelfield, now included within the boundaries of Walsall.

Bloxwich, or "Blocheswic," as it was written by the surveyors of 1086, is set down as a member of Wednesbury, owing, says Eyton, to the wasted condition and obscurity of Walsall. On the revival of Walsall, Bloxwich afterwards became a member, manorially and parochially, of Walsall; thus transferring some 3,000 acres from Wednesbury to Walsall.

Shelfield, or "Scelfeld," is set down in Domesday Book as a member of the Manor of Wednesbury, although it is more remote than even Bloxwich. It is now a township of Walsall-Foreign. At Domesday period it represented 985 acres, now comprised in the the chapelry of Walsall Wood.

It is clear, therefore, that since the year 1086 Wednesbury has lost no less than 3,985 acres. In this connection the following points have a significant bearing:—The boundaries of modern Wednesbury are penetrated zigzag fashion by those of the surrounding parishes. Darlaston had no independent existence at Domesday, and its line of division between Wednesbury is of an extremely artificial character. Wednesbury Oak is now in Tipton parish; and Harvills Hawthorn, named after the Heronvilles, lords of Wednesbury, is in West Bromwich parish. The Hundred of Offlow in 1086 included Burton, Tamworth, and Edingale.

The "demesne" was the home farm, the lord's own lands, which he tilled himself by the aid of his villeins and theows, or slaves; or let out for a money rent if that arrangement suited better, as it might do, if he possessed more than one manor. Nothing is said of the Steward of the Manor ("Prepositus") living on the lord's demesne lands.

The rest of the manor was held in villeinage; the "villeins" rendering certain services in return for the land they held for the lord. Although they held by the lord's will, their holdings were hereditary, the son succeeding to the father on the payment of a fine or "heriot." The villeins were the highest class of villagers, the chief part of the population of the "vill" or manor.

Though actually serfs, as we now understand the term, they formed the jury at the Halimote, or manorial court; they could make wills, and were nearly free-men, except for the services they were bound to render as rent due for their holdings. They were bound to work so many days in each week for the lord of the manor; as in reaping, ploughing, and other services. Then their boon-work ("precariæ") was sometimes part of this, and sometimes extra to it—customs differed in different parts of the country. In some cases, too, money payments had also to be made to the lord; as rent or gafol, hearth-penny, etc. There were other servile customs; but the days on which they were not required to work on the lord's domain they employed in the cultivation of their own holdings.

The "borderers," bordarii, or cottiers (cottagers) were an inferior class to the villeins. Their holdings were the open lands outside the village, and sometimes ranged in size from one to ten acres, according to the quality of the soil. Their services to the lord were more trivial and casual than those of the villein. A "cotarius" or cottager not only had no voice in the deliberations of the manorial court, he put no oxen into the village plough-team; and this was an important considera-tion. The amount of open and waste land occupied by a borderer extended beyond the usual acre if the nature of it were poor and unproductive.

The servus, or slave, or theowe was one whose life was at the absolute disposal of his lord; he was a mere chattel. He had no place in the courts, no rights of any kind. Slavery among the Saxons was hereditary; or a person became a slave through crime or debt.

The "Mill" was an important institution in those days. Every man in the place was com-pelled to have his corn ground in the lord's mill; the lord, of course, taking toll upon it. In the earliest Saxon communities the only houses of any importance in a village were—first the manor house of the lord, then the priest's house, and thirdly the miller's house. The rest of the village would consist for the most part of abodes built of wattles, smeared inside and out with mud or clay; the whole close clustering round the church. The mill was, of course, a water-mill at that period. Situated on the side of the Tame, it was of importance to the life of the community dwell-ing in Wednesbury, and a source of revenue to the lord; the miller borrowed his conse-quence from this.

Mills—their number and their value—are the very best test to apply to ascertain the con-dition of a locality at this period. Mill-value is most significant of population, too. Now in all Staffordshire there were found only sixty-four mills, and the annual value of most of them ranged from one shilling to five shillings. Yet a county like Dorset, with less than a quarter of the acreage of Stafford, possessed 272 mills, some of them valued as high as 25 shillings a year.

The "two shillings rent" at which Wednes-bury mill was valued was then a considerable sum, when so little money was used, and so few coins passed from hand to hand.

After the miller, the next most important craftsmen were the blacksmith and the car-penter. It was the duty of the former to keep in repair the ploughs and other farming implements of the community; while the lat-ter had all the woodwork under his charge. These two were really communal officers, work-ing for the whole community.

Scant as the population of Wednesbury was, it doubtless included such ordinary craftsmen as a smith ("faber") and a mason ("cement-arius").

No direct mention is made in this Wednes-bury return of a single freeholder ("socman"), afterwards known by the name of franklin, and later still as a yeoman. Nor is anything said of a parish priest ("presbyter"), a point noted in "Religious Wednesbury," p. 22.

With regard to the population of England at that time, it has been worked out that there was but one labourer in proportion to every 167 acres registered in Domesday Book; or, worse still, one in proportion to 255 acres of actual surface. But it must be borne in mind that out of the 468,004 acres registered, 319,538 acres, or about three-fourths of the whole, were woods and forests. To the residue of corn and meadow land there would be one labourer to 53 acres; or, again, confining our comparison to lands actually ploughed, namely, 119,100 acres, the single labourer correlates with 42 acres.

Of the Woodlands, it may be said that ordinarily they were of little profit, save for the purposes of exclusive chase or warren; and as hunting grounds they were strictly guarded by the nobles. Under certain con-ditions they also provided pannage, that is, swine food, consisting of the mast of oak and beech.

"Wednesbury Wood," described as two miles long and one mile in breadth, probably com-menced at Old Park and stretched towards Cannock.

The cultivated lands were arranged for a rotation of crops in three divisions, one divi-sion being fallowed each year in its turn. The holding of a villein did not lie all together, but was scattered about in various parts of the three fields; this was to obviate one man holding all the best land, and another all the inferior soil. Each man generally held about thirty acres, ten in each field; this portion was called a "virgate," or a "yardland." Four virgates, or about 120 acres, made a "hide" of land, which, when taxed for scutage, or main-tenance of a Knight, became known as a "Knight's fee." But this acreage was not constant, varying in different parts of the land, according to its accessibility, or the fertility of the soil.

The term "carucate" means the "carved" or ploughed-land. It was generally identical with the hide of 120 acres, and was seldom less than 100 acres. It was really the amount cul-tivable each year by a full ox team of eight beasts. The holding of a villein might not be less than half a virgate, which was designated a "bovate" ("bos," an ox), because each bovate had to contribute one ox to make up the full team of eight necessary for the cultiva-tion of the carucate, or hide, of arable land.

None of the village lands were then cut up into fields enclosed with hedges. The cultiva-ted land were open fields, and presented some-what the appearance of modern allotment gar-dens; the dividing line between the holdings consisted of turf balks or field-paths; there were no enclosures of any kind. The strip of each villein or cottar was about an acre in extent. It was so arranged for convenience of ploughing. Many of our land measure-ments now in use were derived from these primitive arrangements. Thus, a "furlong" is simply "furrow-long"; in the "rood" there were as many furrows as could be made in the breadth of a "rod" (or ox-goad); and four of these rods made up the "acre" or field.

The Wednesbury field-names preserved from this ancient system of tillage to the present time in the Parish TitheTerrier are The "Reding (or Ridding) Field," "Church Field," "Monway Field," "Kingshill Field," and "Mesty Croft." More significant still is a field-name which points directly to the villeinage tenure of ancient Wednesbury; there is a field in this parish which in the Wednesbury Tithe Book is named "The Ten Days Work Piece." It now contains 8 acres 3 roods 4 perches; and its naming probably belongs to the later period of decaying villeinage, when the holder of it had to render to the lord of the manor ten days' farm work in each year as quittance.

. . . .

It has been noted that two large slices of modern Walsall—Bloxwich and Shelfield—were anciently included within the manor of Wednesbury.

Although the estate of Walsall is known to have existed long before the Norman Conquest,

the name of Walsall is not mentioned in Domesday Book. It is known, for instance, that the Lady Wulfruna had designed to bestow her estate of Walsall upon her intended monastery of Hampton—now Wulfrun-Hampton, or Wolverhampton—but that it had now merged into the estates of the King.

But if Walsall is not named in Domesday, Bescot figures therein, and takes its place.

The manor of Bescot (Bresmundescote) is stated to have been of the "old dominions of the crown," and to have contained much "waste." This latter statement seems to tell us in a vague sort of way all that can be known—or unknown—of Walsall at that time.

It would therefore seem that Bescot had by the year 1086 absorbed the whole of Walsall; yet at the present day Walsall, the parochial area of wihch is 7,882 acres, now includes not only Bescot but two other estates which at that period were members of the Manor of Wednesbury; to wit, Bloxwich and Shelfield.

XII.—SIR RALPH BOTEREL, LORD OF WEDNESBURY (1164).

Very little is known of Wednesbury during the period immediately following the Norman Conquest.

In the reign of Henry I. Staffordshire was ravaged by Robert de Belesme, Earl of Alencon and Shrewsbury, and son of Roger of Montgomery, in favour of Curthose. This resulted in a number of changes in the ownership of many properties, but Wednesbury remained a royal manor still.

In the reign of Stephen there were again stirring times in this locality, considerable fighting taking place around Dudley Castle during the Civil Wars of Matilda. This has been described in "A History of West Bromwich," pp. 7 and 8.

Sampson Erdeswick, the county historian, writing his "View of Staffordshire" in 1593, says:—

"Tame being past Bilston, somewhat further north-eastward takes its course to Wednesbury, which at the Conquest was the antient demesne of the Crown; but by the King was afterwards given, about Henry the Second's time, to the ancestors of William Heronville, in exchange for the town of Stuntsfield, which is in Oxfordshire, and is now parcel of the honour of Woodstock," etc.

More recent research has disclosed the name of this ancestor of the Heronvilles. It was Ralph Boterel, a brave and loyal knight, who held the manor of Stonesfield in Oxfordshire, and whose transference to the manor of Wednesbury in Staffordshire, in the year 1164, is associated with one of the most romantic episodes in English history.

It would appear that Henry II. resided very much at Woodstock. The same place had been a favourite residence of the Norman monarch Henry I., who built himself a new palace in

the vicinity of his new park at Woodstock. This park he "had fraught with all kinds of strange beasts, wherein he much delighted, as lions, leopards, lynxes, camels, porcupines, and the like." But the second Henry did not spend so much of his time at Woodstock because he had any particular fancy for strange beasts. He certainly built a very substantial Park Wall round Woodstock, at an expenditure of the enormous sum (for those days) of £30. But this was a measure of precaution; not to keep in wild animals—but to keep out prying eyes. Who has not heard of the romantic traditions connected with the sylvan shades of Woodstock Bower? Who has not read of the Herefordshire beauty, Rosamond de Clifford, or, as she is better known, the Fair Rosamond? To carry on his amours with this "most sightly maiden" Henry II. contrived wondrous labyrinths, and many other strange devices to guard against surprise.

To complete his plans it would appear to have been necessary for the King to acquire the neighbouring manor of Stonesfield, immediately outside the walls of Woodstock. This he did by effecting an exchange with its holder, the complacent and loyal Sir Ralph Boterel, who accepted the manor of Wednesbury for it, thus enabling the gratified monarch to secure greater privacy for carrying on his amours.

The labyrinth of Woodstock had most likely existed before Rosamond's time, for in the Middle Ages all Pleasaunces and Gardens were contrived with this adjunct. There is indisputable evidence that "Rosamond's Chamber" was distinct from Woodstock Palace, yet belonging to its domain, being a building situate beyond the Park wall, and according to credible testimony approached by a tunnel under the said wall. Brompton says that one day Queen

Eleanor saw the King walking in the Pleasaunce of Woodstock, with the end of a ball of floss silk attached to his spur. Coming near him unperceived, she took up the ball, and the King walking on the silk unwound, and thus the Queen traced him to a thicket in the labyrinth of the park, where he disappeared.

Keeping the matter secret, after the King had gone on a distant journey, Eleanor searched the thicket, and came on a low door cunningly concealed. This she had forced open, and found it the entrance to a subterranean path, which led out at a distance to a sylvan lodge in the most retired part of the adjacent forest.

The jealous Queen came suddenly upon her rival, the Fair Rosamond Clifford, who was seated in her bower, intent on her embroidery frame.

Soon after this discovery, the "Fair Ladye' became a nun at Godstow, living a life of penitence for many years.

It is certain that Henry II. knew her before he married his Queen; and it is further believed he even married her. This would have made his children by Queen Eleanor bastards, and such he is said to have called them in his anger. Anyway they repeatedly rebelled against him, and the close of his reign was marked by a bitter feeling between the royal father and his sons.

From the romantic side of this episode we now turn to the commercial, or, more properly speaking, to the feudal aspect of it. Wednesbury thus ceased in 1164 to be of the royal demesne; for Boterel seems to have held it as a fief under his former lord paramount, a higher noble named D'Oyly, whose barony was afterwards inherited by the Earl of Warwick. It may be remarked, however, that D'Oyly held his lands under the great baron of Stafford ("Salt Collections," I. pp. 104, 148, 168).

But Wednesbury was worth more than Stonesfield. So to balance matters it was arranged that Ralph Boterel should still owe service to D'Oyly of one knight's fee for Wednesbury; and also pay to the Crown a fee-farm rent of £1 per annum for the said Manor of Wednesbury. Or as it is put in another form: "The King gave three parts of his Staffordshire Manor of Wednesbury to Ralph Boterel, who happened to be tenant in fee of Stonesfield, holding it as a knight's fee in the Barony of Henry D'Oyly. To Henry D'Oyly the King gave the service of Ralph Boterel and his heirs, in respect of the said fee in Wednesbury."

By the transference of Wednesbury to the barony of a noble, the King's territorial possessions within the county of Stafford, which had never been considerable, were thus further reduced.

The Great Rolls of the Exchequer, otherwise called the Pipe Rolls, inform us of this fact. These ancient national documents chiefly concern the Crown revenues, and the great diversity of sources from which the said revenues were drawn. The Domesday Book has shown us the extent of the Manor of Wednesbury. The Pipe Rolls now inform us of its value a century later. At the Christmas of 1164 the Rolls make allusion to "4 librates blanche* of Crown land in Wednesbury"—which may have been a surplus paid for the whole of Wednesbury—"paying the Crown a fee-farm rent of £1 per annum." The tenant who paid this, was evidently the first tenant who held the Manor under this new tenure, and it would seem that he did not pay the full value for it; in fact, he seems to have got the better of the Sheriff who could not ease his liability to the Crown in this matter.

The Ferm of Stafford was what was known as a blanche ferm; or what was reckoned at the Treasury in purified money; it was a term used in contradistinction to reckoning by tale, or in the ordinary and current standard of circulation. The old Exchequer plan of comparison was effected thus; to reduce a payment by tale to a blanche figure was to deduct about five per cent. value from the former.

Boterel held the Manor of Wednesbury, under Henry D'Oyly, by service of a knight's fee —a variable amount of land, ranging anywhere between one and five hundred acres of cultivated land; it was, in fact, supposed to be as much land as would suffice to maintain him, and to enable him to present himself and his retainers ready equipped for the field of battle. Each knight's fee which a baron held has been valued as an estate worth £20 a year. But money values of this kind convey no adequate idea to the modern reader.

The number of knights that had to be furnished by a great baron was specified in the infeoffment. These knights (like Boterel) in their turn held lands from the immediate tenants of the Crown, which were owned by homage, fealty, and a great variety of tenures, as well as by direct payments in money. Some tenures were merely nominal, such as a grain of cummin, or a red rose; others were of more or less value, such as a pair of white gloves, a tun of wine, a gold spur, or a silver salver; and others by such service as holding the lord's stirrup, keeping a pack of hounds, etc., etc. The Manor of Bescot was held by tenure grand sergeantry, that is, on condition of the providing the King with some trifling matter towards his wars. The manor of Hooknorton—held along with Wednesbury, to which reference will presently be made—was held 12 Edward I. by Ela, Countess of Warwick, by the sergeantry of carving at the King's table on his birthday, "and she was to have the knife the King then uses." The lands of these knights

*That is "£4 white" money, or in silver; which was the Tower pound in use at that time. From the Conquest to 18 Henry VIII. the money "pound" was an actual pound of silver (½oz. less than the pound troy), which maintained its standard well till 28 Edward I. It was divided into twenty shillings, and each shilling into twelve pennies (of silver), of the weight of 24 grains. The coin in use at this time in Staffordshire was exceptionally pure.

were called "fees," and composed the barony of a crown vassal (like Ansculf). The term is also sometimes used for the rent paid to the lord for the fee.

Shortly after, when the Earl of Warwick had inherited the barony of D'Oyly, the Liber Niger Scaccarii, or Black Book of the Exchequer (the Exchequer Court took its name for the Scaccarium, or chequered cloth, which covered its table), alludes to this same transaction. Under the heading of the Barony of Robert de Stafford, the Feodary states that "Wodenesburi was the fief the Earl of Warwick, held of him by service of one Knight for 20 shillings annually to the King, the surplus of the value of the said vill."

Now it may have been that Ralph Boterel considered that he had done quite enough as a dutiful subject, when, to suit the convenience of his liege lord, he had migrated from the county of Oxford to the county of Stafford. Anyway, it is certain that he never troubled himself to pay the one pound per annum. Perhaps the King on his part had not felt disposed to enforce his claims; and, curiously enough, the Sheriff also had manipulated his accounts, year by year, without enforcing payment.

So matters remained till the year 1181, when Boterel died, and the arrears of eighteen years had accumulated. Then William de Heronville came into possession of this manor, presumably on account of having married the daughter and heiress of Boterel; for we read that "Heronville held Wadnesbury jure uxoris, of D'Oyly." In 1182 the Sheriff made Heronville liable for his predecessor's arrears, and actually charged them to him all at once. Again, we find that the Sheriff of Staffordshire "continued to ease his accounts with the Crown, of 3 librates only, as given to Heronville." The Pipe Rolls of 1183 show that Heronville "accounts for a further instalment of his arrears as Fee-farm Tenant of Wednesbury." And it seems clear that he paid the rent of £1 accruing in the current year to the Sheriff, whose due it was. Consistently with this, "the Sheriff discharges his ferm of £3 only in respect of Terræ Datæ in Wednesbury. The fourth pound he had received. It was part of his official income. The King had not given it to another."

By "Terræ Datæ" is meant lands entered on the Sheriff's accounts for the county, as having been granted away from the "Corpus Comitatus" by the King. On this basis the matter was evidently settled.

The tenure of Ralph Boterel was manifestly a good one, and he now felt himself secure in the possession of Wednesbury. He resided within his manor, and in 1166 was bold enough to trespass in the adjoining royal forest of Cannock. This appears to be the only time he was troubled by the authorities. On that occasion a Forest Justice visited with penalties "for transgression of the Forest Laws, or trespass on the King's Forest, Ralph Boterel of the Manor of Wednesbury."

This may be accepted as evidence that Wednesbury Old Park was in existence in 1166; as from a later record it seems to have been in the year 1340. It certainly merged into Cannock Forest.

Little more remains to be recorded of this romantic transaction, except to note the various spellings of the name Wednesbury as they appear in the Rolls—Wodnesberi, Wodnesberia, Wodnesbi, and Wadesburi. The name of Ralph is always rendered Radulfo or Radulphus in the Latin.

WOOD GREEN.

XIII.—WEDNESBURY PASSES TO THE HERONVILLES (1182).

1.—William de Heronville I. (1182-12 . .):—In 1182, presumably on the death of Boterel, William de Heronville, a Norman knight who had evidently married Boterel's daughter and heiress, succeeded to, by right of his wife, the manor of Wednesbury.

In 1183 the new lord of the manor commenced to pay off the arrears of the preceding eighteen years by annual instalments. The Sheriff of Staffordshire seems to have made a determined attempt to rectify his accounts in the matter of this £1 reserved rent belonging to the Crown Estates within his county.

The full fiscal value of Wednesbury was unmistakably £4, and the Great Pipe Rolls record the various payments made unbrokenly by William de Heroville (or Herovilla) from 1189 to 1215; when for two-and-a-half years no Exchequer accounts were kept, owing to the French invasion, brought about by the barons' exasperation at the misrule of King John. The Sheriffs did not resume their functions till 1217, after the death of John, so that there is an interruption in the Pipe Rolls highly significant of the disorganised state of England at that trying period of its history.

After the accession of Henry II., when any one of the "old dominions of the Crown," either in whole or in part, was given or entrusted to a subject, it was necessary that the Sheriff should enter the gift or trust among the "Terræ datæ" of his annual account. This applied to Wednesbury. And, further, in 1186 it is observed that "three-fourths of Wednesbury," being a Crown Estate, which had been given "sine ulla servicio" (without any services), was not subject to Tallage—"tallage" being the name given to those arbitrary rather than periodical levies, which generally were assessable on all the Royal Demesnes, as well as on the King's Escheats.

As this manorial history proceeds, it will be observed that the tenants of Wednesbury claimed various privileges on account of the manor having been previously in the hands of the Sovereign.

2.—William de Heronville II. (1226-12 . .):—The William Heronville, Lord of Wednesbury in 1235-1240, who heads the pedigree printed in Bagnall's "History of Wednesbury," p. 22x, is not the first of that name, as is clear from an ancient law case, a summary of which shall now be given. Harwood's "Erdeswick's Staffordshire," p. 291, notes that Wyrley gives many evidences of the Heronville family, but no pedigree. William Wyrley, by the way, was grandson of William Wyrley, of Handsworth; he was born in Staffordshire in 1574, became an eminent antiquary amanuensis to Erdeswick, and assisted in a survey of Staffordshire churches, 1603.

Considerable light is thrown on the earlier history of this family by the Plea Rolls (Salt, Vol. IV.). In 1227, William de Heronville, and also Joan, his widow, being both dead, there was a dispute between William de Heronville and Philip de Heronville, sons of the first-named William, as to the successor to the manor of Wednesbury.

Philip stated that he was the oldest and legitimate son of William and Joan, and was born at Hooknorton, in the county of Oxford, and maintained there and elsewhere by Joan for a long time, and until he went to Ireland.

Here we have all the usual elements of an unsavoury family scandal. On the face of it, so far as can be judged at this remote distance of time, Philip may have been a natural son born before his father wedded the heiress of Ralph Boterel. She seems to have taken precautions before her death to ensure the succession of her own first-born. The family appear to have resided in Oxfordshire, where the Boterels were originally settled; and Philip may have been one of those military adventurers who at that time found a field for their enterprise in the newly-conquered territory of Ireland. It is recorded that in 1172 the Sheriff of Staffordshire had expended the considerable sum of £50 on military stores for the Irish expedition of Henry II., commonly called the Conquest of Ireland.

Philip further said that his mother Joan died seised of the land; and that if William had at any time seisin there, it was as bailee only of the said Joan, and not in fee (that is, not in perpetual right) Moreover, Philip claimed that he was the eldest son, born before William, and that the land should descend to him as son and heir of Joan. And so he sued William for the manor of Wednesbury.

On the other side, William de Heronville denied that Joan died seised of the manor, and stated that two years before her death she had conveyed the land to him, William, as her son and heir, at Hooknorton, in the Court of Lord Henry D'Oyley, the capital lord. Further, William denied that Philip was the son of William de Heronville and Joan, and stated that they had never looked upon him as their son, and he was not brought up by them as their son.

The first record of this trial is dated 20th January, 1226, and the claim includes not only "Wotnesbiri," but lands in Oxfordshire, namely, at "Hokenorton," and in "Rollendricht" (Rollright?). Later, Philip de "Harunvil" puts in his place Bertram de Heronville in his plea against William. The records are fragmentary, but it is evident that, notwithstanding this vexatious lawsuit, William de Heronville was securely in possession of the manor of Wednesbury. In 1227 we find him selected to act as a juryman at a great assize.

William de Heronville is mentioned under date 1233, in Vol. IV., p. 83, of Salt Collections.

3.—Simon de Heronville (12 . .—1272):—Simon de Heronville is mentioned by Bagnall as holding the manor of Wednesbury 1254-1256 (pp. 10, 11, and 22x). His name appears in the Hundred Roll of 1256 as holding Wednesbury under the Heirs of D'Oyley. Simon appears to have been the third of his family name to hold the manor of Wednesbury.

4.—John de Heronville I. (1272-13 . .): This typical Knight of the Shire appears to have held Wednesbury from about the year 1272 to some date anterior to 1316, when his widow is on record as recovering dower.

From the Staffordshire Assize Roll of 56, Henry III., it appears that on the death of Simon de Heronville, his son John brought a writ of Mort d'ancestor against Sibilla, the widow of Simon, respecting a tenement in "Wodnebyri," which he afterwards withdrew. The purport of such a writ was to direct the Sheriff to summon a jury of assize to view the land in question, and to recognise whether such ancestor were seised thereof on the day of his death, and whether the demandant was the next heir.

At this time we find mention of one Henry de Heronville.

A jury of the Hundred in 1272 names Henry de Herunville among the Valets (that is, young gentlemen of quality and good descent) who hold full Knight's fees, and are of full age, and are not yet Knights. A fine was imposed —possibly an unreasonable one, for such was the custom. Two years later it was enacted that when the eldest son of a landowner, such as of the lord of the manor of Wednesbury, was knighted, the fine payable to his lord superior should not exceed 20s. for each Knight's fee. Nor could the fine be levied till the youth was at least fifteen years of age. This was to remedy the abuse which had grown up.

Henry de Heronville is mentioned in the Plea Rolls of 1280 ("Salt" VI., i, 99) as a deforciant in a suit which Alice Fitzwarine, widow, of Tipton, brought for the recovery of dower. It would appear from another suit (p. 142 of same vol.) that Henry was nephew to Geoffrey Fitzwarine, father-in-law to the widow Alice.

In 1293 John de Heronville claimed the custody of certain properties in Tipton, by reason of the minority of one Henry de Heronville.

As to Sir John himself, he seems to have led so busy and active a life that it will be impossible to compass all the records of it which are still extant within the limits of one chapter, remote as is the date of his life and times.

Sir John de Heronville figures very frequently as taking part in the proceedings of Staffordshire cases tried in Crown Courts.

In 1282 "Sir John de Heronville" is a witness to a convention; in 1283 "Dominus Johannes de Heronville" is again a witness; he appears as a surety in a Walsall case in 1293; the same year he is fined for certain transgressions, and is also surety for a fellow offender; other fines are recorded against him, in 1272 for a trespass, and in 1294 for failing to appear as a "recognitor" when duly summoned to serve on the jury. As one of the four Knights who elected the jury he is named in 1289, in 1290 (as "John de Hermenill"), in 1293 (twice), and 1296. In common with the heads of other Knightly families, he also served as a juror, actually trying the cases as do the petty jurors of the present day. He so served in 1292 and 1293 (several times). In 1302 he was fined for non-appearance; but figures again on the jury list in 1307.

As a litigant Sir John puts in several appearances. In 1280 he won a suit respecting a messuage, 12 acres of land, and two acres of meadow in Wednesbury, because the manor, being of the ancient demesne of the King, the writ would not run there, and his opponent had to withdraw the suit. Two cases relate to Darlaston, and throw some light on the indefiniteness of the boundary between that parish and Wednesbury, and also show that Darlaston was once part of the barony of Dudley. William de Darlaston, in 1288, was said to have unjustly disseised John de Heronville of two acres of land in Wadnesbury. The jury found that the land was not in Wednesbury but in Darlaston. In 1293 a case was tried to prove if John de Heronville and another had unjustly disseised William of Darlaston of common of pasture in ten acres of heath (? Fallings Heath) and 40 acres of arable land in Wednesbury appurtenant to his free tenement in Darlaston. Heronville denied William of Darlaston's right of common because Wednesbury was of the ancient demesne of the Crown, whereas Darlaston was of the fee of Dudley. The jury said William had no right of pasture, and so gave John de Heronville the verdict.

In 1307 William Illary (? Hillary of Bescot) was set down as a "conspirator," for falsely moving a plea against John de Heronville to deprive him of a piece of land.

About this time was proceeding the struggle between Edward I. and the Abbey of Hales Owen for the right of presentation to Wednesbury Church, which is recorded on p. 25 of "Religious Wednesbury." In the Calendar of Patent Rolls, we find, under date 1293, March 4, at Garendon, the "Presentation of Nicholas de Burton to the Chapel of Wednesbury, in the diocese of Coventry and Lichfield." Also, in the same Rolls, and dated Kempsey, May 5th, 1301, is the record of the fine of ten marks, which the monastery was to pay "of pure charity"—as "frank almoin" signifies. It was thus recorded on the Roll:—"Grant in 'frank almoin,' in consideration of a fine made before the treasurer and barons of the Exchequer by the Abbot of Hales Oweyn of the Premonstratensian order, to that Abbot and his convent, of the advowson of the Chapel of Wodnesbury in the diocese of Coventry and Lichfield, which the King sometime ago recovered as his right from Nicholas, predecessor of the present Abbot, before John de Berewyk and his fellows justices, last in eyre in the county of Stafford; and licence for them to appropriate the said chapel."

A verdict returned in 1294 decided that 7½ acres of land in Wednesbury were "the free alms of the church of Nicholas de Burton, the parson of Wednesbury, and not the lay fee of

Philip Bonde of Bromwych, who held the tenement, and that it had been alienated by Nicholas, the Abbot of Hales" (Salt VII., 17).

To leave the ecclesiastical and resume the territorial history : In 1272 some twenty tenants of the manor of Wednesbury, including "Robert, son of Gervase of Wednesbyri, and Richard de Beneytleye," appeared in the Crown Courts in a plea against John de Heronville "that he exacted from them other customs and services than they used to render when the manor was in the hands of the ancestors of the King"—when it was a royal manor.

Apparently the men of Wednesbury vindicated their rights, as eight years later it is recorded on the Plea Rolls that John de Faukener, representing the King, "sued John de Hereville in a plea that whereas the King had commanded him not to distrain his tenants in the manor of Wednesbery, which is of the ancient demesne of the Crown, for other services than they were accustomed to render in former days, and to restore to them their goods and chattels which he had seized ; and, whereas, pending the suit between him and his tenants, the Crown was suing him for the same manor, in which the said John was causing great waste and destruction, refusing to permit his tenants to cultivate their lands" (1280).

The same Rolls, immediately after, disclose how John de Hervile, like nearly every other lord of an English manor, was summoned by that stern monarch to show by what right he held his lands. The lord of Wednesbury successfully pleaded that Richard I.—beyond which monarch the "legal memory" takes no cognisance—had never possessed the manor of Wednesbury, and had held nothing in it beyond a rent of 20s., payable to the Exchequer, according to the term of a certain exchange made with Henry II., and because the manor of Wednesbury was more valubale than that of "Stuntesfeld" given in exchange. In verification, Sir John de Heronville produced an enrolment from the Exchequer to that effect.

When Edward I. issued his writs of "Quo Warranto" to enquire by what title each man held his lands, John de Heronville claimed to have assize of bread and beer in his manor of Wednesbury (1293). Under this franchise the lord had power to regulate the quality, price, and measure or weight of these commodities within his manor. There were various recognised qualities of bread (according to the meal of which it was made), and of ale, which was periodically tasted by a manorial ale-taster.

In 1293 John de Heronville also satisfied a jury of the Hundred of Offlow to the same effect, on which occasion the Sheriff testified that the 20s. yearly had always been paid, and that there were no arrears. De Heronville seems to have been in possession of a "ligula," which was a transcript of the Exchequer Roll. The jury made the necessary presentment as to the validity of his title.

But much more remains to be recorded of the conditions of life among the tenants of the manor of Wednesbury at that time ; also of the social status, official routine, military services, and other daily doings which throw some strong side lights upon the kind of life which was then led by such knightly land-owners as Sir John de Heronville.

It must here suffice to close this chapter with another record on the Patent Rolls of the year 1293 affecting Wednesbury. It is dated from Woodstock Palace, October 11th, and runs thus :—"Pardon to Robert le Webbe, of Wednesbury, for the death of John, son of Robert de Bileston, as it appears by the record of William de Bereford and Robert Hastang, justices appointed to deliver Stafford Gaol, that he killed him in self defence."

XIV.—WEDNESBURY UNDER THE FOREST LAWS.

In mediæval times the greater part of Wednesbury was included for Forest offences, within the jurisdiction of the Royal Forest of Cannock. As the boundary of the afforested area ran from Wolverhampton along the highroad to Wednesbury, about three wards of the modern borough were thus included, the Town Hall Ward alone being almost entirely outside. The "high-road" was not then the Holyhead Road ; at that period it ran through Upper High Street, Oakeswell End, and on past West Bromwich Hall, Stone Cross, and the rear of West Bromwich Church towards Birmingham. In Hydes Lane was Finchpath Bridge, where the boundary of the Forest turned along the brook towards Walsall. The "high-road" did not run through Bridge Street and over Hill Top till much later times.

In 1308 (as recorded in the Plea Rolls 2 Edwards II.), Felicia Neville's claim for dower against John de Swynnerton, included a third of the profits of the "Stewardship of Cannock" ; which stewardship comprised over forty places in Staffordshire, among those named being Wodnesbury, Dorlaston, Wybenhale, and Wodenfeld.

The term "forest" does not signify that the whole area was covered with trees. It simply meant that the afforested area was kept purposely out of cultivation in order to maintains beasts and birds of the forest ; its boundaries were carefully fixed and made known, because there were so many offences against the Forest Laws, within its prescribed limits, for which grievous and oppressive penalties were inflicted.

Even lords of the manors lying within a Royal Forest, as Wednesbury lay within that of Cannock, could not convert pasture into arable land. Nor could they cut down their own woods, or make any enclosure, or do anything whatever which would prevent the larger game passing freely in or out of the land. This might seem a great hardship; but some mitigation of it was found in the right of pasture given them for their cattle within the forest.

Adjacent to the confines of a Forest, as in Wednesbury, freeholders and farmers might keep only one dog (a mastiff) for security, and only this providing his fore-claws were clipped; and greyhounds could be kept only by special warrant. In fact, the whole code made a transgressor of anyone who did aught in the least to interfere with the special privileges of the King and his great barons in the sports of the chase.

The "Forest" had its own officers and magistrates, with its own peculiar courts for the protection of "venison," of "vert" (that is, greensward, as, for instance, where Wood Green opened wide within the forest glade) and of "covert," in which the deer were lodged, as in Old Park and Friar's Park. Offences against "vert and venison" were tried in the Court of Wood-mote every 40 days; the officers being known as Foresters (game-keepers); Verderers (chosen by the freeholders, but sworn to maintain the Forest Laws in every respect); Agisters, who looked after the herbage and pannage; and the Woodwards, the lowest officers, who accounted for the game and the timber. Every third year was held a Court of Regard for the survey of dogs. There were also twelve important officers called Reguarders, appointed by the King or the Chief Justice; they surveyed and valued rights within the forest boundaries; felled the King's timber, slashed the underwood, and maintained his fences; inspected eyries of hawk within the forest; and inquired who kept bows, arrows, crossbows, hounds, nets, or engines to destroy the game. The Court of Swein-mote inquired into forest offences generally. The many barbarous punishments included loss of eyes and limbs; and these were awarded by the Court of Justice Seat before a Chief Justice itinerant, who would summon four knights of the shire to elect twelve freemen as a jury, and these made presentment at the bar of those accused and arraigned for trial. The offences for which Wednesbury men would thus be liable to appear at these courts would be extremely numerous and vexatious, including poaching, keeping unauthorised dogs and weapons, making deer-leaps, stealing firewood, wasting oaks, erecting fences and forming illegal enclosures, etc. These Forest Laws prevailed from the time of Canute; were most oppressive under the Normans and early Plantagenets; and finally disappeared in this district when Cannock was at last deforested, owing to the extensive use of the timber for iron smelting about the year 1600.

Such were the laws under which the inhabitants of this manor were forced to live in olden times. Where it was so easy to offend, many trespasses were sure to occur. The Pleas of the Forest prove this; as will now be made manifest by a few local instances.

One common offence was to make an "assart." An assart was a clearance in the wood by which trees and bushes were uprooted, and the ground brought into tillage. Sometimes an assart might be allowed on payment of a fine, fixed according to the value of the crop; but more frequently the assart was reduced to forest again.

This offence seems to have been most frequently committed by the small freeholders. For instance, it is recorded that in 1271—John de Heronville being one of the Verderers then in office—presentments of new assarts within the Regard of Cannock were made against—

John, the Baker, of Walsall, who was fined for having newly assarted half-an-acre within the fee of John de Heronville in Wednesbury. Another offender who had newly assarted a rood in the same fee was also fined; and John de Heronville gave half a mark to have them back again. He also paid for the "old waste in his Wood of Wednesbury."

Again, in 1286, presentments for both new and old assarts, and for purprestures, were made against certain tenants in Wednesbury. Here are two records—

"Thomas, son of William the Forester, holds half-an-acre (frisca) which is of the fee of Wednesbury."

"Thomas, son of Roger Hillary (of Bescot) holds half-an-acre which was frisca (in Wednesbury)."

In explanation of two ancient law terms in the foregoing, it may be said that "frisca" signifies uncultivated lands, such as added to the natural wilderness. "Purpresture" was an offence in the shape of an encroachment to the detriment of the forest, whether hurtful to vert or venison.

Offenders, such as the two named, were fined; and if the land was their own freehold, it was taken into the King's hands till the fine was paid.

New purprestures, of the Third Regard of the time John de Clynton was Seneschal, were reported at Wednesbury in the fee of John de Heronville. In 1286 a record of the Forest Court was made to the following effect:—

"William the Forester holds 1 acre of the fee of John de Heronville in Wednesbury, enclosed. The enclosure is to be prostrated."

Again, records of new purprestures made when William Trumwyn was Seneschal, are stated in these terms, and refer to Wednesbury—

"Tandy de la Coldelvere ... ... 1 acre.
Richard de la Grene ... ... ½ acre.
William the Forester (and 2 others) 3 acres
All fences enclosing them to be thrown down."

Under the heading "Agistment of Cannock" appears the record—

"For ancient destruction of Woods: John de Heronville, (paid) half-a-mark for waste in Wednesbury."

It is not improbable that this indicates the fact that the lord of Wednesbury manor had been taking in the cattle of others to agist or pasture; which he could do at a profit, after paying the customary fine. It would be by such practices that Wednesbury Wood fell into decay.

Doubtless John de Heronville, as an officer of the forest, knew exactly how far he could go. The Seneschal or Steward, or Chief Forester, was the highest official; then came the Foresters; and next in importance were the four Verderers.

A Perambulation of the two Staffordshire Royal Forests of Cannock and Kinver was made in 1300. John de Heronville was one of the four Verderers taking official part in this strict court of inquiry relating to Cannock; and as regards himself it was found that he held "the vill of Wednesbury and Walstwude (? Walsall Wood) with the woods and wastes appurtenant, of Henry de Plescy, afforested since the time" of Henry II.

An interesting forest incident is recorded of 1282. In that year a buck was killed in Cannock Forest by wolves—at a considerably later period than this wolves were to be found in Gloucestershire and Staffordshire. The foresters came quickly upon the carcase, and finding it fat had it skinned. After it had been "viewed" by the Verderers—of whom John de Heronville was one—the carcase was salted and handed over to the keeping of one Robert de la Putte, while the horns were handed to another person. A presentment which was afterwards made declared that William Trumwyn had taken this venison and consumed it in his own house. Now the accused was a man of importance, being "forester in fee" of Cheslyn Hay; and as he was probably wrongfully fined for the supposed offence, he seems to have appealed against the false presentment with success; for some years later it is recorded in the Pleas of the Forest that both the Seneschal of the Forest and the Verderers admitted that their presentment was wrong, and that Trumwyn had given the venison, perhaps as an act of charity on behalf of the King, to the Lepers of Freford. These officers were therefore all fined for their error in making such a presentment—probably on false evidence—and Trumwyn "quietus est"; that is, he was fully exonerated, or acquitted.

It will be observed that William Trumwyn had once held the position of Seneschal, the highest officer execising authority in the Royal Forest of Cannock; and yet his high position had not saved him from the jurisdiction of the Forest Laws.

At a little later period, when the Forest Laws were still severely pressed, the franchise of "free warren," or right to take smaller game, and which usually belonged to the Lord of the Manor, was the right in "Wodnesbury" of Roger Hillary, lord of Bescot Manor (1345), and who dwelt well within the metes and bounds of the forest. This was granted him by Royal favour, as per Charter Rolls of 18 Edward III.

<hr>

XV.—THE SUIT OWED BY WEDNESBURY TO FINCHPATH MILL.

It would appear that William de Heronville, the grandfather of John de Heronville, had demised his manorial mill to the Abbots of Bordesley. The deed making the grant is in monkish Latin (Salt VI., pt. 1, p. 170), the following being the substance of it:—

"Let the present and future generations know that I, William de Heronville, the son of William de Heronville, have granted etc., for the salvation of my soul, and of the soul of my wife Alicia, and of my heirs, to the Abbot and monks of Bordesley, in perpetual fee, the Mill of my manor of Wodensbury, with all its appurtenances, etc., from the meadow of Robert, the son of Osbert, up to the Bridge of Pynchespath, with all the sequela of the whole vill of Wodensbury (namely), so often as meal is to be carried (?) the men of Wodensbury shall always carry meal to the Mill within the county, and the monks shall carry (?) the other meal. Moreover, the said monks are to be allowed to transfer the said mill from place to place within the same tenement if they so wish, and to direct the water course over my land to the head of the Bridge toward the North up to the pool (or ford or shallow). And be it known that from each house in the whole vill of Wodensbury year by year the said monks shall have one man in the year once for repairing or taking care of the pool of the said mill. Further, I have granted the said water which is between the two bridges to the said monks, of which (bridges) the one is called Wynchespath bridge and the other Wystibridge, etc., for the purpose of making a mill on the Wisti (or at Wisti)."

In the foregoing the "sequela," or more fully the "sequela molendini," is the owing of suit to a particular mill; or put more plainly, it signifies that every tenant on the manor of Wednesbury was bound to have his corn ground at Wednesbury mill, the charges made for the grinding constituting a portion of the lord of the manor's income. This item of manorial revenue was hereby given up to the monks of Bordesley in a fit of pious devotion. "Pynchespath" and "Wynchespath" are, of course, the same place, both mis-spellings for "Finchespath." Finchespath Bridge was evidently in Hydes Road at that time, on the "metes and bounds" of Cannock Forest; and "Wisti" seems to indicate "Mesty," now Mesty Croft. One authority has suggested that "Wisti" was a form of the name "West-town," now known as Witton. But this is highly improbable. It will be observed that at "Wisti," or Mesty Croft, there was a second bridge over the Tame.

At the Hillary Term 1287, Thomas Hillary (? of Bescot) brought an action against John de Heronville concerning the Finchespathe Mill. The plea was that Heronville and his Wednesbury tenants ("his villains of Wodnesburi") ought to "do suit" to the said mill, as they used to do   Thomas Hillary said that the Abbot of Bordesley had demised the mill in fee farm to one Nicholas de Bordesley, who in turn had conveyed it to him, Thomas Hillary; and that de Heronville had withdrawn from the mill the "suit" of himself and his villains.   In other words, everyone in Wednesbury had withdrawn their custom from Finchpath Mill—perhaps because John de Heronville, resenting his grandfather's excess of piety, by which he was now robbed of so much profit, had built another grist mill somewhere on the stream.   Anyway he was forced to concede all that Thomas Hillary now asked, as the grant of his grandfather was held to be valid in law.

From a law-suit a year or two later it would appear that this Thomas Hillary had been given the mill, together with five acres of land and two acres of meadow in Wednesbury, by his father, Roger Hillary (Salt VI., pt. 1, p. 189).

Years later, namely, in 1316, a similar suit was brought into court by William Hillary (doubtless the heir of Thomas) against Geoffrey Henries, Dulcia Underhill, Thomas de Erbury, and eighteen others, to compel them to "do suit"—that is, to take their custom—to "his mill of Fynchspade in Fynchspade," as they formerly used to do (Salt IX., p. 55).

Yet again in 1352 when Roger Hillary had succeeded to the ownership of the mill—which was then described as "of Wednesbury," and not the "Finchpath Mill"—two separate actions of a similar nature were brought into court.   It is interesting to glean the names of the Wednesbury freeholders who were then summoned "in a plea that they should perform suit" to Roger's mill in Wednesbury.   The defendants in the first action, and their respective holdings in the vill of Wednesbury, as proved by Roger Hillary, were:—

John Dymmok, a messuage and 2 virgates of land.

Henry Musard, a messuage and ¼ virgate of land.

Henry de Moxelowe (Moxley), a messuage and ½ virgate of land.

William Heronville, a messuage and 1 virgate of land.

Henry Spryg, a messuage and ¼ virgate of land.

William Golde and Alice his wife, ½ virgate of land.

It was admitted that by virtue of these tenancies they "ought to do suit to his mill, by grinding all their corn growing on the said land up to the thirty-second 'vas,' and they had substracted the said suit for the two years past."   Damages were laid at £40, but Roger, on recovering "the suit of mill," remitted all but 6s. 8d. each tenant.

The term 'vas' would appear to be the monkish name for 'a peck,' the 32nd part of the quarter measure.

In the record of the second suit we obtain the names of still more Wednesbury tenants at that remote period.   They were all freeholders, probably holding by villain tenure. Originally the tenure of a villain tenant had been a messuage and a virgate of land—a virgate, or yardland, varying in size up to forty acres, according to the district.   Except two, all these defendants held but a quarter of a virgate each, in addition to their messuage, which illustrates the gradual sub-division of the land; their names were:—

Robert atte Ee,
Nicholas le Fitere,
Thomas de Erbury,
Robert Dawesone,
John Waters,
Nicholas Aleyn,
Philip Nitengale,
William Corviser,
John Avery,
William Baroun,
Thomas Nityngale,
William Woolrich,
William le Kyng,
Alice la Quene,
William Golde,

and five others, all tenants who had "substracted' the suit they owed to the mill at Wednesbury, and who on admitting their liability escaped with a fine of 6s. 8d. each, although the total damages had been laid by Roger Hillary at £100.

At the dissolution of the monasteries in 1539, it is not at all improbable that it was the value of this "mill suit" which, described as "a rent of 20s. in Weddisburie," was surrendered to Henry VIII. by John Byley, Abbott of the monastery of the Blessed Mary of Bordesley (Salt XII., p. 186).

At this point it is worth calling attention to the way in which the monastic houses in those times acquired property far and near. In this history it has already been recorded that Wednesbury lands were left to an abbey at Burton; that the great tithes of Wednesbury Church were acquired by Halesowen Abbey; and here it has to be recorded that even the mill dues of Wednesbury had passed into the possession of Bordesley Abbey, which is near Redditch.

Difference of opinion has existed as to the exact locality of Finchpath, and it is necessary that some attempt should be made to fix it.   It was either on the site of the present Bridge Street crossing of the Tame, or on that of the Hyde's Lane crossing.   Wherever the mill and bridge of Finchpath were situated, there was an angle in the boundaries of Cannock Forest; it is recorded in 1340 that "the bounds of the Forest of Cannock commenced at Wednesbury Bridge, and, passing down the Tame to Bescote, ascended the stream through the middle of the town of Walsall"; and so the metes and bounds are further defined right away towards Tamworth, King's Bromley, Rugeley, Brewood, Pendeford, through the market-place of Wolverhampton, and then along the King's highway through Bilston to Wednesbury Bridge.

(The stewardship or bailiwick of the Forest of Cannock was at one time held of the King in capite by the Swinnerton family—see previous chapter).

Wednesbury Bridge, spanning the Tame near the modern Wednesbury Mill, belongs to a comparatively new thoroughfare between London and the north. It is often confounded with the ancient road between Wednesbury and Birmingham for many reasons. One source of confusion is the fact that at Wednesbury Bridge an old road ran into this section of the more modern one ; namely, an old Roman salt-way. coming from Droitwich, and on which stood "Old-Bury"; this ancient road crossed Swan Village near the present gasworks, became known as Mollaston's Lane, and ran into the modern highway at the Fountain Inn. At its entrance to Wednesbury was located some well-known place called "the Gate," which is often referred to in ancient deeds. It might have been a town gate in some ancient fortification which admitted to the "Portway." This road then proceeded through Darlaston, Moseley Hole, Wednesfield. Moseley Court, and fell into the present Stafford road near Coven, ultimately reaching Chester.

Another source of confusion is the fact that the region now known as Hill Top has always been a comparatively populous one ; and, further, that the name "Finchpath" has been applied to many parts of it. As this locality was outside the metes and bounds of the royal Forest of Cannock, the dwellers here were free from the irksome rule of Forest law ; a man setting up his dwelling here might keep a dog to guard it without having its feet mutilated ("expeditated") to prevent it chasing the game ("canis apertus et non impediatus"—an unlawed dog with its fore-feet whole).

Such inducements to settle here would undoubtedly attract new comers. But Bridge Street (or Bridge End as it was formerly called) has always been a populous part of Wednesbury ; and it is therefore reasonable to argue that this locality was also outside the arbitrary jurisdiction of the Forest Courts, as it would have been if the Forest boundary ran along Hydes Road, and not along Bridge Street. So that the erection of houses in olden time along the line of Hill Top and Bridge Street was fostered by the same exemption from the restraints of Forest law enjoyed by both localities alike ; and not from their being the line of a King's highway.

As to so many places around Hill Top being described as in or near to Finchpath, it must be remembered that place-names had to do duty for whole districts before specific street-names were in use ; and that Hill Top was then as easily accessible from Hydes Road as it now is from Bridge Street.

Briefly, the history of the more modern highway from London to the north, and now very generally known in this locality as the Holyhead Road, is as follows :—

Before 1752 the coach road from London to Shrewsbury ran through Coventry and Castle Bromwich, and along the Chester Road to Brownhills and the Watling Street.

Birmingham had been missed entirely by this route. But in the said year 1752 the Shrewsbury traffic was first brought through Birmingham and Wolverhampton; the journey of the lumbering caravan occupied four days, and at Birmingham the passengers slept the third night, Birmingham to Shrewsbury being the fourth day's journey.

In 1731 it was announced in Owen and Bowen's Road Book, almost as a great discovery, that "Since the survey of this road by our author, that part of it from Birmingham to Shrewsbury passing through Dudley, etc., is now wholly disused, a much better way having been found both in respect of goodness and shortness, an account of which we have received from a gentleman well acquainted therewith ; viz. 'as soon as you pass Birmingham the new road breaks off on the left acutely, and passes through W. Birmingham (this is a mistake for W. Bromwich), Wolverhampton, Shifnal,' etc."

Four years previously, by an Act of 1727, the route through Wednesbury was turnpiked. This Act was "for repairing several roads leading from Birmingham through the Town of Wednesbury, to a place called High Bullen ; and to Great Bridge, and from thence to the end of Gibbet Lane," etc. It would seem that the "Holloway" was first made at this turnpiking of the road in 1727, although the road was again considerably eased a century later, and is still manifest by the altered levels. Within the next few years, owing to the improvement effected in the roads, the traffic between Birmingham and Shrewsbury was attracted along the route which came through Wednesbury, although it was not till 1784 that the new fast "mail coaches" were put on the road. Till then they had all been "slow coaches," the mail-bags being conveyed by "post-boys" on horse-back.

When this first became the coach route there was no bridge across the stream, the road going through the water (as the levels of the old cottages on both sides still indicate), and the crest of the hill was on the level of the Hop Pole Inn (indicated by the embankment which still rises above the cutting of the road), so that the gradient here was one of the steepest on any coach route in England. In fact, the passengers always got out of the coach at Wednesbury ford to walk to the "hill top."

The road over West Bromwich Heath (now the High Street of that town) was widened and improved by a local Act of 1802 ; no less than 387 acres of common waste lands were enclosed, and the road was cut straight and broad, as it now appears.

In 1810 the Holyhead mail running via Oxford, Hill Top, and Wednesbury, was allowed 40 hours 22 minutes for the 276¼ miles' run. This coach went through Wednesbury market-place.

In 1816 and again in 1826 the Holyhead road was greatly improved by Telford, the eminent engineer, who built Wednesbury Bridge. A footpath alongside the brook then went under the last arch of the bridge, and along the top of the retaining wall by the side of Disturnal's factory. It was at this period the new Wednesbury portion of the Holyhead Road was made; turning out of Lower High Street along Camp-field Lane—as it was then called—in which stood the old chapel, the new "cut" commenced at the site of the Art Gallery, and ran in a straight line over Cock Heath, and through Moxley into Bilston.

(The great antiquity of the Portway Road and of the Camp-field Road, very small sections of each of which were occupied in later times by the coach road, has added to the existing confusion).

Previously the coach road had been along Lower High Street, Market Place, Upper High Street, High Bullen, Old Bilston Road, and Dangerfield Lane.

Enough has been said to show that Finch-path mill was not on the site of the present Wednesbury mill, but somewhere on the stream nearer to Mesty Croft.

The present Wednesbury mill was extended by a "new side" erected for steam-power in 1855, when the old water-power mill was relegated to the grinding of pig-meal. A primitive form of steam-engine had previously worked a part of the "old side." The old portion still stands in the central part of the building, and the internal evidence seems to show that it was built in the 17th or 18th century for an iron forge; in fact, it is known to have been the iron-works of "John Wood, who lived in great splendour at Wednesbury," keeping his hunting stables, and kennels for a pack of hounds there, about 1760-1780. (See "Wednesbury Workshops," p. 116). The wood-work is of hewn oak, and the iron-work is a fine specimen of the durable cold-blast charcoal iron of olden Wednesbury. The scoriæ of the furnaces may still be dug up.

Wednesbury mill was always the highest on this stream, and the right of pounding the water belonged to it till the Mines Drainage Commissioners interfered with the full flow of water in 1878. The mill was finally closed in 1885, owing mainly to the severe competition of imported American-ground flour.

Photo by]   WEDNESBURY MILL   [*T. Stanley*
(The New Side erected in 1855.)

XVI.—THE CUSTOMS OF WEDNESBURY MANOR.

Towards the close of Chapter XIII. allusion was made to a conflict in 1272, between the men of Wednesbury and their feudal lord.

There seems no doubt that the occupiers of tenemental lands in Wednesbury anterior to the lordship of Ralph Boterel had enjoyed many privileges simply because they were tenants of a royal manor, on which there was probably no "mansum capitale" or manor house. It would appear that the presence of a resident lord within the manor had brought about the curtailment, or attempted curtailment, of many manorial privileges, which the men of Wednesbury resisted as a violation of the old Saxon constitution of their ancient manor. The quarrel may have arisen at first from a dispute as to which were the demesne lands and which were not, as to the rent and free services of the tenants, and as to manning ("manopera") or day-work to be done by them (refer back to p. 23). Apparently the tenants went and cultivated lands from which the lord drove them out again, claiming the lands as his own domain.

The result of the differences was a most important lawsuit between the contending parties, the details of which have been left on record. These details of the customs of Wednesbury Manor have a general interest because of the insight they gave into mediæval life and feudal relationships.

The twenty appellant tenants of the year 1272 had probably passed away; but in 1307 the cause was still undecided, as the following law records will disclose (Salt IX., p. 7):—

"It was shown to the Lord the King, 'ex parte,' William Underhull del Hethe, Richard le Rowe, Henry atte Lydeyate, and William, son of Walter, tenants of John de Heronville, of the Manor of Wodensbury, which is of the ancient demesne of the Crown, that whereas the said John had been summoned to appear before the Justices of this Court at the Octaves of Hillary to answer the plea of the said William, Richard, and the others, that he exacted from them other customs and services than they ought to perform, or which their ancestors who were tenants of the same manor had been accustomed to perform, at the time when the said manor was in the hands of the King's progenitors, and the said John had been inhibited, whilst the suit was pending, from distraining the said tenants, the said John nevertheless had grievously distrained them day after day to the manifest contempt of the King, and to the great damage of the said men; and a precept was therefore issued to the Sheriff, that if the said men found security to prosecute their claim against the said John, he should produce the said John at this term, and in the meantime direct him to deliver back to the said men without delay their chattels, to be held by them until the case was fully terminated in this Court. John did not appear, and the Sheriff was again ordered to distrain and produce him at the Octaves of Michaelmas, and to inhibit him in the meantime

from causing further damage or molestation to the said tenants."

By the "octaves" is meant the eighth day after the Feast day (of St. Michael), both inclusive.

This by no means ended the case. The Court records of the year 1310 are much fuller, and as quaintly interesting as they are explicit. In Salt IX., p. 17, the suit is thus stated:—

"John de Heronville was summoned to answer William Underhull, William de Hethe, and three others, the men of the said John, of the Manor of Wodenesbury (Wednesbury), which is of the ancient demesne of the Crown of England, in a plea that he had exacted from them other customs and services than they, or their ancestors, tenants in the same manor, had been accustomed to yield at the time the manor was in the hands of the King's progenitors. And they stated by their attorney that when the manor was formerly in the hands of King Henry, the great grandfather of King Edward, the King's father, their ancestors held their tenements by certain (i.e., by fixed) service, viz., each holding a virgate of land by fealty and services of 5s. annually, and suit at the Manor Court twice in the year, viz., at the feasts of Michaelmas and Easter, and when it should happen a writ of right was in the same Court, then suit at the same Court from three weeks to three weeks, so long as the writ was pending in the Court; and they were liable to be tallaged when the King tallaged his boroughs and demesnes, and those who held more in the manor, they rendered more in proportion; and the tenants had continued in this 'status' from the time of the said King Henry until the time of the King's father, when the said John de Heronville distrained the tenants to do suit of Court every three weeks for the whole year, and by tallaging them high and low ('alto et basso') at his will, exacting from them 'merchetum' for their sons' and daughters' marriage, and other villein services and customs, which they had not been accustomed to perform, he had damaged them to the amount of £40, for which statements they produced proofs. And John de Heronville appeared by attorney, and prayed that the defendants should be required to show that the manor was of ancient demesne, and the Book of Doomsday having been examined it appeared that it was of ancient demesne of the Crown, whereupon the said John denied having inflicted any injury on his tenants, and stated that two of the plaintiffs held new assarts by fealty and by a fixed rent, which were not of the ancient demesne, while as regarded William Underhull he held half a virgate and the fourth of a noke of land by fealty and service of 4s. yearly, and the said William de Hethe held the fourth part of a noke of land and by right of his wife three acres, and that beside the said service, the said tenants by reason of their tenure of ancient demesne ought to do service of Court every three weeks, beside two appearances per annum at the View of Frankpledge at the Feast of St. Michael and at Easter; and that when the King tallaged his demesnes it was lawful for the lord of the manor to tallage at his will, and likewise to appoint Provosts from year to year, and Tything-men ('decennarios') by election of their peers; and each of them ought to plough the lord's land for one day in Lent, and harrow the land after ploughing, and to mow the meadow of the lord for one day and to carry the hay; and, further, that they ought to reap the land of the lord, each of them for three days in the autumn at their own costs, and on the fourth day they had a repast at the cost of the lord; and if any of the said tenants brewed Beer they gave one penny, and if any of them had five pigs at the feast of St. Martin the lord then had the best of them, and if they had less than five then for each pig which was of complete age they gave a penny, and for a hogette a farthing; and, further, they had to give 'merchetum,' viz., each of them for marry- a daughter within the manor 2s., and for license to marry a daughter outside the manor 3s.; and if any of the daughters were carnally known then in the name of Lecherwye they paid 12d.; and if a tenant died the lord had a Heriot and Relief, with half of his pigs, his boar, all his male colts ('pullanos'), and a cart bound with iron ('carettam ferratam'), and the cloth which was not cut ('pannos non taliatos'), and all the hams which were entire ('bacones integros'); and that the tenants of the manor had owed all the above services and customs since the manor had been in the hands of the King's progenitors, he, the said John, was prepared to prove.

The tenants appealed to a jury, which was summoned for the octaves of Hillary next ensuing."

Supplementary to the explanations already given in parentheses a few more may be necessary to the full understanding of the foregoing extract from the ancient Plea Rolls.

The term "tallage" has been referred to on p. 29; it would almost appear that Wednesbury manor had anciently enjoyed the privilege of being exempted from the payment of such tolls. In the Rolls of 22 Richard II. (1399) the men of Wednesbury were eventually declared to be free from "thelonio," which was the right of a lord who held a royal demesne in fee-farm to recover reasonable toll there, if his demesne had been accustomed to be tolled —of which precedent there seems to have been considerable doubt in Wednesbury at this date. Hence the raising of this issue in the law courts.

There was no question at law that tenants of an ancient demesne—that is, of a manor which had passed like Wednesbury from Edward the Confessor to William the Conqueror—really possessed many immunities and privileges which had been granted them in Saxon times. Among such were certainly exemptions from arbitrary toll and tax; and afterwards, when the House of Commons came into existence, this exemp-

tion was extended to mean a non-liability to contribute to the expenses of the "Knight of the shire" sent to represent the county in Parliament.

By the term "alto et basso" is also sometimes meant the absolute submission of all differences to the lord of the manor.

"Merchetum," or "the maid's fee," was a strange custom once common to England, Scotland, and Wales, by which every tenant at the marriage of his daughter paid a sum to the lord of the manor. In ruder and more ancient times it had been the custom for the lord to claim the privilege to lie the first night with the bride; but as the three several nations emerged from that state of semi-barbarism which the existence of such a custom implies, a money fee was substituted for the prerogative. In Scotland the custom was abrogated by Malcolm III. at the instance of his queen; but in England the period of commutation was so remote that some authorities have denied the very existence of a custom so repugnant to modern ideas.

Th "noke" was a quantity of ploughed land, being the fourth-part of a "carucate," a measurement previously explained on p. 24.

The "decennarios" or "deciners" were the men who had the oversight at "views of frankpledge" for the maintenance of the King's peace; the limit of their jurisdiction was called "decenna" because it usually consisted of ten households (or a "tithing"); they were the petty constables or the deputies of the constable of the manor in his absence.

"Lecherwye," sometimes written "lecherwite," was a fine anciently imposed on adulterers and fornicators—if they were discovered and brought before the manorial court.

The allusion to St. Martin's Day is made because that was the period of the year (November 11) when it was customary in olden times to kill off all surplus stock and salt the meat for winter use; root crops had not then been introduced into England, and as there was but little "winter keep" for farm stock, only just sufficient beasts for breeding purposes could be maintained till the grazing time came again. It was on account of eating so much salted meat in olden times that the people suffered from scurvy, and, as some think, with leprosy. The nearest leper-house to Wednesbury in those times was at Freeford, Lichfield, now the seat of the Dyott family; the "lepers of Freford" were mentioned at the close of Chapter XIV. (p. 33).

Nearly a century later, namely, 5 Henry IV. (1405), certain tenants of Wednesbury manor maintained their prescriptive right to be free of tolls in all markets and fairs. Among these privileged Wednesbury men were Richard Lydegate, John Hounte, William Grene, and John atte Lynde. They with others from Wednesbury, three years previously had attended a fair held at Birmingham on the Feast of the Invention of the Holy Cross (May 3), and another fair held there the following Michaelmas-day, when they refused to pay for each beast sold or bought 2d., viz., one penny from the buyer and one penny from the vendor; and on the Thursday when the market was held, for each beast sold and bought a penny, viz., one half-penny ("obolum") from the vendor, and a half-penny from the buyer. They were sued by William de Bermyngham, lord of the manor of Birmingham, for the tolls on 60 oxen, 60 steers, and 60 cows, and for the tolls on their merchandise, viz., for linen and woollen cloth, iron, "calibe," and brass sold or bought in the markets. and for 40 oxen, 40 steers, and 40 cows sold and bought at the said fairs.

The defendants, without admitting any of the quantities specified, pleaded that Henry de Heronville was lord of the manor of Wednesbury, which manor was of ancient demesne of the Crown, and that each of them held a messuage and 20 acres of land in the said manor, by certain services according to the custom of that manor, that they were resident within the manor, and that their tenements were only sueable by the King's lesser writ of right, and that they and all other tenants of that manor, according to the custom of the kingdom hitherto obtained and approved ("optentam et approbatam"), were quit of toll throughout the kingdom, and that they had bought and sold cattle and merchandise in the said markets and fairs for their own use, and they asked for judgment whether William de Bermyngham could maintain the action against them.

One of the defendants, William Grene, was charged with breaking into the close and house of the said lord of Birmingham at Barre, and treading down and consuming his corn and grass with his cattle to the value of £10. This was evidently a spiteful sequel to the privileged cattle dealing at Birmingham. (Salt XV., pp. 110-111). Under his prescriptive privilege of "thelonium," William Grene might have been justified in defying the "thelonmannus," or toll-man of Birmingham, but he surely had no right to add insult to injury, and commit a trespass on the same individual!

Photo by]   FOUNTAIN INN, ON THE ANCIENT ROAD-LEVEL,   [*Stanley.*
                    WEDNESBURY BRIDGE.

XVII.—THE HERONVILLES (CONTINUED).

4.—Sir John de Heronville I. (1272-1315)—continued:—

How full of incident was the busy life of John de Heronville, who became lord of Wednesbury in 1272, is evident from the recorded facts which this history commenced to set forth in Chapter XIII. (See p. 30), and of which the tale is not yet fully told.

On December 21st, 1291, we find Sir John sitting on an important jury at Dudley (Salt IX., pt. 2, p 33; also see IX., p. 17).

In 1307 (Plea Rolls, 1 Edward II.) John de Heronville and Juliana his wife were sued by Alan de Wednesburi for trespass. The following year John de Heronville and Simon his son were attached to answer the plaint of John le Someter that they had beaten, wounded, and ill-treated him at Wednesbury on the Sunday, the Feast of Palms of the previous year, and for which they claimed 100s. damages. This Simon de Heronville does not appear in Bagnall's pedigree of the family.

Also in 1312 John de Heronville and Juliana his wife were defendants in a plea of trespass brought against them by William Underhull, of Wednesbury. Two years later the same two defendants denied a trespass alleged against them by Richard Justiceman of Birmyngeham, namely, that they had illegally seized two horses worth 40s. on the high road at Wodnesbury and impounded them. This is the earliest allusion to the parish pinfold (1314).

Full of years, some honours, and perhaps not unmarked by many cares, Sir John de Heronville, lord of Wednesbury, died in 1315. According to Bagnall his widow was named Eleanor. But in Salt, Vol. IX., 53, it is "Joan, formerly wife of John de Heronville," who sued for dower in 1316. The eldest son of this John was Henry de Heronville, who at the time of his father's death was 50 years of age (1315). The second son was also named John; the wife of this second John de Heronville was named Juliana, who, the same year (1316) also sued for dower, which she recovered. The same "Juliana, formerly wife of John de Heronville," was defendant in another case, the same year. She was living in 1325, and is evidently the person meant by the name of "Joan" aforementioned.

John de Heronville and Juliana his wife were named in a lawsuit (1392) over lands and rents in Wednesbury, Tipton, and Brereley (Sedgley), which had been given by John Dymmock and Felicia his wife to them and their heirs, and which were to descend to Sybil their grand-daughter, as cousin and heir of John. Sybil's father was Thomas Heronville.

Towards the close of the 13th century there was a Sir Hugh de Heronville, who was Sheriff of Staffordshire (Salt VIII., p. 152); so far no other trace of him has been met. Doubtless the Heronvilles had many collateral branches in and around Wednesbury by this time, some of whom had sunk in the social scale, whilst others had risen (Salt IX., p. 17).

5.—Henry de Heronville I. (1315-1316):—

Sir John de Heronville the First was succeeded by his eldest son, Henry de Heronville the First, in the lordship of Wednesbury. Henry was 50 years of age when his father died, and his tenure of the manor was a short one. An Inquisition Post Mortem was taken at his father's death in 1315, and a similar inquiry had to be undertaken the following year upon his death.

"Inquisitiones post mortem," or Escheats, were inquiries on oath before a local jury, summoned by writ of the County Escheator, or of the Sheriff. They were held upon the decease of a Crown tenant to show (1) what lands he died seized of; (2) by what rent and services such lands were held; (3) who was the next heir, and of what age he was; and (4) whether he was attainted of treason, was alien, or was otherwise disqualified to hold land, etc., etc. These enquiries were held from the reign of Henry III. to that of Charles I., and the finding of the district jury was made to Chancery, and a transcript was sent to the Exchequer. These documents are preserved in the Record Office in London.

The documents relating to the passing of the manor in 1315 and in 1316 are given in Bagnall's History of Wednesbury, pp. 13-18. It is interesting to note the ancient forms of some local names contained therein:—

Richard "le Rugaker," Nicholas Golde, and Richard "lee Grete" were freeholders, whose lands were doubtless in West Bromwich, and to-day may be severally identified at Ridgacre, Gold's Hill, and Greet or Great Bridge. Thomas Attedelf evidently lived "at Delves." Some place was called "Wedneswalle"; more easily recognised are the names Kyngehullefforlong (King's Hill furlong—part of the ploughed lands of the ancient Saxon community); Moniweyffeld (Monway Field); Leybrocke (Lea Brook); le Rudynnge (Ridding Lane); Kyngeshullstone (King's Hill Stone); and Mockeslowe (Moxley).

6.—John de Heronville II. (1316-1355):

When John II. succeeded to the manor he was but 12 years of age. When, in due time, he married, his wife's name was Joan. Very little else is known of their personal history.

There is a law court record of his time which is rather interesting, inasmuch as it alludes to the Steward of the Manor, and exemplifies the judicial powers possessed by that official. This is the substance of the record:—

John de Alne having been indicted before Henry de Derlaston, the Steward of Wednesbury, for breaking at night into the cellar of John de Heronville, the lord of Wednesbury (17 Edward III.), and feloniously stealing a maser (a carved bowl of hard wood), worth 6s. 8d., two mappas (napkins) worth 6s., a towel worth 18d., a silver spoon worth 12d., and a "primarium" worth 2s., at a gaol delivery held at Stafford in 1348 was found guilty, and hanged as a common robber.

John de Heronville II. died June 8, 1355, and was succeeded by his son John.

7.—John de Heronville III. (1355-1403):

John the Third was 24 years of age when he succeeded to the lordship of Wednesbury. For his wife he married Alice, daughter and heir of John de Tynmore, an alliance which introduced new interests. Tynmore, or Timmore, is a place on the Tame beyond Tamworth.

From the Originalia (public records consisting of extracts transmitted from the Court of Chancery to the Exchequer, of all grants of the Crown, where any rents are reserved, and salary is payable, or any service to be performed) is to be gathered the extent of the feudal payments made on behalf of Wednesbury Manor in the reign of Edward III. It is there recorded that the Sheriff of Staffordshire "having received security from John, son and heir of John de Heronville concerning his Relief" (a sum of money payable to the King for entrance upon the ownership of the manor upon the death of the previous holder), the said heir was allowed "full seisin," or complete possession on the payment to the King, of whom he held "in capite," of 21 pence yearly. "And of the fifth part of the manor of Tipton with its belongings, which he holds from another, he is not to be interfered with."

The Heriot and the Relief, those ancient "succession duties," as payable by the manorial tenants of Wednesbury, were noted in the previous chapter (p. 38).

This John de Heronville II., lord of Wednesbury, is probably the one who is often quoted by writers on Heraldry as affording a rare instance of a knight entitled to bear arms trafficking in his heraldic honours. He is said to have transferred his coat of arms, no doubt for a consideration, to Roger Wyrley, lord of the manor of Handsworth. This very uncommon transaction is sometimes dated 1442 (20 Henry VI.) by local historians, although the deed by which the grant of the said escutcheon of arms was made is believed to be extant, and dated at West Bromwich, 41 Edward III. (1368), the names of the contracting parties being given as Thomas de Heronville and Robert de Wyrley respectively (see Nineteenth Century Magazine for June, 1896).

John Heronville III. died about St. Valentine's Day, 1403.

8.—Henry Heronville II. (1403-1406):

Henry Heronville the Second succeeded to the lordship of Wednesbury when he was 30 years of age. He evidently held Tinmore also, in right of his mother.

The Inquisition Post Mortem taken on his father's death is recorded as follows:—

"Inquisition made at Walsall (Walshale) before William of Walsall, Escheator of our Lord the King in the County of Stafford, by virtue of a certain writ of our Lord the King

directed to the same Escheator to make this Inquisition on the day of March next after the Feast of St. Gregory the Pope, in the fourth year of King Henry the Fourth after the Conquest, on the oath of John Wilkes of Darlaston, Thomas Chilterns, Richard Harper of Darlaston, Laurence Happeford, John Hoget, William Harper, John Simcox, William Collins, William Sweetcocks, Roger of Norton, John Peart of Bromwich, and Thomas Gilks of Brereley: Who say on oath that all which John Herville so called in short, [for Heronville] held of our Lord the King on the day on which he died, the manor of Wednesbury with its belongings in the aforesaid County of Stafford, gift and feoffment having been made by certain [persons, viz.,] Henry of Tynmore parson of the church of Elford, and John of Tynmore, to the same John Herville, and to a certain Alice wife of the same John Herville and to the heirs issuing from the bodies of the same John and Alice Herville, by the license of our Lord Edward, lately King of England, and grandfather to our Lord the King now [reigning] then obtained by the service of twenty shillings (XXs.) to the same our Lord the King, paid for all services into his treasury on the Feast of St. Michael yearly by the hands of the Sheriff of the aforesaid county for the time being: which manor is of the annual value in all demands, about the true value of the same after deductions. And they say that the aforesaid John and Alice Herville had issue between them a certain Henry, and that the aforesaid Alice died afterwards, and that the aforesaid John Herville died on the Friday, next after the Feast of St. Valentine, in the year of the reign of the King aforesaid, and further they say that the aforesaid Henry is son and next heir of the same John Herville and thirty years old and more; and that the aforesaid John Herville also held no other lands or tenements in the said County of Stafford of our Lord the King, or of any others in demesne, nor in service, on the aforesaid day on which he died. In witness of which the aforesaid jurors have affixed their seals. Given on the day and year aforesaid."

One Henry de Heronville in 1388 was sued for taking goods by force from Sir Thomas de Thomenhorne at Horton; in the following year he sued Henry Stoupere of Tynmore and another for cutting down his trees and underwood at Tynmore, taking timber from his houses, fish from his fishponds, and other trespasses (Salt XV., pp. 7, 10, 19).

Then there was a "Richard le Heronville," who was sued in 1374 for forcibly breaking into the close of John in le Lee at Fynspathe, and consuming and treading down corn and grass to the value of £10. Richard did not put in an appearance, and as it was reported that he possessed no property in the county, the Sheriff was ordered to proclaim and call him, and if he came not on the last court day to outlaw him, and if he did appear to arrest him and produce him for trial. This Richard may have been a younger son, or he may have belonged to a collateral branch of the family

Henry Heronville, lord of Wednesbury, married Margaret, the daughter and heir of William Sperner. He died about St. Matthew's Day, 1406, after holding the Manor only three years. More than twenty years afterwards his name, his marriage, and his untimely death, transpire in the course of a long lawsuit.

From the records of a prolonged trial over the manor of Frankley in Worcestershire, still proceeding in the year 1430, it would appear that Margaret, the wife of Henry Heronville, was a daughter of William Spernore, and that Joyce, wife of William Swynfen, was another daughter, and that they claimed the right of remainder in the manor of Frankley, which should descend to them on the death of their mother Alice, they being their deceased father's only heirs. The two heiresses, and Swynfen, the husband of one being under age,

prayed that the suit should remain till they arrived at full age; and strangely enough Henry Heronville, the husband of the other heiress, died while the trial was pending.

With this death is brought to a close the direct line of a family of typical Anglo-Norman knights, in whose hands the lordship of Wednesbury had remained for upwards of two centuries (1182-1406). At first these lords of Wednesbury had held also the manor of Hooknorton; the last two representatives of the family held, in addition to the manor of Wednesbury, the Timmore estates. The two estates were held by their representatives till Tudor times, more than a century after the name of Heronville had passed away.

Their bones are dust, their swords do rust,
Their souls are with the saints, I trust.

"CASTLE RINGS,"
The Remains of an Ancient Camp, Cannock Chase.

From " Historic Staffordshire."]   [*By permission of the Midland Educational Co.*

XVIII.—WILLIAM LEVENTHORPE, LORD OF WEDNESBURY, "BY RIGHT OF HIS WIFE."

Shakespeare makes Henry V., upon his succession to the crown of his father (1413), discard all the boon companions of his rollicking youthful days—Falstaff, Bardolph, Pistol, and all the rest of that riotous crew.

But there was found in the circumspect Court of the reformed monarch one favourite who not improbably knew something of Madcap Harry's exploits in those unregenerate days of his irresponsible youth. This was John Leventhorp, one of the Squires of the King's Household.

John de Leventhorp belonged to Thorley and Sabridgecourt, co. Hertford, and was a favourite esquire of Henry V. This is proved by the fact that when the King made his will shortly before his memorable departure for France, Leventhorp was appointed one of his executors. The will was dated 14th July, 1415; on October 25 following, Henry V., with a loss of only 1,600 men, had won the glorious battle of Agincourt, in which the Constable of France and 10,000 French soldiers were slain.

But what concerns this history more closely is another mark of the royal favour which was conferred upon Leventhorp. As recorded in the previous chapter, the death of Henry Heronville occurred in 1406; and as he left no son, the direct male line failed with him. But he left three daughters; Joanna, the eldest, who was then four years of age; Alicia, the second, who was two; Margareta, the third, who was one.

Wednesbury, being held of the King "in capite," the wardship of the three co-heiresses, so long as they remained under age was vested in the Crown. Henry V. gave his guardianship to his favourite squire, John de Leventhorp.

In his capacity of "custos," or guardian of the infant heirs of the Heronvilles, the name of John Leventhorpe, "armiger" (esquire), occurs in a number of records.

As the custos of the lands and of the heirs of Henry Heronville he is found in 1415 suing a number of Wednesbury colliers, who had broken into and damaged the manorial lands. The same year he sued one Richard Lowe, yeoman, of Walsall, to compel him "to give up a bag containing deeds and muniments which he unjustly detained."

Still in his capacity as custos of the land and heirs of Henry Heronville, John Leventhorpe in 1417 attached Robert Nyghtgale, "bocher," whom, with John in the Lee, Henry Hancokes, and John atte Lydyate, "colyers," and all described as of Wednesbury, he sued for breaking into his close at Wednesbury and doing damage. As plaintiff he accepted nominal damages, sufficient to vindicate his rights in the manor; and the suit was thereupon dismissed.

The next Staffordshire lawsuit in which he engaged was a very similar one in 1419; but in this instance the offence was committed by Whittington men on the Tymmore estate, of which he also had the custody on behalf of his wards. (Salt XVII., pp. 50, 52, 58 65).

In 1420 the two younger daughters of the deceased Henry Heronville became nuns, Alice being over seventeen years of age, and Margaret under seventeen at the time of taking the veil. At the formal inquiry, which was then taken on oath (exactly as if each girl was dead to the world), it was given in evidence that they were co-heiresses in the manor of Wednesbury, the manor of Tymmore, and lands in "Tibyton," with their "sister Joan, wife of William Leventhorpe," who was their nearest heir.

From this passage it is clearly manifest that John de Leventhorp had given his oldest ward Joanna (or Joan) in marriage to his own son; and that her two sisters, either voluntarily or under pressure, had very conveniently retired from the world. Having accomplished this very desirable family arrangement, John Leventhorpe, the father, drops out of our records, which presently show us William Leventhorpe in full possession of Wednesbury manor, holding it by the right of his wife.

To William Leventhorpe and John Harper were directed Letters Patent, dated 18th May, 1421, in the matter of certain disputed properties, of parts of which they had the custody. This property in its entirety consisted of the manor of Darlaston, the adowson of Darlaston Church, and lands in Bentley. There was a protracted lawsuit over the succession of Darlaston manor at this time.—See History of Darlaston, pp. 22-28, and Salt, Vol. XVII., pp. 132-135.

In 1432 William Leventhorpe and his wife Joan were concerned in an action for lands and property in Rushall, belonging to the family of Bowles, the heiress to which, one Eleanor, had been married to the aforementioned John Harper.

Of the Wednesbury branch of the Leventhorpes but little more is known. The family seem to have derived its name from a Yorkshire estate; but under the history of Hertfordshire are to be found genealogies and the bulk of the family records.

It is possible that William Leventhorpe was not the eldest son of his father; and as to John himself it is by no means improbable that he was but a cadet of this important Hertfordshire family. If so, the wardship of the infant Heronvilles was a welcome slice of good fortune, of which he failed not to make the most by marrying his son William to the eldest, and securing the whole of the Wednesbury and Tymmore estates undivided, to his own family. The very youthful age at which the two co-heiresses were induced to enter a convent and abandon their worldly rights savours strongly of the scheming efforts of a mature mind.

But the name of Leventhorpe was not fated to be handed down in connection with the manorial history of Wednesbury. Again the male line failed, for the only issue of the marriage of William Leventhorpe with Joan Heronville (who was living in 1435) was one daughter, who was named Joan.

Joan Leventhorpe in due time married and carried Wednesbury and all the other family estates to her husband, Sir Henry Beaumont, Knight.

The noble family of Beaumont was one of the most distinguished with which the manor of Wednesbury was ever associated .

.   .   .   .   .   .

About this time, or rather soon after the close of the Leventhorpe period, there is found living in Wednesbury a man named Charles Nowell, who was evidently a person of some position.

Thus in 1454 it appears that Charles Nowelle " within in his fee of Wednesbury," had impounded the cattle of a " husband-man," named William Haukes, " for customs and services owing to him "; whereupon the said William had violently and forcibly " broken into his pound " and carried off the cattle. A lawsuit followed thereupon. (Salt III., N.S., p. 218).

Again in 1460 the same Charles Nowell, described as an " armiger " (that is, an esquire entitled to bear arms), is found suing a Wednesbury " bocher " (butcher) named Thomas Whyng " for breaking into his close at Wednesbury," and digging and carrying away " earth " (evidently coal for fuel) to the value of £10.

It is suggested that as Sir Henry Beaumont was dead by 1452, and that his heir being a minor in 1454 and 1460, this Charles Nowell had his wardship during the period of his minority.

AN OLD VIEW OF STAFFORD.

From " Historic Staffordshire "]   [By permission of Midland Educational Co.

XIX.—THE BEAUMONTS OF WEDNESBURY.

The family of Beaumont derived its name from the seigniory of that town in France. According to Glover's "Derbyshire" (1829), the distinguished and highly-allied family of Beaumont deduce their origin from the early sovereigns of France.

The first mention of their connection with this country appears in the marriage of Richard, Viscount de Beaumont, to Constance, a natural daughter of Henry I.

In the twelfth century Eremengarda, the grand-daughter of Richard de Beaumont, espoused William, King of Scotland, and became the mother of a line of kings; and in the next generation, we find the possessions and honours of the Beaumonts vested in a female (Agnes, Viscountess de Beaumont and Mayne), who married Lewis de Brienne, surnamed of Acon.

The family of Brienne was extensively and powerfully allied. Their names are celebrated in the Crusades. Gauthier de Brienne became King of Naples and Sicily by his marriage with the daughter of Tancred; his brother John succeeded him, and, by espousing Yolanda, the daughter of the famous Conrad de Montserrat, became one of the early nominal sovereigns of Jerusalem.

Lewis of Acon, who married the heiress of the Viscounts de Beaumonts, was the second son of the King of Naples, and his children took the name of Beaumont. The eldest of these accompanied the famous Isabel (termed by Gray, "she-wolf of France"), wife of the unhappy Edward II., to England; and John, another of the sons of Lewis d' Acon, became the ancestor of the French branch of the Beaumonts.

In the next generation, the Beaumonts became doubly connected with the reigning royal family, by the marriages of John, Lord Beaumont, and his sister Isabella; the latter with Henry of Lancaster, and the former with the sister of that prince.

Beaumont, the knight errant who had found his way to England in the reign of Edward II., had a barony conferred upon him by that monarch in 1309.

In a publication entitled "Our noble and Gentle Families of Royal Descent" (London, Hatchards, 1885), there is given, on p. 366 of the Library Edition, the "Descent of Sir George Howland William Beaumont, Bart., of Cole Orton, Leicestershire, from the 'Blood Royal of England.'" In tracing the Genealogy, we find on p. 368, references to the Beaumonts of Wednesbury.

It would appear that Eleanor, daughter of Henry Earl of Lancaster, and great granddaughter of Henry III., married for her first husband one John, Baron Beaumont, who died in 1342. This Beaumont was Constable of England 12 Ed. II., and might have used his Scottish title of Earl of Buchan; by his marriage into the royal blood there was issue Henry third Baron Beaumont, whose son John the fourth Baron, was a K.G., and admiral of the

King's fleet northwards, warden of the Scotch Marches, and warden of the Cinque Ports, &c., &c., dying full of honour in 1396. This great noble left among other children Henry, the fifth baron, and Sir Thomas, his third son, through whom the pedigree of the present Sir G. H. W. Beaumont is traced, and with whom Wednesbury has no connection.

Referring to the eldest son, Henry, the fifth Baron Beaumont, we find that he had two sons; the eldest was lord John, constable and great chamberlain of England, K.G., created Count of Boulogne in France, 27th July, 1436, and Viscount Beaumont 12th February, 1440, being the first of that dignity in England. He fell in the cause of the House of Lancaster, at the battle of Northampton, 10th July, 1459. The second son of Henry, the fifth baron, and the brother of John, the powerful Lancastrian noble, was Sir Henry Beaumont of Wednesbury.

1.—Sir Henry Beaumont I., Knight (about 1440):—The first Sir Henry Beaumont, lord of Wednesbury, acquired the manor by his marriage with Joan, daughter and heir of William Leventhorpe, of Wednesbury. He also held the manor and lordship of Thorpe, in Balme, Yorkshire, by his father's will.

By his wife Joan he had three children; two were daughters, namely Margaret, a nun of Dartford, and Agnes; his only son, named Henry, after himself, received the honour of Knighthood, and succeeded him.

The first Sir Henry's tenure of Wednesbury must have been a very brief one of a few years only, for he was dead in 1446. At the Michaelmas term of that year we find that Joan Beaumont, "wydowe," formerly wife of Henry Beaumont, Knight, of Wednesbury, and executrix to his will, was sued by Roger Holbeche for a debt of £16 10s. 6½d. (Sa:t III., N.S., p. 172).

There is another record of her, in which she is again described as a "widow," of the year following (See Bagnall's "Wednesbury," pp. 49-50). In 1447 the Rev. Richard Marchald, priest, was presented to the vacant chantry of St. John the Baptist, at Walsall parish church, the presentation being "in the gift of the noble-woman Joanna, widow of Henry Beaumont, Knight, and of Richard Whithill, 'domicelli,' true patrons of the same chantry." A "domicelli," it may be explained, was a higher servant in a monastery; this Whithill evidently held some office of importance in Halesowen Abbey.

2.—Sir Henry Beaumont II., Knight (1446—1471):—The second Sir Henry Beaumont who held Wednesbury with the other family estates married Eleanor, youngest daughter of John de Sutton, K.G., Lord of Dudley, one of the greatest feudal barons of those warlike times (See "Sedgley Researches," p. 18).

By this marriage there were two sons and a daughter. The younger son was named James, whose wife was named Elizabeth; their arms were formerly in the windows of Wednesbury Church—see Bagnall, p. 146. The elder, who succeeded to the estate, was John Beaumont, born about 1470 .

Sir Henry was High Sheriff of Staffordshire during the year in which he died, 11 Edward IV.

Sir Henry made a will dated 14th November, 1471. Reference to it may be found in the Index to the Wills at the Prerogative Court of Canterbury, thus:—

"1472: Beamount, Henry, Weddesbury, Stafford; Derby; Yorks."

The testator died 16th November, 1471, and his will was proved 30th November, 1471. According to his testamentary dispositions, he was buried in the parish church of Wednesbury, to which he bequeathed the sum ot one hundred shillings (Bagnall's "Wednesbury," p. 58).

An abstract of the will (Testamenta Vetusta I., p. 322) runs:—

"Henry Beaumont, Knight, November 14th, 1471—my body in the church of Wednesbury, in the County of Stafford—I will that a chaplain celebrate for me in the said Church for three years after my decease—I will that the Lady Eleanor, my wife, have my lands in Eginton, in the county of Derby, and elsewhere, for the term of her life, with remainder to John Beaumont my son, and heir, by the said Eleanor—And I constitute Eleanor, my said wife, my executrix."

The usual Inquisitio Post Mortem was taken at Willenhall 28th June, 1472 (Bagnall, p. 25 from which it appeared that Sir Henry Beaumont held no lands, but that John Hampton, of Stourton Castle, esquire, was seized for the use of the said Henry Beaumont and his wife Eleanor, of Wednesbury manor, and lands in Tipton; and he had by deed granted them to the aforesaid Eleanor to be held by her for life, with remainder to the heirs of Sir Henry and his said wife Eleanor. The jury also found that Eleanor had survived her husband and was still fully alive (" in plena vita existit "); and that John Beaumont, the son and next heir, was of the age of two years and more.

Possibly John Hampton was a trustee under some deed of settlement. He was lord of Stourton and Kinver, and died in 1472; his alabaster monument in Kinver Church showed him in full armour, with spurs on heels, a collar of SS about his neck, a chaplet round his helmet, a crest of a black wolf's head issuing from the tilting helmet upon which his head rested: and curled at his feet was the sculptured full figure of a black wolf.

A few years after this there died at Frankley —with which place Wednesbury seems to have had some connection (see p. 42) — another eminent personage, whose will discloses that he owned lands in Wednesbury at this period. This will is that of Sir Thomas Lyttelton. Kt., the celebrated judge, and author of the well-known treatise on Tenures, which was written at Frankley 22nd August. 1481. It is a long document (Testamenta Vetusta I.. 362). in the course of which he bequeaths to his third son. Thomas (seated at Spechley, and from whom des-(see p. 42)

cended the Lord Keeper Lyttelton of Charles I.'s reign, and the Sir Thomas Lyttelton who was Speaker of the House of Commons in the reign of William III.), certain "lands, rents, reversions. and services that I have in Spechley, Cuddeley, Bradicot, and White - lady Aston, with the lands and tenements in Weddesbury in co. Stafford."

And now the family history of the Beaumonts may be resumed.

Eleanor, the young widow of Sir Henry Beaumont, re-married, her second husband being George Stanley, of West Bromwich, founder of a family who afterwards held that manor (See "A History of West Bromwich," p. 29). According to another extract from the Episcopal Register, printed on p. 50 of Bagnall's "Wednesbury," "George Stanley and the Lady Eleanor, wife of the same," were two of the "vice patrons" who made a presentation to the aforementioned chantry at Walsall, on 29th March, 1485.

3.—John Beaumont, Lord of Wednesbury (1471—1502):—At the death of his father, John Beaumont was more than two years old—see Inquisition Post Mortem on p. 22 of Bagnall's History. It has been mentioned that he had a sister; her name seems to have been either Eustace or Constance.

According to Salt I., p. 363, "Sir Richard (sic) Beaumont, of Wednesbury, in the county of Stafford, Knight, had a daughter Eustace, who married John Mitton, of Weston, esquire, and had by her one daughter, Joyce; the said John departed this life February 16th, 1552." according to a tablet in Weston Church. The date should be 1532; and a further correction is to the effect that his wife was Constance, daughter of Sir Henry Beaumont, of Wednesbury," etc., etc.

John Beaumont, of Wednesbury, married into the same family as his sister. His wife was Joan, daughter of John Mitton, of Weston, co. Stafford, or, as it is stated in the Harleian MS., 810, p. 23, "Eleanor, daughter of Weston, or Weston-under-Lizard, co. Staff." Whatever was the name of his wife, the Wednesbury Beaumonts became extinct at his death, 21st September, 18 Henry VII., as he left three daughters, but no son to inherit and perpetuate the name.

Bagnall's pedigree omits the name of the wife, simply describing her as a "daughter of Mitton, alias Harpesfield."

Joyce had previously married (1505) John Harpesfield ,of London. By an Indenture dated 20th November, 1533, "Richard Jenyns, Vicar of Wadesbury," and others who had been jointly enfeoffed "with James Beamont since deceased," remitted to Joyce Herpesfield, "daughter and heir" of John Mitton, the manors and estates in Salop, co. Stafford, and elsewhere. which had formerly been held for the said John Mytton's "son and heir." (Salt II., N.S., p. 129).

In 1493 John Beaumont with Sir Henry Vernon made presentation of a chantry priest at Walsall Church (Bagnall, p. 51, and Willmore's "Walsall," p. 129).

The Index of Wills at the Canterbury Prerogative Court has one of—

"1513: Beaumonte, John, Esq., Wednesbury, Stafford."

By this will of John Beaumont (1502) he appointed "Richard Wrottesley, Esq., and Humphrey Swinnerton, Esq., to make 'stat' (sic) to James Beaumont his brother of the lands in Wednesbury, to him and his heirs for ever; and also after the decease of Elenor his mother to make 'stat' (sic) of the manor of Tymore to James and his heirs for ever, and likewise of Eginton"; which "John (continues Shaw's "Staffordshire," II., p. 84), dying that year (1502), and James having no issue, his three daughters were his heirs," etc.

So that John's eager desire to perpetuate the name of Beaumont through his brother James failed altogether.

Although the Wednesbury Beaumonts soon became extinct, this was not the case with other branches of this great and important family. The Beaumonts have distinguished themselves in many ways; as soldiers, there was Sir John Beaumont of Cole-orton, who was slain at Towton, fighting for the Red Rose faction: while in the Civil Wars of Charles I. another Sir John fell at the siege of Gloucester, and a number of titled Beaumonts had to pay fines for their loyalty to the Royalist cause. Sir Francis Beaumont, of Gracedieu, was one of the judges of Elizabeth's reign. Two of his sons, John and Francis, distinguished themselves as poets; the dramatic works written by the latter in conjunction with his friend Fletcher, son of the Bishop of London, will ever be ranked among the highest classics of the English language.

The interesting fact has been recorded that a Beaumont was the first to bear the title of "Viscount" in England; but he was the first and last of his race to do so. In the reign of James I. a Beaumont petitioned for its revival; but without success. In 1840, however, the barony of Beaumont was restored to Miles Stapleton, who became the eighth baron Beaumont; this gentleman (who represented the ancient family) importuned the House of Lords till he succeeded in being restored to the rights of his ancestors, evidently sustained by the family motto "Things will be better." The crest of the Beaumonts, which is a Saracen's head, connects the family with the Crusading period; and it may be worth mentioning that the supporters of the family arms (and in England none below the grade of Banneret were allowed supporters) are two talbot-dogs, with slit ears dropping gouts of blood. The arms of the Wednesbury branch, which were entirely different, were formerly emblazoned at Wednesbury Old Church, on its

"Storied windows richly dight."

AN OLD VIEW OF WOLVERHAMPTON.

From "Historic Staffordshire"]　　　　　[By permission of Midland Educational Co.

XX.—SOME LOCAL EVIDENCES IN THE DECLINE OF FEUDALISM.

Feudalism was that system of military government which held sway in England for some five centuries, its iron grip of the nation being firmest under the Norman monarchs; and relaxing very slowly, yet none the less surely, under the Plantagenets. It was a form of constitution which sapped the industrial vitality of the nation, and barred the way to all commercial progress. As such it proved particularly irksome to the enterprising English spirit; and as the Englishman emerged from serfdom to freedom he gradually broke down its barriers one by one, till in the spacious times of Queen Elizabeth he was free to turn aside from the private squabbles of petty lordlings, and go forth to the conquest of new worlds, to expend his energies in the building up of new empires across the seas.

In this place the workings of feudalism can be noted only so far as they relate to Wednesbury and its vicinity. Of the earlier workings of the system there are but few local records. Here is one:—

Edward I. having formed an alliance with the Flemings and the German Emperor against the French King in 1297, took an army to Flanders on August the 21st of that year. In this expedition the active John de Heronville I. and his tenants took part, rendering the usual military services (Salt VIII., p. 19). But as Sir John's name is scheduled under the heading of Oxfordshire, it would appear that the lord of Wednesbury was serving for his Heronville estates in that county.

If this may be accepted to signify that Sir John Heronville was doing feudal service for Hooknorton, a short digression dealing with that subject may be made here.

As previously mentioned, the Heronvilles inherited some interest in the Oxfordshire manor of Hooknorton. But while Wednesbury manor was held by them "in capite" directly of the King, the manor of Hooknorton was held under a great baron.

The D'Oylys, who came over with the Conqueror, held the barony of Hooknorton first. Sir Foulk D'Oyly, the Crusader, mentioned in Scott's "Ivanhoe," was a son of the fourth baron of Hooknorton. Some portion of Wednesbury seems to have been held by Ralph Boterel under the D'Oylys (see p. 26). Then, in 1232, the barony passed to a nephew, Henry de Newburgh, fifth earl of Warwick. Thus (p. 26) we find Ela, Countess of Warwick, holding it. Then in 37 Henry III. the D'Oyly baronies passed by marriage into the hands of the family of the De Plessets (or De Plescy—see p. 33).

The county historians of Oxfordshire ignore this matter of the subinfeudation of the manor of Hooknorton to the Heronvilles. Only once in Kennet's "Oxfordshire" is the name of Heronville mentioned, and then merely as a witness to a deed. Yet it is certain, as recorded on p. 29, that at one time the Heronvilles were seated at Hooknorton.

It will be interesting to note in a future chapter that another family connected with Wednesbury, though somewhat remotely, had also interests in the same Oxfordshire estates. These were the Babingtons of Oxfordshire. Robert Babington, in 1464, left Lower Kiddington, Asterley, and Hoke (? Norton) to his son and heir. He was hereditary Keeper of the Palace of Westminster, and the first Warden of the Fleet Prison.

To resume our main subject, perhaps the earliest sign of decay in the ancient feudal system is where money payments are accepted side by side with military services.

In 1327, on the accession of the youthful Edward III,. the Scots took advantage of the King's minority to invade England. The English parliament at once granted a subsidy to carry on a war of defence; the tax was one-twentieth part of all movable goods, as valued by the elected assessors in every vill or township. The villeins in each manor seem to have been taxed equally with the freeholders, which may be accepted as a sign of the growing emancipation of the serf. Armour and cavalry horses were exempted from the impost, because, when there was no standing army, these added to the military strength of the country. Agricultural implements went free, as did also the goods of the poor, if they did not reach ten shillings in assessable value. On the other hand, the nobility obtained exemption for their plate and jewels.

The returns on the Subsidy Roll (1327) for this parish stands as follows:—

Wednesbury.

De—

	s.	d.	
Juliana de Hervile	iiij	iiij	qu.
Matilda de Grete ...		xxij	ob.
Rog'o de Brynghul ...	ij	iij	
Ric'o de Erbury		xxij	
Galfrido Henrys	iij		qu.
Joh'e Attyate	iij		ob. qu.
Henr' Attelideyate	iij		ob. qu.
Hugon'e Aleyn	ij		ob.
Joh'e atte Grene	ij		ob. qu.
Joh'e Dvmoke		viij	
Joh'e Hanrys		x	
Joh'e de Hervile	ij		qu.

Summa ... ... **xxvijs. jd. Pb.**

In the foregoing list the name of Hervile is, of course, Heronville: Grete is a family name still seen in Greets Green and Great (or Greet) Bridge; the Henrys or Hanrys, the Erburys, the Dymokes or Dimmocks, and the Greens seem to have been the names of yeomen families in mediæval Wednesbury; and it is supposable that as one John lived "at Green" (Wood Green or Delves Green), there was another John, a Wednesbury freeholder, who lived "at the gate" ("Attyate"), a well-known landmark in the parish, either a town-gate on the Portway, or that described in 1628 as "Monway Gate" (Bagnall, p. 59)

The whole of the circumstances connected with the levying of this ancient war tax have been explained rather fully in "A History of

West Bromwich " (pp. 19 and 20); a few glossarial explanations will suffice here to make this piece of mediæval accountancy intelligble to the general reader.

The " De " in front of the first item, and understood to be repeated all the way down the other items, is equivalent to the modern commercial expression " received of." The abbreviation " r̄b " at the end of the account stands for " Probata," signifying " proven," or, as the modern expression stands, " audited and found correct." The " ob." is the abbreviated form of " obolus," or " halfpenny," as " qu." is of " quarter-penny " or " farthing " —the silver pennies then in use were literally cut into " halfpence " and " forthings," and circulated in such fragments. A simple piece of addition will show that the " summa " or " total " actually amounts to the twenty-seven shillings and one penny.

A few years later (1332) the country was taxed for the same king's Scotch Wars. The method of levying and collecting this war tax is also explained in " A History of West Bromwich " (p. 20). Cities, boroughs, and ancient demesnes of the Crown were assessed at one-tenth; while in vills or parishes outside these limits the tax-payers escaped with the payment of only one-fifteenth assessed on all goods and chattels valued at 10s. and upwards. Wednesbury came under the former category, and is included in the same collection as Walsall, the " summa " for the two amounting to 114s. 1¼d. This is the Wednesbury list of tax-payers in 1332-3:—

Wednesbury.

De—

	iij	viij	ob.	qu.
Joh'ne de Hereville ...	iij	viij	ob.	qu.
Juliana de Hervill	vj	iiij	ob.	qu.
Joh'ne Dymoke	iij	ix	ob.	
Thomas de Brynghull ...	iiij	vj		
Ric'o de Erbury	ij	j		qu.
Joh'ne Henrys	ij	x		qu.
Hug' Aleyn	ij	v		
Joh'ne Averey	ij	iiij		
Will'o Underhull ...		xviij		qu.
Henr' de Derlaston		xiij	ob.	
Thoma le Rede		xij		qu.

In the division of Offlow Hundred paying on the lower assessment of one-fifteenth appear Darlaston and Bentley, with a number of other parishes: the next one being Elford, where a freeholder named William Hacwode pays a tax of two shillings and a farthing. (Salt X., p. 105).

So much for taxation, or money payments, on behalf of feudal warfare. There is an entirely different kind of incident recorded of the year 1415, which is highly significant of the declining state of feudalism at that period. It is recorded (Salt XVII., p. 20) that a fine of £20 was imposed upon " John Broun, of Lychefeld, squyer, for giving Liveries against the Statute to John Baker, of Wennesbury, and four others named, at Christmas 12 Henry IV." (1411). Fines of 40s. each were also forfeited by " the same John Baker and the others named, for receiving the same Liveries."

Who these Wednesbury men were who accepted the Liveries is immaterial. But the incident itself illustrates a great constitutional change which was then being slowly effected.

The great feudal barons had been accustomed to distribute liveries amongst their dependents and retainers. The wearing of such liveries was not confined exclusively to menial servants of the household (as at the present time); and in a military system like that of ancient feudalism it was no more degrading to wear a baron's livery than it is at the present day for a colonel or other high officer to wear the king's uniform.

Feudal barons were as kings in their own domain, and when right was might, each noble tried to furnish himself with the largest number of swords and spears, and strong right arms to wield them. It is not surprising, therefore, that the nobles, and afterwards the gentry in imitation of them, should try to enlist as many mercenaries as possible to serve under their respective banners. These were supplied with liveries the same as their lawful retainers, the colours being consistent with the armorial bearings of the employer, and carrying his heraldic device as a distinguishing badge.

This dangerous practice, which made for tumults and disturbances rather than for peace and quietness, had prevailed to such an extent during the 14th century that Richard II. determined to try to check it by most severe enactments. He ordered that " no varlets called yeomen, nor none others of less estate than esquire should should use, nor bear no badge or livery called livery of company of any lord within the realm, unless he be menial or familiar or continual officer of the said lord."

It is probable that the five Wednesbury offenders were " varlets called yeomen "; and it is manifest they were not the tenants or feudal retainers of the man who employed them to wear his livery. He was, admittedly, only a " squire," and not the head of a great barony.

The statutes against Liveries were allowed to fall into abeyance till Henry VII. put them into force again with the heaviest penalties he could possibly impose. This broke up the feudal power of the nobles so effectively that the Tudors reigned almost as absolute monarchs.

Coming to the Wars of the Roses, which dealt Feudalism its death-blow, there can be little doubt that this locality sustained its full share of misery and suffering during the thirty years of that civil strife. The Battle of Blore Heath was fought on Staffordshire soil in 1459.

As already recorded, Lord Beaumont, brother to Sir Henry Beaumont, of Wednesbury, was slain at the Battle of Northampton, 1460, in which Henry VI. was defeated and taken prisoner Among other nobles with interests in this locality who fell on that disastrous day was Buckingham, who held the great barony of Stafford, of which Darlaston formed a part.

Of this great battle, in which 10,000 Lancastrians were slain, there is a quaint account in " Hall's Chronicle," published in 1548 · that is, within 90 years of the event. The King had assembled his army at Coventry, and possibly men from this locality were drawn amongst the rest, by " ye lord Beaumond." " At this battayl were slain, Humfrey duke of Buckingham, Ihon Talbot erle of Shrewsbury, a valeant person, and not degenerating fro his noble parent; Thomas lord Egremond, Ihon viscount Beaumond, and syr William Lucy.

* * Diuers others gentlemen were slayn in this ciuile battail, whose names were not remembered nor published by any aucthor that I have redde."

Mention was made in the last chapter that this John, Viscount Beaumont, was an elder brother of Sir Henry Beaumont, of Wednesbury; and that another knightly Beaumont was slain at the Battle of Towton (1461), yet another Lancastrian disaster.

Our records now leap forward almost another century. In 1539 the Pope, Paul IV., excommunicated Henry VIII. for his heretical opinions, and endeavoured to induce the Emperor Charles V. and Francis of France to make war upon him.

Alarmed at this, the King and his privy council ordered a muster to be made of the entire force of the kingdom. The levies were never called up, as Henry's diplomacy was sufficient to disconcert the Pope's plans; but Letters Patent appointing Commissioners of Array for each county were issued 1st March, 1539, among those for Staffordshire being Sir George Gresley, Knt., John Vernon, and William Wyrley, Esq., in Offlow Hundred.

Strangely enough, the published Muster Rolls for this Hundred are as yet incomplete as regards Wednesbury, although the names of nearly all the surrounding parishes are to be found. All that can be noted is the name of Comberford, which is the name of a family at that time in possession of Wednesbury manor, as will be noted in due course.

Thus it occurs in the Returns then made (Salt IV., N.S., p. 226):—

Under "Wyggentun and Comberford" appears the name of "Humfray Cvmborford, horse, harnes, bill, able"; meaning thereby that he was able to take the field, equipped with all kinds of defensible armour for man and horse.

Under the heading of "Rowlston" appears a similar return (1539) respecting Thomas Rowlson, with whom the family of the Wednesbury Rollasons are said to be connected.

Harking forward yet another century, our local records will disclose the last phases of decaying feudalism. It will be manifest to the reader that the land being no longer made to bear the full burden of the national defence, the age of standing armies was clearly within sight.

A Muster Roll was made in 1640 to repress the Scotch Covenanters. The evil genius of Charles I. led him to undertake heavy liabilities in a conflict with his own subjects. The trained bands were employed, and in Staffordshire an additional body of 300 men were impressed for the occasion. The cost of the first equipment of the men, and their maintenance till they reached the place of rendezvous (Selby, in Yorkshire), was found by the county. This was called "coat and conduct money": on their arrival at the rendezvous they received their arms, and were then paid by the King at the rate of 8d. a day—a sum quite equal to 2s. present money.

The levies were made on the various Hundreds of Staffordshire, for military service to commence on 1st July, 1640, at Uttoxeter. In the list of the soldiers called up on that occasion occur the following names in Offlowe Hundred:—

Traine.

Wedgbury.—George Maydewe,
William Paskin,
Thomas Siluster.
Presse.
Richard Wyatt,
William Shelnocke.

In addition to the men raised in this manner, a force of cavalry was procured under the old feudal law dating from Edward III., and which was still in force. It was enacted that all who held land of a clear annual value of £10 up to 20 marks should find a hobelar (light-horseman), and those who held £20 of land two hobelars, and those assessed at £25 a man-at-arms—a lancer completely covered with armour. Although these feudal levies could not be constrained to take the field unless the King placed himself at the head of the army, there were never lacking volunteers when hard fighting was in prospect. It is interesting to note that on this, the last occasion of raising a national force of feudal retainers, a Wednesbury gentleman, William Hopkins, of Oakeswell Hall, was commissioned in his "division" to purchase 6 of the 50 Horses required to carry the ammunition. Under the heading of Offlow Hundred, the return of purchases made on 14th July, 1640, was as follows:—

Mr. Hopkys diuicon:—

	li.	s.	d.
Wednesbury...1 bay nagge baught of Rich. Haukes; price	5	0	0
eadm ... ... 1 bay nagge baught of John Carter; price	8	0	0
in eadm ... 1 sorrel nagge baught of Rich. Tunke; price	5	0	0
Rushiall ... 1 white gelding baught of Nich. Ward; price	6	10	0
Walsall Forren 1 daple gray nagge baught of John Byrch; price	7	10	0
West Bromwich 1 bay gelding baught of Thomas Groves; price	6	10	0

Omnes sine Condicone.

The trained bands were armed with pikes and firelocks, and the impressed men with pikes only; and when the army came in contact with the Covenanters at Newburn on the Tyne, the whole of the infantry behaved very badly. The fact was, the service was highly unpopular. The cavalry, however, did good service.

In the same Muster Roll is an earlier list, which appears to have been used on this occasion (1640). Headed "A list of the Travned horse of the County of Stafford, taken at Stafford 5th June, and at Litchfei'd 2nd October, 1634," it contains among the 20 landowners in Offlow Hundred liable for providing "Curiasiers" these names:—

Sr. Richard Shilton, Kt.	1
Sr. Thomas Whorewood, Kt.	2
Simon Mountford, Esq.	1
Humfrey Wyrly, Esq.	1
William Cumberford, of Cumberford, Esq.	1
William Cumberford, of Tamworth, Esq.	1
Mrs. Lane and her sonne.	

—the estates of the foregoing gentry being respectively at West Bromwich, Sandwell, Bescot, Hamstead, Comberford, Tamworth, and Bentley.

XXI.—GLEANINGS FROM THE LAW COURTS (14TH & 15TH CENTURIES).

From the records of proceedings in the mediæval Courts of Law, many interesting items may be gleaned which throw strong sidelights on the social life of Wednesbury at that period.

First of all, it will be noted how the landed interests always stood first and foremost with our forefathers. The search for wealth and position in those days resolved itself almost exclusively into the acquisition of lands and estates. Many extracts from the old records will illustrate this, and show how strictly all rights in the proprietorship of the soil were guarded. Feudalism, as will appear from the previous chapter, had at least one great merit —it made such ownership of the land bear the entire burden of the national defence.

John Heronville II., in 1369, sued John Dymmok, of Wednesbury, for forcibly breaking into his close at Wednesbury, and allowing his cattle to consume and tread down his grass and corn. Trespass was always resolutely resented, in whatever form it appeared. (Salt XIII., p. 69).

In 1344 the same John de Heronville sued Robert de Wynnesley (clerk), and John Henryes, of Wednesbury, and Joan de Wyrley (widow), for forcibly taking fish from his fishpond at Tipton. Two of the three parties, namely, John de Heronville and Joan are concerned with others in a law suit three years later. (Salt XII., 24 and 53).

Fishponds were useful adjuncts to land when Roman Catholicism prevailed, and made compulsory the observance of so many fast-days throughout the year.

Henry Heronville (afterwards lord of Wednesbury) had to sue a man in 1401 for forcibly breaking into his close at Tymmore, and taking fish from his fishponds there. (Salt XIII. 152). A similar trespass of the year 1388 has already been recorded on p. 41.

A case of the year 1416 reveals the name of Bond as that of a landed family in Wednesbury, holding in demesne. One Richard Bonde sued his father's executrix for the possession of three "pyxes" (caskets for holding coins or precious articles), containing the family deeds and muniments. One was a deed by which the Abbot of Halesowen had conveyed to Richard's great-grandfather a messuage, 10 acres of land, and a piece of moor in Wednesbury. Another deed was that by which his grandfather had acquired 30 acres in the same vill, and the third was the document by which John Heronville had remitted and quitclaimed to his grandfather all rights in the said lands and tenements. However, it was pleaded that his right of action was barred by a deed in which, under the name of "Richard Bowde of Wodesbury," he had previously abandoned every claim to the said properties, and that therefore he had no claim to the deeds.

The Heronvilles were in some way connected with a West Bromwich lawsuit of the years 1360-3, from the records of which it appears that John Heronville acted as Bailiff to William de Heronville and Joan his wife, to John de Alrewas and Alianora his wife, and certain others; these were defendants in the case, and among the others it is interesting to note the name of John Tymmesone, of "Finchespathe."

The property at stake was the considerable sum of 100s. of rent in Bromwich. The dispute arose out of the second marriage of the original possessor of this property, one William Goide (? of Gold's Hill). By his first marriage he had two children, Thomas Golde and Christiana, a daughter, who became the wife of John Bonde, of Wednesbury. By his second wife Agnes he had two daughters, Alice and Isabel.

William Golde, by a deed dated at Fynspathe, Friday after the Feast of St. Hillary 5 Ed. III., granted the said rent of 100s. under the title of all his lands and tenements in Bromwych, to his son Thomas Golde. But Thomas died before his father; and when the father, William Golde, died, John and Christiana Bonde, of Wednesbury, entered into possession. Then arose other claimants, including Alice and Isabel, sisters of the half-blood to Thomas Golde, whose claims led to lengthened litigation.

In 1374 it appeared that Richard de Heronville and Margaret his wife held lands of the inheritance of one Roger Golde, of which they refused to make partition with John atte Lee and his wife, "according to the law and custom of the kingdom." (Salt XII., p. 171, XIII., pp 5, 28, 104: ante p. 41).

Another Richard Hervill and Juliana his wife were concerned in a lawsuit over lands in West Bromwich in 1373. If these names are correct the parties may have been a collateral branch of the Heronville family; and it is interesting to note that "Harvill's" Hawthorn in West Bromwich parish borrows its name from that of the Wednesbury Heronvilles, or some branch of them. (Salt XI., 180).

The next few extracts introduce the name of Hancocks. This family was evidently one of some importance, as they lent their name to a locality; High Bullen being anciently called "Hancock's Cross."

John Hancokes, of Wednesbury, served on a jury for the Hundred of Offe (Offlow) in 1377. (Salt XIV., 143).

John Heronville and Margaret his wife, in 1390, sued Richard Hancock and others for breaking into their close at Wednesbury, and doing them a large amount of damage, for which damages were claimed.

Four years later a number of Wednesbury tenants, who had not rendered him their feudal services for two years, were sued for their holdings; among the defendants was Joan, daughter of William Hancokes.

Henry Hancokes, of Wednesbury, "husbondman," and a "bocher" named Robert Nightgale, were sued for debt in 1416. These were parties in another suit, mentioned on p. 43. Some years earlier, according to the Plea Rolls of 1402, Henry Hancokkes, and a Juliana, widow of a Richard Hancokkes, of Weddensbury, appear on opposite sides of a trespass suit. At the same Assizes this Henry Hancokkes was charged with breaking into a house at Wednesbury, and taking four quarters of bee), worth 40s.; and at the following Assizes with damaging and consuming with his cattle the crops of John Heronville, at Wednesbury. (Salt XV., pp. 18, 54, 102, 104, 105).

Here we trench upon the criminal as well as the civil side of the law. Some further examples of ancient criminal proceedings may now be given to illustrate the moral and social condition of Wednesbury in those times.

In the first three, the place-name Finchpath recurs again.

For the murder of Alice, wife of Roger le Cok, at Fynchespathe, one Roger de Borleye was in 1337 found guilty before the Coroner, and hanged.

For an act of felony, one Richard Courson, "yeoman, of Fynspade," was in 1415, threatened with the punishment of outlawry.

In the following year Richard Dudley, Prior of Sandwell Monastery, sued John Ford, of Fynspade, husbandman, for breaking into his close and houses at Fynspade, and taking goods and chattels valued at 100s., and for treading down and consuming his grass with his cattle.

Two sons of Simon Heronville, of Wednesbury, whose names were John and Richard, together with several other defendants, were charged in 1363 with beating, wounding, and ill-treating at Wednesbury, John Marshall, the servant of Roger Hillary, Knight.

Three years later the same John Heronville, son of Simon, was sued by Hugh de Wrottesley for forcibly abducting his "native," Alice Hitchcokes, who was in his service at Wrottesley. Alice was a "native" born bondservant on Wrottesley manor, and, under feudal law, had no right to go away from it to work in Wednesbury or any other place. She was a serf, and therefore tied to the soil. (Salt XIII., 25, 48).

John Heronville, lord of Wednesbury, in 1373 charged Sir Roger Hillary, Knight, and William Sagowe, chaplain, with abducting four men from his service—doubtless "natives," or the born serfs of Wednesbury soil. Sir Roger was lord of Bescot manor, and was evidently taking some high-handed proceedings against his neighbour; for at the same Court John Heronville accused the same two offenders with coming to Wednesbury and beating, ill-treating, and wounding Alice, his wife. (Salt XIII., 92).

Strangely enough, in 1406, another John Heronville had to bring an action against Richard Frebody, of Dudley, and several others, for insulting and assaulting his wife Margaret, at Dudley. (Salt XIII., 185). The same John Heronville and Margaret his wife have just been mentioned as suing Richard Hancock in 1390.

In 1442 four men were prosecuted by Richard le bard for insulting, wounding, and beating him at Wednesbury, and keeping him a prisoner there until he paid a fine of 6s. for his release. It would be interesting to know who this unfortunate "bard" was! He seems to have fallen into the hands of men little better than brigands. (Salt III., N.S., 161, 224).

One Elena Roggers in 1457 brought a charge of rape against Thomas Robyns, "late of Waddesbury, yeoman," and a number of other men from Enville and Alveley, in Salop. Ten years later John Smyth, another Wednesbury "yeoman," broke into the houses of one William Harpur, at Darlaston. And so the tale of crime and outrage might be continued. But enough has been adduced to convey an idea of the condition of life in feudal Wednesbury.

The frequent recurrence in the pleadings of such terms as "husbandman" and "yeoman," indicate that it was an age of agriculture. Then the repeated allusions to "meadow," "pasture," "common" lands, "moor," "furze," and "wood," convey some idea of the rurality of olden Wednesbury, in the days of the Merrie England of long ago. In 1553 "twenty acres of wood in Wednesbury" formed part of a claim in an action at law.

The population of the parish could have numbered but a very few hundreds; perhaps not a couple of hundreds. Even at that figure it would probably be higher than that of any of the surrounding parishes, inasmuch as Wednesbury had very early begun to develop a new industry—that of coal-getting, to which due attention will be given in the next chapter. Nail-making was another local industry, but no direct allusion to its existence in Wednesbury is found till about the year 1500.

Whatever importance Wednesbury had attained in the Saxon period, when Ethelfleda's castles were always combined with burghs—and so eminent a writer and antiquarian as Dugdale, writing of Aston, says that its name was originally Estone, that is, the town east of Wordsbury (Wednesbury), a town of some note in Saxon times—it was a place of no importance whatever in the Middle Ages. There are ancient references to a "Gate" near the lower end of the town, and to places called "Bradeswall" (1315), and "Springswall" (1315), and on p. 40 "Wedneswall" was mentioned; but no shred of evidence exists that ever Wednesbury was a walled or fortified town after the Norman Conquest.

Of woods and wastes around Wednesbury there was a vast extent. The sparseness of the population during three centuries may be inferred from much of the foregoing. War and pestilence did much to keep down the population in those times.

It has been recorded that wolves existed in the neighbourhood of Wednesbury in the thirteenth century. At the end of that century (1281), Sir Peter Corbett was commissioned to destroy all the wolves in the royal forests of Staffordshire, and the adjacent counties of Salop, Hereford, Worcester, and Gloucester, and the Bailiffs of those counties were directed to give him every assistance.

Concerning the Royal Forest of Cannock there is a legend which shows it to have been hunted by the King down to the fifteenth century. The ballad of "The Tanner of Tamworth" chronicles how Edward IV. was hunting in Drayton Basset, when the tanner met him, and after some bargaining they exchanged horses, the King giving his valuable hunter for the tanner's mare, "Brocke," a sorry beast worth but four shillings. But the poor tanner soon found that he could not ride the fiery spirited animal, and was glad to forfeit a good sum to get back his own gentle mare. Then the King wound his horn. and when the scattered courtiers came riding up, the poor tanner expected nothing less than to be hanged. But the King "in merry pin" gave him the manor of Plumpton Park with 300 marks a year. As

thus it reads in the "Percy Reliques":—

"Nowe, out, alas!" the tanner he cryde,
- "That ever I sawe this daye!
Thou art a strong thiefe! yon come thy fellowes
To bear my cowhide away."
"They are no thieves," the King replyde,
"I sweare, sae mate I thee;
But they are the lordes of the north countrey
Here come to hunt with mee."

XXII.—THE ASPECT OF WEDNESBURY ABOUT 1500.
ITS EARLY COAL MINING.

Mediæval Wednesbury was but a small place, but doubtless pretty, and prosperous withal. Let us glance at it as it appeared towards the dawn of the Tudor period.

The little town lay chiefly on the southern and western declivities of that eminence which was crowned by its stately parish church, the architectural beauty of which bore testimony to the devotion of many past generations of pious parishioners.

The houses were for the most part irregular and ill-designed, yet not without a picturesqueness of their own. Most of them were old, strongly framed in timber, and well thatched; this state of good repair bearing witness to the general prosperity of the town.

The houses of this little straggling township were built in clusters, rather than in continuous lines along the main streets and cross lanes. Of street-names there were but few; possibly not one was then in use except that of the ancient 'Portway"; not even the King's highway through the town had as yet appropriated the proper name "High Street." But to the different quarters of the parish had been applied many place-names which are still in use; these residential parts, where the houses clustered in groups were known respectively as "Town End," "Oakeswell End," "Hall End," and "Bridge End." Near the last-named locality were "Finchpath" and the "Ridding," both on the brook-side between Mesty Croft and Wednesbury Bridge.

The open space now known as High Bullen was then called "Hancock's Cross"; possibly because a wayside shrine had been erected there at the cost of this well-to-do family, of whom some account was given in the last chapter. (In 1728 the lane now called Ladbury's Lane was described as leading from Hancock's Cross, alias High Bullen, to "Spicers Stock," or "Spicers Street Stock").

The most important residence in the parish after the Manor House was that quaint old mansion which is still standing, Oakeswell Hall. The Manor House, known as Wednesbury Hall, seems to have been re-built in the Tudor period. The remnants of it have now been converted into a farmhouse.

Near the centre of the main street would be a sprinkling of burgages, the class of larger houses in which resided the few tradesmen, such as nail-factors, and well-to-do yeomen.

These burgages were much newer, and considerably taller buildings than the bulk of their neighbours, consisting of over-hanging storeys, the topmost surmounted by high-peaked gables ornamented by quaintly-carved barge-boards, above which peeped clusters of ornamental chimney pots on the tops of their massively built chimney-stacks.

The majority of the houses, however, were old low-built cottages, consisting simply of one storey. But every house, large or small, had its slang of garden land attached to it; and behind every burgage was an orchard, or an enclosed paddock, or just as often, both.

Of the existence of any public buildings besides the church, the evidences are but shadowy and vague. It can only be surmised that "Monway Gate," mentioned in old deeds as a well-known landmark in the parish, was an ancient watch-house on the Portway—perhaps a rude but massively built gate-house.

It has been suggested that the neighbourhood of the High Bullen was anciently the site of two mediæval institutions; one was the "Spital," or manorial hospital for the reception of travelling friars and other poor wayfarers, and believed to have been situated in that narrow thoroughfare once known as "Beggars' Row"; the other, a Bethlehem Hospital for lunatics, situated in the adjacent lane, which therefrom acquired the name of "Bedlam."

Although the dwelling-houses were all detached, and often well separated from each other by gardens, closes, and sometimes open fields, the insanitary principles upon which they were all constructed, and the absence of any recognised system of drainage. invited those visitations of pestilence which in olden times made periodical appearances in every part of the country. It was when the neighbourhood was once plague-infected that, according to traditional local history, Wednesbury and Walsall markets were removed to Stone Cross: at the buying and selling there carried on, it is said that the buyer first approached a great hollowed stone filled with vinegar or other potent liquid, and deposited therein the price of the wares or provisions which the vendor from a safe distance had agreed to accept, and which he fetched out of the disinfecting fluid when the purchaser had again retired.

So much for the appearance of the old town. Now to consider the people who lived and moved within its little sphere of social life; and, first of all, how they employed themselves. Practically, it was an agrarian population; but it was not purely so.

Except on market days and at Fair-time, there was but little of life and animation to break the stillness of the streets of olden Wednesbury. Beyond the townsfolk themselves, but few people ever passed along its sleepy High Street or its less-frequented by-lanes. The strangers who excited least interest were the shaven friars, who trudged about in couples, clad in hooded and wide-sleeved frocks, girded up with thongs of black leather, and who asked of all well-to-do burghers the alms with which they were enabled to perform their acts of charity. "Friars' Park" names a retreat from which the good brothers were wont to set forth on their errands of mercy.

Yet, though so few folk were to be seen out of doors signs of human life and activity were not entirely wanting to the ears. Up and down the parish, near at hand and subdued by distance, were to be heard the tinkling of many busy hammers and the ring of resounding anvils. For from a very early period of its industrial history, Wednesbury had been the home of the nail-making craft.

Nailers' workshops were attached to not a few of the cottages. The flooring of them was merely mother earth trodden hard; and the light of day was admitted to them through unglazed casements, the appertures of which could be closed only by shutters of wood.

It was in domiciliary workshops of this type that master and 'prentice plied their arduous trade; living together in the adjoining apartment, which communicated directly with the smithy, and which in fittings and furniture bettered it but little; the dwellings of the poor affording few comforts or conveniences, and, indeed, scarcely providing for the ordinary decencies of life.

In an age given over to feudal militarism, there were but few industrial callings to occupy the time and attention of the good folk of Wednesbury, the majority of whom in times of peace followed man's primal pursuit, the tillage of the soil. But doubtless there were others.

The town possibly contained an armourer or two, a cutler, and a chape-maker or harness-smith, among its other workers in "the metal of war."

The woods in and around Wednesbury found occupation for a few swineherds; a barker or two, who obtained the oak-bark for supplying the numerous tan-pits in and around Wednesbury and Walsall: and on the same side, towards Cannock Forest, not a few would follow the trade of charcoal burning.

At one time mention is made of a "coupere" —the coopering craft is an ancient and a useful one to thirsty civilised man.

Besides "bochers," tanners, and fellmongers, glovers are recorded to have followed their calling on the Darlaston side; and as weaving as well as domestic spinning was done in every town and village (was it not mentioned on p. 38 that the lord of Wednesbury manor took as a Heriot every uncut piece of cloth standing on the loom of a deceased tenant?), there would most probably be fullers and dyers also plying their industrial arts in the vicinity.

The milling interest was well represented in Wednesbury. Besides the water-mill on the brook at Finchpath, there were by this period two, if not three, windmills. The site of one was known to be in Windmill Lane, a second in Reservoir Terrace, and a third at King's Hill.

But in this history, the calling which demands the greatest amount of notice is that connected with coal-getting. The earliest allusion to "cole-pits" in Wednesbury is dated 1315, when a piece of land is described as "lying near bradeswalle, over against the cole-pits."

Ere the fourteenth century had closed, it is quite manifest, from a number of law court proceedings that the people of Wednesbury had satisfied themselves of the practical usefulness of the new mineral fuel, which was to be found so abundantly on all sides of them.

Doubtless the good folk of Wednesbury at first regarded the coals, which could be obtained so readily below the turf, or at most for digging only a foot or two below the surface, as something which might be appropriated for the mere getting of it. It must be remembered that as tenants of the manor they had the right of Turbary (that is, of digging turf), and also the right of Estovers (that is, of collecting sticks for fuel). Here was a strange kind of black "earth," which could be dug up like turf, and burnt on fires like wood faggots!

As a knowledge of the value of the new mineral fuel spread, the demand for it increased; and consequently its value became enhanced. Then the lord of the manor, and other Wednesbury freeholders, began to set a price on their mines and minerals—Wednesbury "dirt" became a marketable commodity.

The Plea Rolls of 1377 afford evidence that coal was extensively mined at Wednesbury, and that considerable value was even then attached to the newly-discovered fuel. The record (Salt XIII., p. 127) sets forth that John Walters, of Wednesbury, sued Sir Roger Hillary for taking away "by force and arms" sea coal ,or "carbones maritimos," as it is written, to the value of £40, from his mines at Wednesbury. Mineral coal had been dubbed "sea-coal" in contradistinction to "char-coal" because that first used in London was sea-borne to the Thames from Newcastle, in the north of England.

In 1392 (15 Richard II.) John Wylkys sued Roger Norton, of Derlaston for digging and carrying away sea-coal from his several soil at Wednesbury to the value of £10.

At the Easter Assizes of 1405 Henry Heronville, lord of the manor, sued John Hykeman, of "Wedesbury," and two others, for digging in his several soil at "Wenesbury" and carrying away "earth" to the value of £10 (Salt XVI., p. 47). A similar carrying away of "earth" has been noted on p. 44.

Most interesting is it to note when the workmen employed in the Wednesbury "coalworks" or "coalrys" were first designated by the craft name "colliers," or "colyers"—as on p. 43.

So early as 1415 a number of men, who were charged with breaking into a close at Wednesbury (where evidently they were employed), were described as "colyers." Their names appeared in the record as "Robert Nyghtgale, of Wednesbury, colyer; John atte Lydyate, of Walshale, colyer; and Richard Bonde, of Bromwyche, colyer." When, two years later, Robert was attached, he was then described as a "bocher" (a "butcher")—doubtless all men of substance in Wednesbury killed their own meat at that period; other offenders named with him on this second occasion were "John in the Lee, of Wednesbury, colyer; Henry Harcockes, colyer; John atte Lydyate, colyer, all of Wednesbury." Robert Nyghtgale offered to pay 40s. damages, and got off at that. (Salt XVII., p. 50.)

Two West Bromwich men, who are described as "laborers," and three Wednesbury "yeomen," respectively named John Watson, John Plummer, and Thomas Hopkyns, were, in 1471, sued for breaking into the close of William Freebody at Wednesbury, and digging and taking away his coal (or "carbones"), to the value of 100s. The Freebodys were an important family in Dudley and West Bromwich, and had certainly owned lands in Wednesbury in 1457 (Salt XI., p 241.) See ante. p. 52.

The coal-getting of that early period was simply quarrying—a mere scratching of the surface; deep mining only became a necessity when the measures so near the surface had become exhausted. The area of this ancient mining in the parish was restricted for a long time to Wednesbury Old Field, lying along the Lea Brook from its source near Bradley to its embouchure at the Blocks, where it discharges into the Tame on the Tipton boundary.

It will thus be seen that even so early as the fourteenth century, there was already a goodly sprinkling of colliers in the town. But the bulk of the population, amounting only to a few hundred. were unquestionably engaged in the cultivation of the soil.

As before remarked, the evidences of a pastoral and agricultural Wednesbury abound. Landowning was then almost the only source or sign of wealth. Consequently the records of the law courts teem with suits for the possession of lands and tenements. So many of these records are there, it would be tedious to reproduce them all. Those given in the last chapter will suffice as fair samples of the bulk.

In a later chapter it will be shown how the tenants of Wednesbury, in the reign of Queen Elizabeth, went to law with the lord of the manor to vindicate their claim to a right of digging coals for their own use. How the conversion of pastoral and agricultural lands into mining lands affected the Wednesbury tithes is dealt with in "Religious Wednesbury," p. 111.

Of the upper classes of society, Wednesbury could boast about the time of Sir Henry Beaumont, all three of the personages characteristic of a mediæval parish, as described by Chaucer. In the lord's own person—

"A Knight there was, and that a worthy man,
That fro the time that he first began
To riden out, he loved chivalry,
Truth and honour, freedom and courtesy."

In the person of his heir, John Beaumont,—

"With him ther was his sone a yonge Squier,
A lover, and a lusty bacheler.

. . . . . .

Singing he was, or floyting (fluting) all the day,
He was as fresh as is the month of May.
Short was his gown, his sleves long and wide,
Wel could he sit on horse, and fayre ride."

While in John Brownfield, the vicar of Wednesbury—

"A good man there was of religoun,
That was a poore Parson of a town,
Who Christe's lore, and his Apostles twelve,
He taught, but first he followed it himselve."

XXIII.—THE BEAUMONT ESTATES "IN CUSTOS."

The manorial history may now be resumed from the point where it was dropped at Chapter XIX., recording the death of John Beaumont in 1502.

But first it may be necessary to go back some half-century from that date.

In 1451-2 (30 Henry VI.) a 'Fine was levied' (that is, there was an amicable agreement in Court by leave of the King's justices transferring the freehold estates and assuring possession of the said land), by Joan, widow of Sir Henry Beaumont, in favour of the heirs of John Knyght and certain other complainants; and, in the opinion of Mr. A. A. Rollason, it was doubtless on this Fine being levied that the manor of Wednesbury was re-settled in such a way as afterwards enabled John Hampton to make the grant of 1471 to Lady Eleanor Beaumont, as mentioned on p. 46.

John Hampton was certainly a party, as was also Charles Nowell, mentioned on p. 44, to this 'Final Concord' (Salt XI., p. 247), as the legal name is for the full recognition and acknowledgment of the rightful ownership in the property thus amicably disposed of.

In the last-named Deed of 1471, by which John Hampton granted to Lady Eleanor Beaumont for her life, and afterwards to the heirs of her husband, the properties scheduled included the manors of Wednesbury and Tynmore, and 120 acres of land, 20 acres of meadow, 40 acres of wood, and £10 rent in Wednesbury, Walstoode, Finchpathe, and Tibinton; and 10 acres of meadow and 10 acres of land in Wirkesworth and Kirke Ireton, and the fifth-part of Egginton, in the county of Derby: truly a goodly heritage to pass to John Beaumont, and one by which he had hoped to establish his name in the land.

On the death of John Beaumont in 1502, however, the rights in the manor of Wednesbury became very complicated. His mother, the Lady Eleanor, by the will of her husband, and the aforesaid grant of her trustee John Hampton, had a life estate therein; and she had taken to herself a second husband in the person of George Stanley, Esq., of West Bromwich.

The arms of George Stanley and Eleanor his wife were formerly in the windows of Wednesbury Church; their great-grandson, Walter Stanley, left a dole to the same church in 1613.

John Beaumont, by his will, had directed that the Wednesbury lands should go to his brother James and his heirs after him; but fate forbad.

The date of Lady Eleanor's death is uncertain; but James Beaumont, her brother-in-law, was alive 10th October, 1521 (13 Henry VIII.), as he was then a party to a deed relative to the Mitton estates. James, however, was dead before 1533.

Now, although John Beaumont, lord of Wednesbury, died in 1502, his will was not proved till 1513. It would almost seem that the delay was caused by the hope that the testator's brother James would have male issue, and so continue the name of Beaumont in the lordship of Wednesbury. But this hope disappeared and the will was proved—possibly on the death of Lady Eleanor Stanley.

It also seems probable that for some years after 1513 the Beaumont estates were held in custos for the three youthful co-heiresses, the youngest of whom would come of age about the year 1520.

The student of this manorial history, having threaded its mazes so far, is here confronted by greater difficulties than ever. The two great problems to be solved at this point are—Who was the legal guardian of these Beaumont heiresses? How and when was the partition of the Beaumont estates effected among these three co-heirs?

To these two queries no decisive and final answers can be given. But from ascertained facts very strong inferences may be drawn, which dovetail together into a hypothesis that is very fairly satisfying, if not altogether conclusive.

Answering the second query first, there is evidence that the partition of the Beaumont estates was effected about the year 1541, and not on the marriage of the co-heiresses, or at their coming of age—say, about 1520.

Even after this date there were several settlements and re-settlements of the Beaumont estates; from which it would appear that certain interests were retained in the Wednesbury property by the representatives of the co-heir other than the one to whom Wednesbury had fallen in the division

of the estates; till all such outstanding interests were eventually bought up fifty years after the partition by the then holder of the manor, who thus became sole and undisputed lord of Wednesbury; as this history will duly disclose when the year 1590 is reached.

The Lady Eleanor Stanley doubtless acted "the Lady Bountiful" in Wednesbury during the period she held the property as lady of the manor. But on her death, and on the marriage and dispersion of her three daughters to the homes of their respective husbands, there seems to have been an interregnum so far as a resident lord of the manor is concerned.

The three daughters of John Beaumont being co heiresses to a fairly extensive property, there was no difficulty in providing them with husbands suitable to their rank.

The present writer's hypothesis is, that all three husbands were provided, as was often the case in those times, by the custos who had the legal guardianship of the three wards.

The identity of the custos or guardian cannot be stated with certainty. Probability points to one of two men, who were already related to each other by marriage (they had married sisters, two daughters of Ralph Fitzherbert, co. Derby), and whose closer relationship would be effected by intermarriages between their sons and the Beaumont wards. As such convenient marriages were actually effected, the guardian in question might have been either Thomas Babington, of Dethick, co. Derby, Esq., or Thomas Comberford, of Comberford, co. Stafford, Esq. Each was a gentleman of landed estate, ancient name, and high position. The present writer inclines to the opinion that it was Thomas Comberford who held custos of the manor of Wednesbury during the minority of the Beaumont wards. His son and heir became lord of the manor of Wednesbury; and his younger son, John Comberford, lived and died in Wednesbury.

The marriages arranged for the Beaumont girls were these:—

Joan Beaumont, the eldest sister, became the (first) wife of William Babington, seventh son of the aforementioned Thomas Babington, Esq., and nephew to the wife of the aforementioned Thomas Comberford, Esq.

Dorothy Beaumont, the second sister, was married to Humphrey Comberford, son and heir of the said Thomas Comberford, Esq.

Eleanor Beaumont, the youngest sister, became the wife of Humphrey Babington, of Rothley Temple, co-heir and fifth son of the same Thomas Babington, Esq.

It will be noted that the younger sister Eleanor married the elder brother Humphrey. Humphrey Babington, of course, was also a nephew of Thomas Comberford, Esq.

The Comberfords owned estates in Northamptonshire, and as an instance of their nepotism it is worth mentioning that in 1510 this Thomas Comberford presented to the rectory of Yelvertoft in that county, Thomas Babington, B.A., who was another son of his wife's sister.

It becomes necessary here to introduce some notice of the Comberford family.

The ancient family of Comberford took their name from Comberford, a manor standing on the east side of the Tame, near to Tamworth, where they long had their principal seat.

The pedigree of the Comberfords is given in Bagnall's "Wednesbury," in Shaw's "Staffordshire" (1. 434), and in Salt, Vol. V. pt. ii, p. 92.

Alanus de Comberford was lord of Comberford in the time of Henry I. William de Comberford was a man of some note in the reign of Henry VI.; and they long continued a family of repute in this place.

The Comberfords had another residence at Tamworth, a curious old mansion called the Moat House, built in the reign of Elizabeth, and in the carvings of which were displayed the Comberford arms—

"Gules, a talbot passant Argent."

Dr. Plot, in his "Staffordshire," records among those traditional forerunners of dissolution in which our superstitious ancestors firmly believed, one such warning signal always given by the approach of death to the members of the Comberford family—"three knocks being always heard at Comberford Hall before the decease of any of that family, though the party dying be at never so great a distance."

Of Wednesbury Manor House very little now remains. Its architecture was in the Tudor style; it was built of small red bricks with heavy stone-mullioned windows; it was severely plain, but somewhat high; its open entrance porch had a stone seat on each side similar to those in the adjacent church porch. Enumerating the residences of the Comberfords, Harwood's "Erdeswick" (p. 326), after mentioning those at Comberford and Tamworth, says: "and the hall at Wednesbury." From which it is conjectured that the Comberfords built Wednesbury Hall as it appeared in its final form.

Thomas Comberford, of Comberford, having provided well for his family, died about 1532, a date about mid-way between the period of the three marriages (say 1520) and that of the partition of the Beaumont estates (1541).

Besides his eldest son Humphrey, already mentioned, and who by his marriage became lord of Wednesbury, Thomas Comberford had two other sons, Henry and John. Although Henry was not directly connected with Wednesbury, a brief sketch of his career may be interesting.

Henry Comberford, D.D., was made Precentor of Lichfield Cathedral 19th December, 1555. This was in the reign of Queen Mary, and the very month in which Cranmer was convicted of heresy by the Pope. In 1558 Queen Elizabeth, champion of Protestantism, ascended the throne, and in 1559 Henry Comberford was deprived of all his benefices on account of his adherence to the old faith. He was at first ordered to remain in Suffolk, at a great distance from his friends.

Later we find him described as "a mass priest."

According to the Calendar of State Papers, No. 32 of date 10th November, 1570, is Archbishop Grindall's letter to Sir William Cecil:—
"Had given orders for searching the Countess of Northumberland's home and for mass priests that might be found therein to be sent to him. Three had been sent, one of whom was Henry Comberford." Accompanying, under date 8th November, 1570, is the examination of Henry Comberford before the Ecclesiastical Commissioners for the county of York: "He defends the service of the Mass, and supposes the Countess of Northumberland to have been possessed of evil spirits."

So dangerous to the State were the religious opinions of Henry Comberford considered, that at the age of 80 he was still detained a prisoner at Hull, 1579 (Bagnall, p. 130).

Allusion will presently be made to Anthony Babington's connection with the Queen of Scots' conspiracy (1586). The Comberfords, or at least some of them, as witness Henry the ecclesiastic, and another named Thomas, refused to join the Reformers, and remained Roman Catholics. As such, their sympathies would be with the imprisoned Mary Stuart, as against Queen Elizabeth. Writing to Lord Burleigh from Sheffield Castle, under date 20th January, 1572, Lord Shrewsbury says:—
"I caused my man to apprehend one Thomas Comberford, of Comberford, gent. He was concerned in the conspiracies of Queen Mary against Queen Elizabeth."

John Comberford, the other son of Thomas, unquestionably took up his residence in Wednesbury, and lived and died within the manor of which his eldest brother Humphrey held the lordship. In the Index of Canterbury Wills he is described:—
"(1560). Comberforth John, gentleman, Wednesburie, Staffs."

By this will, dated 23rd April, 1559, "John Comberford, gentleman, of the parish of Wednesbury, gave to the churchwardens six-and-eightpence to bestow on the church; also another six-and-eightpence to the church for his burial." As directed, his body was interred at Wednesbury Church (1559).

Within the chancel rails of Wednesbury Church is a monumental slab bearing the figure of a man in armour, and also the effigy of a lady, and one son and four daughters at their feet, with the marginal inscription, quoted on p. 41 of "Religious Wednesbury," as a strange example of a post-Reformation invitation to pray for the souls of the dead. It is the monument of "Ihon Cumberfort. Gentylman, and Em' hys wyffe," 1559. Apparently John Comberford and his family adhered to the ancient faith.

According to "Wyrley's Church Notes" (1597), the painted windows of the Church bore the arms of the same "John Cumberford et Em. sa. feme. 1559," which were:—
"A Cross charged with five roses, impaling on a bend three stirrup irons."

Emma, the widow of John Comberford, of Wednesbury, was concerned in lands at Halesowen, Rowley, and Dudley in 1563 (Salt XVII., 212). According to her marriage licence, dated 13th February, 1548-9 (in the Faculty Office), her maiden name appears to have been Emma Bellet.

XXIV.—PARTITION OF THE BEAUMONT ESTATES: THE BABINGTON FAMILY.

Before tracing the manorial history of Wednesbury through Dorothy, the second daughter of John Beaumont, and who on the partition carried this estate to her husband, Humphrey Comberford, it becomes necessary to deal first with the other two daughters, who married the brothers Babington.

Joan, the eldest, born about 1496, carried to her husband, William Babington, as her share of her father's estates, the manor of Tymmore, then valued at £13. In right of his wife, his description then became "William Babington of Tymmore."

Tymmore was near to Comberford. It was also on the Tame, close to Tamhorn; wherefor the country people often mis-called it Timhorn. Tymmore Mill was till recently known as Elford Mill; Elford is bounded on the south by Comberford, while the river Tame forms its western boundary. But the name Tymmore is no longer to be found on the maps.

From this Wednesbury woman Joan Beaumont, by her marriage with William Babington, was descended the historic character, Anthony Babington, who was attainted in 1586 for participation in a conspiracy on behalf of Mary, Queen of Scots.

The issue of the marriage of Joan Beaumont with William Babington was Anthony Babington, their heir, who held Tymmore after them. According to Shaw's "Staffordshire" (I., p. 339), his tomb at the east end of the south aisle of Lichfield Cathedral bore this inscription:—

"Here lyeth the body of Anthony Babington, of Tymore, in the county of Stafford, esquire, and of Joyce, his wife, which Anthony died the 18th day of March, anno domini 1579."

The arms at the head of the monument were:—

"1. Quarterly, 1 and 4 Argent, 10 torteux, 4, 3, 2, 1, with a label of three points azure (Babington); 2 and 3 semee of fleurs-de-lis, a lion rampant (Beaumont)."

It is stated in Wyrley's Church Notes, written in 1597, that the arms of John (? William) and Joan Babington, impaling Beaumont, and also of Humphrey and Eleanor Babington, were then in the windows of Wednesbury Church (Bagnall, p. 146).

This Anthony Babington had issue, a son, Thomas, who died in 1579; his son was Henry, whose son was the Anthony Babington, of Dethick, the conspirator of the year 1586. He had sold the Staffordshire property long before he perished on the scaffold (Nichol's "Leicestershire," III., 954-967).

Another pedigree of the Conspirator traces his descent from a brother of William and Humphrey Babington aforementioned.

The Babingtons owned very extensive properties in Derbyshire; and it is interesting to note that Queen Elizabeth granted a considerable parcel of the possessions of Anthony Babington, forfeited on his attainder, to Sir Walter Raleigh.

Eleanor Beaumont, the third and youngest daughter, was three years younger than Joan, the eldest. This co-heiress married Humphrey Babington, afterwards of Rothley Temple.

In 31 Henry VIII. (1539-1540), a Final Concord seems to have been effected in the Law Courts by way of attempting some re-settlement of the estates; Humphrey Babington and Eleanor his wife acknowledging the rights of Edmund Knyghtley, Esq., and certain others.

In 1541 Humphrey Babington and Eleanor his wife presented to the rectory of Eginton. Eginton was among the Derbyshire properties of the Beaumonts. In the same year Humphrey Babington would appear to be in possession of Tymmore.

Humphrey Babington died 22nd November, 1544, leaving two sons and three daughters. His wife Eleanor may have predeceased him.

Their eldest son and heir was Thomas Babington, of Rothley Temple and Cossington, both in Leicestershire. He married Eleanor, daughter of Richard Humfrey, of Barton, Northants.

This Thomas Babington joined in that historic episode, the fruitless attempt to place Lady Jane Grey on the throne of England, 1553. He only escaped the consequences of his rashness by the payment of a large fine, his pardon passing under the great seal in the first year of Mary's reign. Here we must leave him for the present; he will re-appear in our next chapter.

XXV.—THE MANOR OF WEDNESBURY PASSES TO THE COMBERFORDS.

(1)—Humphrey Comberford, Lord of Wednesbury (152.-1555):—

The second daughter of John Beaumont, of Wednesbury, was Dorothy, who married Humphrey Comberford, of Comberford. She was a co-heir with her two sisters, and in the division of their father's estates, the manor of Wednesbury fell to her portion.

In her right Humphrey Comberford, of Comberford, became lord of Wednesbury; the official valuation of the manor at that time being £13 4s. 4d., and therefore slightly in excess of that of Tymmore.

Humphrey Comberford was also the heir to his father's large estates, comprising Wigginton, Hopwas, Coton, Tamworth, and Comberford, with extensive appurtenances thereto, in the shape of water-mill, fishery, rents, cattle, sheep, messuages, cottages, wood, meadow, pasture lands, and commons, all set forth at large at the Inquisition Post Mortem when his father died in 1531. Humphrey then being 40 years of age. Humphrey is mentioned as "Lord of Wednesbury" in 1550 (Bagnall, p. 156).

Humphrey "Cumbreforde" acquired certain lands in "Wednesbury and Walstede Delves" by a Final Concord made in the year 1543-4 (Salt XI., p. 285). The place-name Walstead has been commented on in "Olden Wednesbury," p. 44.

Humphrey Comberford, Esq., made his will, dated 1st December, 1555, and died the December following, at the age of 65. At the Inquisition taken at Tamworth in relation to his extensive Staffordshire properties, it was found that Thomas was his son and heir, aged 32 (1556). (Shaw I., p. 431—see also under "Wednesbury"). A similar Inquisition at Daventry relating to the Northamptonshire properties found that Thomas was heir to those also; but mentions that there was another son Humphrey—not the elder of the two, as represented in Bagnall's pedigree.

The Prerogative Court Indexes his will thus: "1556. Will of Humfrey Cumborforthe, Esquier, of Cumberfode."

Of Humphrey Comberford's brothers, Henry the Precentor, and John, who resided at Wednesbury, biographical sketches were given in Chapter XXIII.

In the old painted glass of Wednesbury Church (1597) appeared the arms of "Humfry Cumberford et Dor," his wife; that is, of Comberford imposing Beaumont on a Shield of Pretence.

(2)—Thomas Comberford, Lord of Wednesbury (1555-1597):—

Thomas, the eldest son of his father, succeeded as lord of Comberford and Wednesbury. He married Dorothea, daughter of William Wyrley, of Hamstead.

The issue of the marriage was three sons and one daughter.

His brother Humphrey probably held the family estates in Northamptonshire, and is perhaps the one whose name thus appears in the Wednesbury Parish Registers under date 1566—"Homfrey Comberford was buried the xiith day of August"; the entry next to it being—"Elizabeth Comberford, the xiith day of August."

His elder sister, Mary Comberford, married Walter Harcourt, of Tamworth. No authority is given for the statement quoted in "Olden Wednesbury" (pp. 3 and 44) that Walter Harcourt was "of the family of Lord Harcourt, of Nuneham, Oxfordshire," and that he "died in the year 1636 as he was passing through Wednesbury." It is clear that Walter Harcourt had married a Wednesbury woman; and Erdeswick's "Staffordshire" states also that the Harcourts of this county married "with Noel's heir and intruded themselves into the Noel's armoury." The Noels were of Ellenhall, Staffordshire; and it is interesting to note that the Noels or Nowells have already appeared in this history (ante p. 44), and further that the Noel arms were anciently emblazoned on the windows of Wednesbury Church—"Or, frette gules, a canton Argent."

In 1605 "Walter Harcourt, Knt., William Comberford, armiger, and others, are mentioned in a Final Concord in respect of lands in Tamworth, etc.

Sir Walter Harcourt was buried in Wednesbury Church. According to Shaw's history of the county, his monument (which has strangely disappeared since 1798) was below the altar rails, and bore the following inscription:—

"Hic jacet Gualterus Hercourte, stemmate pernobilis, virtute nobiliori qui Dominum suum assassinatorum gladiis obsessum stupenda magnanimitate (etiam in pueritia) munivit et liberavit."

This may be translated:—

"Here lies Walter Harcourt, though of noble birth he was yet of more noble courage, who (when but a youth) with marvellous valour shielded and freed his master when hard pressed by the swords of assassins."

Isabel, the younger sister, married Gervase Rolleston, who was of the ancient Staffordshire family owning Rolleston. When Gervase died, and his relict "Isabella" administered to his will in 1577, the following interesting Inventory of his goods was made out:—

"Two oxen ... ... 17 nobles
Two kyne, one carven and the other
    with calve ... ... 5 marks·
One barren heyfar ... ... 30s.
Two heyfers ... ... 4 marks
Five calves ... ... 4 marks
Three fyllies, mares, 5 swyne, 3 hyves 1 mark
Tyrtle henne and a tyrtle cocke ... 2s.
Locks and keys about house ... ... 16d.
Cutting sawe ... ... 16d.
A sword and dagger ... ... 2s.
7½ acres of pease £5
2 acres of barley and dredge ... ... 40s.
Parte of wheate croppe 7½ acres ... £4 16 8
etc., etc., etc."

Thomas Comberford seems to have inherited Wednesbury subject to a number of outstanding charges upon it, many of them having no doubt been created at the death of John Beaumont, and subsequently at the division of the Beaumont estates.

Thomas Comberford would appear to have set himself resolutely to the task of buying out all other interests in, and arising from, the manor of Wednesbury, and making himself sole proprietor and lord of every right or interest whatsoever within the said manor.

In support of this view important transactions within the Courts of Law may be adduced, from which it will transpire that Thomas Comberford became sole lord of Wednesbury in 1564-5, and "levied a Fine" for a re-settlement of the estate 1566-7.

The Thomas Babington mentioned in the previous chapter, in 1563-4 acquired from his cousin Anthony, son and heir of William and Joan Babington, £9 10s. 1½d. of rent in Wednesbury (Salt XIII., p. 227).

The same year the said Thomas Babington, armiger, and Eleanor his wife, remitted all their right to a "third-part of the manor of Weddisburye, and of 1,000 acres of land, 500 acres of pasture, 200 acres of wood, and £11 0s. 1d. of rent in Weddesburie, also of a third-part of all mines of sea-coal and of other mines whatsoever in the said 1,000 acres of land, 500 acres of pasture, and 200 acres of wood in Weddisburie," to Thomas Comberford, and Dorothy his wife.

Commenting on the two foregoing transactions, Mr. A. A. Rollason says that there would seem to have been an outstanding right in the heirs of Joan Beaumont as regards the rent. Thomas Babington having secured the right from his cousin Anthony, re-sold it to Thomas Comberford. This re-sale was confirmed by a Final Concord in 1564-5 (Salt XIII., p. 252).

Thomas Comberford having got into his own hands all the outstanding rights in the manor, levied a Fine 1566, perhaps with a view to a re-settlement (Salt XIII., p. 267).

A Final Concord (upon a re-settlement of the estates on the marriage of Humphrey) was made in 1591, when William Comberford was stated to be "the son and heir apparent" of Thomas Comberford and Dorothy: the properties then enumerated embraced the manors of Wednesbury, Wigginton, and Comberford, and 41 messuages, 12 cottages, 4 water grain mills, a wind mill, 2 dovecotes, 100 gardens, 40 orchards, 810 acres of land, 404 acres of meadow, 820 acres of pasture, 800 acres of wood, 1,500 acres of furze and heath, a mine of coals, a quarry of stones, and £7 of rent, and a rent of two pounds of pepper in the three places aforementioned, and in Westbromwiche, Typton, Tamworthe, Hopwas, and Cotton; free warren in Comberford, Wednesbury, and Hopwas; and the Hay of Hopwas, with appurtenances in the Forest of Cannock; also of chattels waived, estrays, chattels of felons and fugitives, tolls, pontage (bridge toll), chimmage (toll for having a way through a forest), and other privileges appurtenant to the afore-said Hay; and also a free fishery in the water of Tame.

Thomas Comberford died in 1597. Sampson Erdeswick, writing his "Survey of Staffordshire" a year or so before, says of him:—

"Thomas, who had issue William, who had issue Humphrey, who had issue William Comberford, all four living anno 1596; the Comberfords are now lords of Wednesbury." From this it appears that four generations were alive at the same time in 1596, Thomas lord of the manor, being about 73 years of age, and his great-grandson William being about 5.

Shaw's "Staffordshire" says that Thomas "died 20th December 40 Elizabeth, seised of this manor with the appurtenances, held of the King (sic) by fealty and 20s. rent; and William was his son and heir, aet. 60, by Dorothy his wife, daughter of William Wyrley, Esq., which William (says Wyrley's Church Notes) is now lord of this manor, 1597, my very good friend and kinsman."

At the Inquisition Post Mortem taken at Shenstone on Thomas Comberford's Staffordshire lands, it was proved that William, his eldest son and heir, was 46 (sic); his second son was named Humphrey, and his third son Edward.

Dorothy, the widow of Thomas, appears to have died a year or two later, as administration was granted at Lichfield in 1599-0 of the estate of one "Dorothy Cumberford." A Dorothy Comberford was buried at Wednesbury 6th January, 1600.

XXVI.—WILLIAM DE COMBERFORD, LORD OF WEDNESBURY (DIED 1625).

3.—William de Comberford and Wednesbury (1597-1625):

William, the eldest son of his father, succeeded to Comberford and Wednesbury.

The other children of Thomas Comberford were Humphrey, second son; Edward, third son; and a daughter, Elizabeth, who married William Stamford. Humphrey Comberford, gentleman, owned lands in Sedgley and Bradley (1599), and his family seem to have remained settled at Bradley in after years.

William de Comberford, for his first wife, married (about 1567) Mary, the daughter of William Skeffington, of Fisherwick.

Sir William Skeffington was a distinguished political personage in Ireland in the reign of Henry VIII.; he died Lord Deputy of Ireland in 1535. A descendant of the Skeffingtons married the only daughter of Sir John Clodworthy, who was created by Charles II. Viscount Massarene, with remainder, in default of male issue, to his son-in-law Skeffington, and his heirs by Clodworthy's daughter. These Skeffingtons continued their seat at Fisherwick; and their title of dignity became Marquis and Earl of Donegal in the peerage of Ireland, and Baron Fisherwick of Fisherwick, co. Stafford, in the peerage of Great Britain.

In 1594 William Skeffington and Elizabeth his wife conveyed the Bonditch Meadows at Bustlehome, on the borders of Wednesbury, to the Symcocks. The latter were a very old local family, Sybil Heronville, mentioned on p. 40, having married a Thomas Symcokes.

By this first wife Mary, who died in 1598, and was buried at Wednesbury Church on 18th March, William Comberford had eight sons and three daughters. For his second wife he married Anna, daughter of — Watson, and relict of — Spencer; by whom he had two other sons and three more daughters. Some of these children doubtless died in infancy, but there can be little doubt that it is this William Comberford who is commemorated in Tamworth Church by a fine Gothic tomb, on which he is shown in effigy surrounded by figures of twelve children. (Further allusion will be made to this monument later on).

The eldest son was Humphrey; of whom more presently.

The second son was Thomas. The third and seventh sons were both baptised by the name of John; the Wednesbury registers record the baptism in 1588 of—"John Comberford, son of William Comberford, Esq."

The fourth son was William, and the fifth

son was Francis. In 1629 administration was granted at Lichfield to the estate of one Francis Comberford.

Two other sons by the first wife were Richard and Henry. The daughters by this marriage were Anna, Johanna (or Mary), who married Thomas Lewzon, and Dorothy, who married Walter Colman.

The will of a Richard Cumberford was proved in 1618 at the Canterbury Prerogative Court.

By the second wife there was another son named William, and another named Humfrey, and three daughters, respectively named Anna, Elizabeth, and Dorothy. The duplication of the names John, William, Anna, and Dorothy is somewhat noteworthy, and undoubtedly confusing.

In 1591 William's eldest son and heir, Humphrey, married Mary Stamford, eldest daughter of Robert Stamford, of Perry Hall.

The Marriage Settlement then drawn up throws a great amount of light on the descent of Wednesbury Manor; the uses and limitations are so very elaborate.

The said Settlement declares that at that date (1591) William Comberford (the father of the bridegroom) possessed the manors of Wednesbury, Comberford, and Wigginton.

That the jointure then settled upon the bride comprised the Manor House at Comberford and its extensive domains, which were to be for the use of the said Mary (after her marriage) for her life:

And after the said Mary's decease the said property was to go to Humphrey, and his heirs male by the said Mary; and in default thereof to the heirs male of Humphrey; and in default of heirs male then to William Comberford (his father) for life, with power of appointment by him, by deed or will, in default thereof:

With remainders to Humphrey's brothers in succession according to age, and to their respective heirs male; namely, to Thomas, John, William, Francis, Richard, John, and Henry; and to Humphrey's father, William, and his heirs male; and failing heirs male of William, to Edward Comberford, his brother; and in default to Humphrey Comberford his uncle; and in default to the use of Francis Comberford, son of a certain Richard Comberford, deceased; and in default thereof, to the heirs female of the body of the said William (the father), with ultimate remainder to the right heirs of William (the father).

The Manors of Comberford and Wigginton were for the use of William (the father) for his life, and then to the use of his sons Humphrey and the heirs male by his marriage with the said Mary Stamford, with remainders as before.

The manors, messuages, lands, etc., in Wednesbury (except the Mansion House of the said manor, together with the orchards and gardens there, and certain parcels of pastures called the Vineyards and Sarisalles) were for the use of William (the father) for his life, and after his death to such uses as he should appoint; and in default of appointment to the use of his son Humphrey and his heirs male by the said Mary, as above.

"The said Mansion House of the Manor of Wednesbury, and the said orchards and gardens and parcels of land" were reserved to the use of the father (William) and Mary his wife for their lives; and after the decease of William to the use of William's father, Thomas Comberford and Dorothy his wife (for Humphrey's grandparents were still alive); ultimately descending to Humphrey and Mary's heirs, as before.

But it was carefully provided in this Marriage Settlement that it should be lawful for William Comberford (the father) to make leases for terms of years or three lives of all the premises, except the Mansion House and the premises limited to the jointure of Mary, the intended wife of Humphrey, at the highest rents obtainable; John Wyrley and the other trustees agreed that after such demises, for the respective terms thereof, the premises so leased should revert to the uses of the Settlement. A "Fine was levied" in due form, etc.

From the foregoing arrangement it would appear that the grandfather, Thomas Comberford, was residing at Wednesbury Manor House; that the newly married pair were to reside at Comberford Hall; leaving the Moat House at Tamworth as the residence of William Comberford (1591).

Humphrey Comberford died 5th April, 1610, in the lifetime of his father; at the Inquisition taken at Stafford it was found by the jurors that the Manor of Wednesbury and other premises there were held of the King by fealty, and by service of paying yearly into the Exchequer 20s.; and that the same were worth per annum clear £26 10s.; and that Humphrey's son and heir was William, then aged 17 years.

During the period of national danger caused by the Spanish Armada, the lord of Wednesbury gave the then considerable donation of £25 to the national defence fund. A Staffordshire list, dated 6th April, 1588, gives his name as "William Comberford, gent." His official description after this date, although in the lifetime of his father, ceases to be "gentleman," and rises to the rank of "armiger" (or "esquire").

It must be kept in mind that William de Comberford did not succeed his father till 1597: by which time his father, Thomas Comberford, had accomplished much in the way of consolidating all outstanding rights and interests in the Manor of Wednesbury (see ante p. 60).

At the dissolution of the monasteries, first in 1527, "Woddesbury" lands are enumerated among a number of estates which were given to the Deans and Canons of Wolsey's New College at Oxford, and by a Fine "warranted to them against all men." (Salt XII., p. 183).

And at the final suppression of the religious houses in 1539, the manor of "Weddesbury," and the advowson of the church "of Woddesbury," figure in another extensive list of properties, which the Abbot of Halesowen surrendered to Henry VIII. (Salt XII., p. 186). The Wednesbury tithes were purchased for 200 marks of silver by William Orme, in the year 1576; while later (1612) it is recorded that Richard Jevons acquired the tithes of sheaves and lambs in "Weddesbury."

It is the opinion of Mr. A. A. Rollason that whatever these interests in Wednesbury were, the re-sale of them, or the grant of them, at that period, led to the Chancery proceedings between the Comberfords and Sheldons so many years later, at the period we have now reached.

At the same time it must not be forgotten that both the manor of Wednesbury and the advowson of the church in 1539, fell into the hands of Sir John Dudley—a fact quoted from the Patent Rolls 30 Henry VIII., on p. 38 of "Religious Wednesbury." Sir John became the powerful Duke of Northumberland, who was attainted, and perished on the scaffold in 1553. How his Wednesbury property was dealt with cannot be discovered; but his temporary possession of it certainly tended to further complications in the manorial history.

Anyway, it is apparent that throughout his tenure William de Comberford was involved in a considerable amount of litigation, as is testified by the recorded Chancery Proceedings during the reign of Elizabeth. Here are no less than six cases in which William de Comberford figures as Plaintiff:—

1. "A claim by Purchase," Richard Sheldon and Thomas Sheldon, Defendants. The Premises were: "The manor of Wednesbury, formerly the estate of John Beaumont, Esq., and purchased by Plaintiff of his descendants."

2. "Bill for Deeds to support title by Purchase," William Jennyns and Thomas Jennyns being Defendants. The Premises were: "A Messuage called New Hall Place, and lands in Wednesbury, sold by defendant W. Jennyns to the Plaintiff."

3. "A claim by Lease." Richard Jennyns and Isabell his wife being Defendants. The Premises: "A messuage and land in Wednesbury, demised to Plaintiff by John Jennyns, the owner of the inheritance."

4. "Bill to ascertain Tenants' rights," against Elizabeth Nicholls and several other Defendants. The Premises: "The Manor and Lordship of Wednesbury, the inheritance of Plaintiff, and in which the Defendants the Tenants claim a right of digging coals for their own use."

5. "Title by lease," Nicholas Bretton being Defendant. "The Manor of Wygginton and divers lands in Wygginton—Disputes between Plaintiff and tenants of the Manor."

6. An action to recover from William Cockayne rent due under a Lease. Premises:

"Land parcel of the Manor of Wednesborough or Wednesbury held under a Lease granted by Thomas Comberford, Esq., the Plaintiff's late father, and Dorothy his wife, to Thomas Comberford, and which afterwards vested in the Defendant."

The second Thomas Comberford in the last case was evidently a relative—perhaps William's next brother. In one case it is stated that the manor of Wednesbury was "purchased" by William Comberford, and in another that it was inherited by him. The "purchase" possibly refers to the manner in which some old outstanding interests had been acquired. The site of "New Hall Place" in Wednesbury is not known, unless it refers to the Manor House, which the Comberfords had probably re-built (ante p. 57). In another Chancery Suit, Thomas Jennyns being Plaintiff, and William Jennyns being Defendant, there was "a claim under a gift on marriage" of a tenement "called New Hall and land in Wednesbury, the estate of Plaintiff's father."

In another Chancery Suit, Thomas Jennyns was again the Plaintiff, suing to obtain admittance to copyholds, the Defendants being William Comberford, John Baggeley, John Averell, and Elizabeth Carter. The Premises were: "A tenement and land held of the manor of Wednesbury, sold to the Plaintiff by John Jennyns his brother, the defendant Comberford being lord of the said manor."

William Comberford, in another Chancery Suit, is styled "farmer or owner of the lordship of Wigginton." It was an action brought by one of his "free tenants" to establish and protect rights of common, and against surcharging common in Wigginton, supported by a decree granted from the Court of Star Chamber in the reign of Henry VIII. during the time Thomas Comberford, Esq., was lord of the manor, and which set out the different portions of the lord, and those of the tenants, in that lordship.

William de Comberford survived his firstborn some fifteen years. On the 8th bell of the peal in Wednesbury Church appears the inscription:—

"X. William Cumberford, Lord of Wedgbury. 1623."

In 1622-3 William Comberford, Esq., Lord of the Manor of Wednesbury, was High Sheriff of Staffordshire. Among his possessions would appear to have been a considerable estate at Kingesberrow, co. Warwick. His will, proved at London, 8th March, 1625, contains the following clauses:—

"I, William Comberford, of Tamworthe, in co. Staffs., Esq., late High Sheriff of the said county:

"I desire to be buried in the north side of the church at Tamworthe.

"I leave to the use of the Poor of Wednesburie £20, to be employed by Anne, my wife, and the interest thereof to be bestowed yearly on Good Friday, in Bread, on the said Poor; and after her death the said £20 to be employed to the same use by my sons William and Humfry Comberford by the said Anne, and their heirs for ever; and also £20 to the use of the Poor of Tamworthe, to be employed in like manner by the said Anne, and after her death by the said William and Humfrey Comberford and their heirs for ever, which of them shall enjoy the Mott Hall in Tamworthe.

"Legacies to my servants, etc.,

"The residue of my goods to my wife Anne, whom I appoint my sole executrix."

Among the witnesses to this will appears the name of "William Comberford, jun." On 21st February, 1631, there issued a commission to "William Comberford, son of Anne Comberford, late of Tamworth, in co. Staffs, widow, deceased, to administer her goods, etc.

THE OLD TOWN HALL, DUDLEY.

From " Historic Staffordshire." By permission of Midland Educational Co.

XXVII.—THE MANOR OF WEDNESBURY UPON LEASE.

The county historian, Shaw, says of William de Comberford that the manor of Wednesbury continued in his posterity until it was sold by one his descendants.

When William de Comberford died in 1625 there were probably three William Comberfords still living.[*] Another of the same name and family was but recently dead, as is gathered from the Wednesbury Parish Registers recording the death of one—

"William Comerford, gentleman, 19th January, 1619."

Much confusion has arisen in the attempts to identify the various William Comberfords concerned in the complications of the family history which followed 1625.

Researches have but recently disclosed the identity of the two chiefly concerned.

The first of these William Comberfords resided at Moat Hall, Tamworth, and during the Civil Wars became known as Colonel Comberford. He was a son of William de Comberford by his second wife Anne; his wife was named Anne, and he had a daughter Anne.

The second William Comberford was nephew to the last-named, being son and heir of Humphrey Comberford, who died in 1610. He resided at Comberford Hall, and into his hands the manor of Wednesbury and the other paternal estates should have descended in 1625.

These two, uncle and nephew, could not have been very widely divided in their ages; for the former was the son of a second marriage, and the twelfth child of his father, while the latter was the son and heir of the eldest of that large family.

It was this relationship which brought about the complications in the ownership of the Comberford family estates which are found to have existed after the year 1625, when William de Comberford died. The last-named seems to have fallen completely under the influence of his second wife; and it was doubtless at her instigation that he took every advantage of the leasing proviso in the Marriage Settlement of 1591 (quoted in the last chapter) to the benefit and best advantage of her own son William, and to the manifest detriment and disadvantage of the grandson William, in anticipation of whose rights of heirship the said settlement had been effected.

Reference to the said Marriage Settlement of 1591 (see previous chapter) will show that the manor of Wednesbury, except the Mansion House and certain appurtenances thereto. William de Comberford (the father of the bridegroom) had reserved to himself for life with power of disposal afterwards; but in default of so disposing, the said manor was to go to Humphrey (the bridegroom) and his heirs male. As to the Wednesbury Manor House and its appurtenances, the same were limited to the use of the said William (the father) and Mary his wife for their lives, and then to the use of Thomas and Dorothy Comberford (grandparents of the bridegroom) for their lives; and after the determination of the before-mentioned life estates, to Humphrey and his heirs male.

It would thus seem on the face of it that William Comberford, the son and heir of Humphrey, for whom the Marriage Settlement had been made, had every prospect of enjoying a goodly inheritance.

But the Settlement of 1591 contained a most material and over-ruling proviso, namely, that it should be lawful for William Comberford (the father) to make leases for terms of years or three lives of all the premises (except the Mansion House and the premises limited for the jointure of Mary Stamford, the intended wife of Humphrey), so that the highest rents should be reserved upon the same, and that after such demises John Wyrley and the other trustees should stand possessed of the specified properties to the uses set forth in the Settlement (Fine, 33 Elizabeth—Salt XVI., p. 110).

When Humphrey Comberford died (1610), in the lifetime of his father, his son and heir William was then aged 17; his other children were Thomas, Humphrey, John (afterwards of Handsworth), Robert (afterwards of Comberford) and four daughters.

Unfortunately for William, the heir of Humphrey, his prospects in life were very considerably modified after his father's death by the advantage so freely taken by his grandfather, William de Comberford, of the afore-mentioned proviso in the Marriage Settlement.

As stated in the last chapter, and repeated here for greater clearness and intelligibility, William de Comberford, on the death of his first wife, Mary (nee Skeffington), married again. His second wife was named Anne, and the first son he had by her, was the "William Comberford, junior" to whom letters of administration were granted in 1631, as stated at the conclusion of the last chapter.

Whether for favouritism to this son of his second wife, or whether by the influence of his second wife, William de Comberford seems to have changed the whole aspect of the affairs of his grandson William, the heir-at-law

---

[*] In those times it was not an uncommon practice in certain families to duplicate baptismal names: thus the will of John Rowlston, of Etwall, Derbyshire, 1592, mentions John (his eldest son) and "John the younger." another son; and among his daughters he names Mary, and also "Mary the younger." The purpose of a name is to distinguish the bearer from all other things of the same kind; consequently this confusing practice defeated the very object of naming. Allusion to this practice was made in the previous chapter—the grandfather was named William; he had two sons named William; and his grandson was another William Comberford (son of his eldest son Humphrey)—to say nothing of two other sons called by the same name John.

of his eldest son Humphrey. For it is evident that he exercised to the full the powers of disposal and leasing vested in him by the Settlement made at the marriage of his son Humphrey, greatly to the prejudice of the right heir.

From the death of William de Comberford in 1625, and for many years afterwards, the manor of Wednesbury was under lease for lives; and that lease was not only mortgaged, but subject to that mortgage, was again leased by way of Settlement for the life of Anne, the wife of William Comberford.

During all this time the real heir-at-law, William Comberford, son of Humphrey, was only entitled to the rents reserved by the leases granted by his grandfather under the proviso aforesaid.

It is even doubtful whether the said heir, William Comberford of Comberford, ever got these rents; for in 1649 there was due to him the sum of £1,246, being 23 years' arrears; and a suit was commenced in the Court of Wards to compel the heir at common law to accept of such arrears of rent.

Colonel Comberford, the favoured son, had become possessed, upon lease from his father, of the following properties:—

1. The estate of Alder Mills for lives (two lives being in existence in 1649), at a yearly rental of £30.

2. The estates of Wigginton, Comberford, Hopwas, Coton, and Tamworth, upon lease for lives (two of which lives were in existence in 1649), at a yearly rental of £128.

3. The estate of Hopwas Hay and a parcel of land called the Deane, upon lease for two lives, at the yearly rental of £14.

4. A Frank Tenement, etc. (probably Wednesbury Manor), for two lives upon several leases made by the said father, whereupon the ancient yearly rents of £86 10s. 2d. were reserved to the heirs-at-law, and which in 1649 were of the yearly value of £71 9s. 10d. above the reserved rents.

Beyond these deprivations suffered by William Comberford of Comberford, the heir-at-law, William de Comberford, his grandfather, appears to have granted (1621-2) an annuity of £30 to one Humphrey Comberford (? another son of the second marriage, and younger brother of Colonel Comberford), out of certain lands in which he was interested, and subject thereto disposed of them to his son William also. The latter sold these paternal lands, whereupon Humphrey obtained a decree in respect thereof in the Court of Wards (1631-2), and in pursuance of that decree William was compelled to charge the annuity upon some of his other lands, which he did upon his Bolehall estate, by a deed dated 17 Charles I. (1641-2).

For some reason or other this William Comberford, of Tamworth, who had managed to obtain most of the lands and estates which his father had reserved power to lease, commenced to raise money on his property. In 1636, by deed and fine duly levied, he leased to John Curzon for 16 years, at a yearly rental of 10s.

the manors of Wednesbury, Wigginton, and Comberford, and all his lands in Staffordshire, to secure a sum of £1,000, and he gave a bond for £2,000 as further security.

On April 20th, 1637, by way of Settlement, he granted a lease to Michael Noble and John Langham (his wife's trustees) of divers lands and tenements in the counties of Stafford and Warwick for 60 years, if his wife Anne should so long live, at a rent of 1d. per annum, to secure £150 a year to his wife as alimony. The fine levied at Michaelmas, 13 Charles I., shows that the manors of Wednesbury, Wigginton, and Comberford were included in this lease.

In 1642 the Civil War broke out; in this great civil strife William Comberford, of Moat Hall, Tamworth, took a very active part, and became a colonel in the Royalist forces.

It is not known for certain what part the other members of the Comberford family took in the nation's fratricidal struggle, but it is not at all improbable that some of them arrayed themselves on the opposite side as Parliamentarians. There was perhaps little cordiality at any time between the Colonel, and the nephew he was keeping out of his inheritance.

When the Civil War drew to a close Colonel Comberford, of Tamworth, found himself among the "delinquents" whom the victorious Parliamentarians despoiled of some of their possessions for the part they had taken. Among the Royalist Composition Papers preserved at the Record Office in London are those of Colonel William Comberford; it is from this source alone that it has been possible to glean the disposition of Wednesbury Manor and the other Comberford estates after 1625, as stated in this chapter. The text of these Composition Papers may be given more fully in a later chapter, when the local incidents of the Civil War are recorded. Suffice it to say here that it was in 1649 that Colonel William Comberford petitioned Parliament to be allowed to "compound" for his delinquency; when his sworn declarations upon that occasion enlighten us as to the extent, value, and situation of his various properties.

It has been surmised that these two William Comberfords were about the same age as each other; they certainly died within two or three years of each other. The nephew's will, proved 1653, contained the following clauses:—

"I, William Comberford, of Comberford, Esq., aged 54. [? In 1647, the possible date of the will.]

"I desire to be buried in the parish church of Tamworth or Wednesburie, if dying within 10 miles of the same, otherwise in the parish where I die.

"I leave to the poor of the parish where I shall be buried £5.

"I appoint my brother, John Comberford, of co. Staffs., gent., and John Birch, of Cannock, in the said county, to be my executors.

"Whereas, by Fine, Recovery, and other assurances, especially an Indenture dated 16 May 16 Car. I., between me, the said William

Comberford, of the one part, and Sir Richard Dyott, Knt., the said John Birch, gent., and Thomas Wollaston, gent., of the other part, I settled my Manors [not here specified] lands, etc., to certain uses, I hereby confirm the same except as regards the said Sir Richard Dyott, Knt., all trusts, etc., limited in him in the said Indenture or other Conveyances being hereby revoked.

" I leave to my brother Robert Comberford, £100, etc.

" To my brother John Comberford and to his wife, 20s. each.

" To my kinsman Francis Comberford, of Bradeley, in co .Staffs., 20s.

" To Thomas Wollaston, gent., Robert Sankey, gent., Joseph Gorway, gent., John Wollaston, son of Thomas Wollaston, and to my uncle George Hawe, jun., 20s. each.

" To my 7 god-children [named] legacies," etc.

" Witnesses: F. Comberford, Robert Sankey, Nath Worswick, Joseph Gorway, William Jervis."

" Proved at Westminster 10 March, 1653, before the Judges, by John Comberford, John Birch, and Thomas Wollaston, joint Executors " (sic).

The John Birch mentioned in the foregoing will was " Mr. John Birch, of Cank, who in his time was accounted the ablest attorney-at-law in England." Robert Sankey was his clerk, and " married Mr. Birch's daughter, a proud passionate dame as ever lived. He went for a soldier in the Parliament army, and was made Colonel "—says Gough's " History of Myddle, co. Salop." Thomas Wollaston, described as a gentleman, of Walsall, was afterwards made an executor to act jointly with the others.

The uncle's will, dated 6th June, 1656, and proved at London in the October of the same year, alludes to his impoverishment by the Civil Wars, and contains the following clauses :—

" I, William Cumberford, of Mott Hall, in the parish of Tamworth, in co. Staffs., Esq.

" I desire to be buried in or near the place where my father and mother lie buried in the parish church of Tamworth.

" And touching my estate, which was greatly devastated of a considerable part by reason of the late sad distractions, as concerning debts due from Robert Arderne, late of Park Hall, co. Warwick., I am content to accept certain lands in Derryton and Bardsley (Deritend and Bordesley), or those of them near Birmingham in co. Warwick, which are valued at the yearly rent of about £62, and which were to be settled upon me and my heirs, the same to be settled on my wife Anne or others, and sold for the satisfaction of my debts, and the surplus, if any, to go to my daughter, Anne Comberford, but if the sale of said lands fails to satisfy my debts the same are to be satisfied by the sale of my other lands ; but in case the said lands at Derryton and Bardsley be not settled in such manner as aforesaid, only so much of my own land shall be sold as shall satisfy Sir John Curzon and Francis his son of my debts to them.

" The residue of my lands to my said wife Anne and my said daughter Anne, and the heirs of my said daughter.

" The rest of my debts to be paid out of the money due to me from Mr. Arderne as aforesaid, the same amounting to £2,000.

" I give the Book of pedigree of the Earles of Warwick to the Marchioness of Hertford.

" My goods and chattels to my said wife and daughter, whom I appoint to be my Executrices," etc.

OAK HOUSE, WEST BROMWICH.

From " Historic Staffordshire."]   [By permission of Midland Educational Co.

XXVIII.—THE LAST OF THE COMBERFORDS.

We now approach the termination of the Comberford tenure of the manor of Wednesbury.

Notwithstanding the statements in Chapter XXV. (ante p. 59), it does not appear from the Inquisition Post Mortem, taken at Tamworth on the death of Humphrey Comberford in 1555 that he, the said Humphrey, held absolute possession of the Manor of Wednesbury. Whatever interest he had in Wednesbury at the time of his death was through his wife, as a co-heir of Wednesbury Manor.

At the Inquisition Post Mortem, taken at Shenstone on the death of Thomas Comberford in 1597 (ante p. 60), it is quite clear that he, Thomas, held the said manor.

This Inquisition is also interesting because it discloses the existence of a Marriage Settlement, drawn up in August, 1566, in anticipation of the marriage of William de Comberford with Mary Skeffington (ante p. 60), which took place in 1567.

The Marriage Settlement of 1567 had no such far-reaching proviso of that of 1591. Among the Trustees appointed in 1567 may be noted the names of Walter Harcourt and John Skeffington; and the properties settled therein included the Manor of Wednesbury, together with certain other lands and tenements in Wednesbury.

These tenements are referred to thus:—
—"namely four messuages or tenements with the appurtenances situate and standing in the manor or lordship of Wednesbury aforesaid, then in the separate tenancies or occupations of Richard Syddowne, John Stephen, William Ley, and James Hunt. And also divers other lands, meadows, pascagia [woods in which pigs were fed], and pastures, with the appurtenances in the Manor of Wednesbury, in the separate tenancies or occupations of Richard Hoppkisse, Henry Sheldon, John Leveson, Roger Haddenbrooke (sic). Richard Stone, John Rastell, Roger Horton, William Crompton, and Thomas Dorleston": also "a certain Capital Messuage [that is, the Manor House] of the Manor of Wednesbury aforesaid, with the appurtenances": and, further, "lands, meadows, pastures, and hereditaments in Wednesbury aforesaid, with the Capital Messuage, etc.": and 46s. 6d. Chief Rents arising from certain lands and tenements in Wednesbury.

All these properties were settled upon William and Mary Comberford from the date of their marriage, in 1567, with remainders to the heirs of their bodies lawfully begotten, and in default to the right heirs of William, for ever. On the death of Thomas Comberford and his wife, Dorothy (grandparents of the bridegroom, who would be but 16 years of age at the date of his marriage), other Wednesbury properties were to devolve upon William Comberford and his wife Mary.

This Settlement discloses that William de Comberford—whose tenure of Wednesbury has been fully recorded in Chapter XXVI.—had a brother named Edward. The complications which ensued upon the death of William

de Comberford have occupied the whole of the previous chapter.

In 1635 it is clear that [Colonel] William Comberford was lord of the Manor of Wednesbury; because in that year (12 Charles I.) a fine was levied upon the grant of a lease for 60 years to Michael Noble, trustee to Anne, William's wife (ante p. 65). Doubtless a mortgage was at that time created to secure the £1,000, which the lord of Wednesbury then raised; and it is by no means impossible that the mortgagee was the "Mr. Gilpin," to whom the county historians have erroneously supposed that Wednesbury Manor was sold about this time.

Again, in 1637 (13 Charles I.), there was levied another fine, wherein John Birch, gentleman, and Edmund Beresford, gentleman, were the complainants, and William Comberford, armiger, was deficient of (inter alia) the Manor of Wednesbury.

By deeds dated 1636 to 1638 (Final Concords) it is disclosed that [Colonel] William Comberford had raised £1,000 by a sub-lease of the Manor of Wednesbury, which was to run 16 years, and expire in 1652.

All "manors, lands," etc., which were settled in the Comberford family about 1640, were unquestionably those properties (the Manor of Wednesbury among them) settled by the Marriage Settlement of 1591, and were subject to the leases then running.

The only known facts concerning "Mr. Gilpin" are that he was dead in 1649, and that he had had a "statute" (i.e., a mortgage) for £1,000 on certain Wednesbury "lands" (not the "Manor") belonging to Colonel Comberford. The Royalist Composition Papers refer to Mr. Gilpin as the purchaser of the Compounder's "lands in Wednesbury." That these lands, over and above the manorial estate, were considerable, will be evident from a Final Concord of 1656, which will presently be quoted. It is the opinion of Mr. A. A. Rollason that Mr. Gilpin was merely a mortgagee—possibly in possession. If he were a bona fide purchaser, a bond which was given for the £1,000 requires explanation. Or, alternatively, it is suggested that Gilpin had purchased the life estate of Colonel Comberford in the Manor of Wednesbury.

There is no shred of evidence to show that "Mr. Gilpin" ever held the Manor of Wednesbury in fee. On the other hand, it is as difficult to discover whether Colonel Comberford was, in the later years of his life, actually lord of the Manor of Wednesbury. His estates had been sequestrated early in the Civil Wars.

In 1649 Sir John Curzon (ante p. 65) was not only in receipt of the profits of the lands in Staffordshire, but also those in Warwickshire, in which Colonel Comberford had an interest.

Sir John's Curzon's lease ran out in 1652, but whether he got his moneys is not clear. Nor is it quite clear whether the sequestration of the Staffordshire properties (discharged by order 3rd December, 1647) was against Curzon or against Comberford.

On the death of Colonel Comberford, in 1656, the Comberford estates passed, under the Marriage Settlement of 1591, to the heirs of his eldest brother (of the half-blood), Humphrey.

William Comberford of Comberford, his nephew, was already dead (? 1653), without male issue, and as Thomas and Humphrey, the next brothers of William (the nephew), were also dead, without male issue, the manors and estates passed, under the limitations of the 1591 Settlement, to the next brother, John Comberford, of Handsworth, as the heir male of Humphrey, his father.

By a fine duly levied, Michaelmas, 1656, John Comberford, with the concurrence of John Birch and Thomas Wollaston, who were the then trustees of the Settlement made by his eldest brother, William, 16 May, 16 Charles I., granted, remised, and quitclaimed the Manor of Wednesbury, with its appurtenances unto Thomas Willoughby and William Booth.

The consideration money was £480, and the properties granted are described as—"the Manor of Wednesb. y with the appurtenances; and eleaven messuages, seaventeen cottages, two water-mills, one forge, thirty gardens, two hundred acres of land, one hundred and eleaven acres of meadow, two hundred and ten acres of pasture, and thirty acres of land covered with water, with the appurtenances in Wednesbury and Delves."

The distinction made between Wednesbury and Delves (the latter being now a portion of the former) is noteworthy. The extensive area under water was Broadwaters.

It is manifest from this that John Comberford, of Handsworth, had become possessed of an interest in the Manor of Wednesbury

The presumption is that, though William de Comberford had exercised his powers of leasing to the fullest extent, and to the detriment of his grandson William (son of Humphrey), he was powerless (under the same Settlement, of 1591) to vary the ultimate uses of the Settlement; and that the estates had now passed, not to the grandson William, who had died before this, but to his brother, John Comberford, his heir, pursuant to the limitations of that Settlement.

John Comberford, of Handsworth, upon whom the Manor of Wednesbury devolved as the next heir-at-law, was aged 58 in 1654.

In that year he gave evidence in the matter of the Petition of Thomas Turnor, of Deephome, co. Monmouth. The examination of witnesses took place at Northwich, 26th September, before the Commissioners for Sequestration within the County of Chester, and according to the orders of the Commissioners for "mannageinge the estates under Sequestracion at Habberdashers' Hall, London."

The will of John Comberford, dated 20 October, 1657, and proved at Exeter Hall, in co. Middlesex, 5 February, 1666, contains the following:—

"I. John Comberford, of Handsworth, co. Staffs., gent., aged about 60.

"I give to the poor of the parish where I shall be buried 40s.

"Whereas by Indenture dated 30 March and 4 April, 1653, I have settled all my lands in Wednesbury, in co. Staffs., to my cousins Anthony Stanford and John Leveson, and to Charles Stanley and their heirs to and for several uses and trusts, since when I have sold the Ironworks therein mentioned to John Shelton, esq. I now hereby confirm the said indenture, the intent of the same being that the said lands shall be conveyed to the use of the heirs of my body, and in default of such issue the said lands shall be sold, and my trustees to whom I formerly assured my interest in a lease of the said lands, which lease was made by my grandfather [not named], to my uncle, Thomas Comberford, and which afterwards came to me, shall release all their interest therein, and the money raised by such sale shall be used for the discharge of my debts, etc. The residue, if any, to be equally divided amongst my wife, Mary, and my sisters, Agatha, Elizabeth, and Hester.

"I give to the use of Katherine Comberford, wife of my brother Robert, and to the use of Mary and Anne, their daughters and their heirs, and for default to the female issues of the said Robert and Katherine, and for default to the said Agatha, Elizabeth, and Hester, and their heirs, my messuage and lands in Hoppas, my cottage in Coton, and the holme, or orchard below Hoppas bridge.

"I give to William Packard, late bailiff of Tamworth, a parcel of ground called Wall-furlong, in Tamworth.

"To my brother, Robert, £10.
,, ,, cousin, John Levison, £20.
,, ,, aunt, Levison, £5.
,, ,,   ,,   Comberford, £5.
,, ,, cousin, Ann Comberford, her daughter, 20s.
,, ,, sister, St. George, £5, and brother St. George, 20s.
,, their daughter Elizabeth, £5.
,, Colonel Stanford, £5.
,, my cousin, Purcell, of Ildfields, 20s.
[And other legacies to cousins and others named.]

"To my wife the residue of my personal property.

"I appoint my said wife, Mary, and the said Anthony Stanford and Charles Stanley to be my executors, and in default of them my cousin John Leveson, Mr. George Hawkins, grocer, of London, and Mr. William Packard," etc., etc.

A codicil [not dated] is to the following effect:—

"The said William Packard having died I give the said parcel of land called Furlong Wall and 3 other lands, which I lately purchased, to the said Katherine Comberford and her two daughters."

It does not appear that any other member of the Comberford family possessed the Manor of Wednesbury, or retained any interest in it, after the death of John Comberford.

The Comberford family estates were unquestionably impoverished, perhaps by the money advances which the Colonel had voluntarily made to the King's cause, and afterwards by the fines imposed upon him by the Court of Sequestration.

John may have sought to curry favour with the Parliamentarian Government, if only in retaliation upon his uncle, the Royalist Colonel.

It is by no means impossible that John Comberford had secured some of the family estates through the Sequestration Courts. In those troublous times so many broad acres changed hands in this way.

Whatever the nature of John Comberford's possessions in Wednesbury, or in whatever manner he may have acquired them, it is clear they were transmitted to no other member of the Comberford family.

About this time the Manor of Wednesbury was acquired by the Shelton family of West Bromwich: and it only remains here to deal briefly with the fortunes of this famous local family of Comberford.

The will of Colonel Comberford's widow, dated 20 February, 1669, was proved at Exeter Hall, co. Middlesex, 3 May, 1670; it contained the following clauses:—

"I, Anne Cumberford, widow of William Cumberford, late of Tamworth, co. Stafford, esq., deceased.

"Whereas several sums of money are due and owing to me by one Gilpin and others, some whereof have been in dispute in the Courts of Law and Equity, part whereof are due upon mortgage of lands and other securities, I give the said lands, tenements, etc., and one parcel of land called Moore Close, in the parish of Amington, in the counties of Warwick and Stafford, or one of them, heretofore the estate of Sr. John Reppington, and all my other lands and tenements, and all my estate in the same, and all moneys due upon the same to my nephew, Mr. Edward Langham, and his heirs for ever, and also my estate whatsoever, on condition that he discharge all my debts, etc.

"I appoint the said Edward Langham to be my only executor," etc.

Elizabeth Comberford, one of the sisters mentioned in John's will, had married George Hawe, of Caldmore.

Robert Comberford was a brother to John, and presumably younger. He had married Katherine Bates, of Sutton, co. Derby. By her he had two daughters—Mary, who married a Giffard, and Anne, who married a Brooke (of Salop).

Robert Comberford, in a certified Pedigree, declared he was the son of Humphrey, by Mary Stamford, yet he was unable to state the Christian name of his own father-in-law (Bates). His age is then given as 69 in 1663, which is also manifestly wrong, as that would make him older than his brother John.

Shaw's "Staffordshire" says that in Tamworth Church, under a beautiful Gothic arch in the north chancel, is the effigy of a man in armour, recumbent on an altar tomb, while in richly sculptured niches underneath are twelve small figures representing his sons and daughters. All this beautiful work is broken and much defaced, evidently the spiteful work of the Parliamentarian faction during the Civil Wars. It follows that the monument must have been erected before the war broke out in 1642; presumably it is the memorial of William de Comberford, who died 1625 (see ante p. 60).

Shaw, writing in 1798, said that over the said Gothic arch a small "modern" mural tablet has been recently inserted; the inscription upon it he gives in its original Latin form, a free translation of which would run as follows:

Here is erected a Monument,
But defaced by the lapse of time,
And more so during the Civil War,
To a Family
Not so long ago of an Eminent Race,
Rich and Honourable,
Namely, the
COMBERFORDS,
Who deserved the highest thanks from this Township,
Both in the Building of this Church and others.
The Lords of Comberford were
Illustrious for a space of 700 years,
But in the case of
ROBERT, of Staffordshire,
The last of the English line,
Who died A.D. 1671,
An extinct stock is lamented;
And he, together with his wife,
The Lady Katherine Bates,
And his two Children,
Mary and Anne,
Is buried in this Tomb.
The name still flourishes in the Irish Line,
Who followed King James II. to France,
And there is distinguished in the
Notable lordship of Anglunia,
In the Province of Champagne.
1725."

The Comberford Arms appear above the inscription, the crest to which is heraldically described thus:—

"Out of a ducal coronet, or, a peacock's head."

It is interesting to note that to the many quarterings on the Wortley shield, as sculptured in Wednesbury Church, the crest there given is:—

"On a helmet crowned, or, a peacock."

The will of Joseph Comberford, Esq., Lord of Anglure, and living in Paris, was admitted to Probate in the Prerogative Court of Ireland in 1729. This branch of the family evidently adhered to the Roman Catholic faith, and followed James II. into exile, where the spelling of the name seems to have been modified by the omission of the letter "b," or sometimes it appears as Cumberfort.

Little else is to be gleaned concerning the Comberford family. Blome's "Britannia," published in 1673, gives a list of the Nobility and Gentry "then" or "lately" related to each county. Here is a selection of the Staffordshire names therefrom; but the first name is manifestly anachronistic:—

William Comberford, of Comberford, Esq.
Sir Simon Degge, of Callow Hill, Kt.
The R. Hon. Humble Ward, Baron Ward of
Dudley and Birmingham, etc.
Walter Giffard, of Chillington, Esq.
John Hoo, of Bradley, Gent.
William Hopkins, of Wedgbury, Gent.
Thomas Lane, of Bentley. Esq.
Edward Mountford, of Bescote, Esq.
Thomas Parkes, of Willingsworth, Esq.
Thomas Parkes, of Wedgbury, Gent.
Samuel Pipe, of Bilson, Esq.
Thomas Scott, of Barr, Gent.
John Shelton, of Bramwech, Esq.
William Stanley, of Stanley, Esq.

— Stanley, of West-Bramwech, Esq.
Richard Wilkes, of Willinghall, Gent.
Among the Wills, etc., at the Prerogative
Court of Canterbury are:—
1611 Comberford, Francis, Staffs.
1626 Comberford, William.
1654 Comberford, William, ? Worc.
1670 Comberford, Robert, Staffs.
1673 Cumberford, Edward, parts abroad.
(Admin.)
The Index to Chancery Proceedings, 1625-
1649, discloses the following cases:—
Comberford v, Dickenson, etc.
Comberford v. Mitton, etc.
Comberford v. Stanford, etc.

XXIX.—WILLIAM PAGET, WEDNESBURY'S MOST ILLUSTRIOUS SON.

In the reign of bluff King Hal flourished a native-born son of Wednesbury, who, by the exercise of his own brilliant talents and the aid of a sound education, raised himself to one of the most exalted positions in the whole realm of England. Beginning life in a Wednesbury nail-smithy, he came at last to dwell among the "haute monde" in the palaces of princes and emperors.

In 1505 was born William Paget, the son of a Wednesbury nailer. Ere the boy grew up he was taken away from Wednesbury by his father—presumably to escape that life of "white slavery" which has ever been associated with the pursuit of the local nail-making industry.

Fleeing from the sordid surroundings of the family calling, the two wayfarers seem to have set their faces, Whittington-wise, towards London.

With what capital beyond a stalwart frame and a good address, the elder Paget arrived in London, will never be known. History first reveals him installed in the comfortable post of Serjeant-at-Mace to the Lord Mayor. By the influence of his official position, William Paget was enabled to place his beloved son in that famous city of London School, St. Paul's, of which the clever boy failed not to take the very fullest advantage.

In after years, when the boy had risen to great eminence, it was sought to connect his father with an old Staffordshire family; but it is significant that although the Pagets came to acquire large estates in their native county the parish of their actual origin, where the family name still lingered, was always studiously avoided.

William Paget became the close Counsellor of four English sovereigns, the esteemed personal friend of three of them, and the executor of one. But, like Wolsey, never did he once escape the pointed objections raised to his lowly birth and humble origin by the envious high-born nobles with whom he associated in the English court.

"In full-blown dignity see Wolsey stand,
Law in his voice, and fortune in his hand "—
exclaims Dr. Johnson, in "The Vanity of Human Wishes": and in the slight parallelism between Wolsey and Paget, it is remarkable that Wolsey was the patron of that other historic character, Gardiner, and that Gardiner in his turn became the patron of Paget.

"Magna Britannia et Hibernia" (Vol. V.), published in 1730, under the heading of Weedsbury or Wednesbury" has the following:—

"This place is render'd famous by the Descent of William Lord Paget from the Pagets of this Town, who were Persons of mean Condition. His father was one of the Serjeants at Mace in the City of London; and this his Son being a Person of excellent Parts, attained great Preferments by his great Abilities, for from being one of the Clerks of the Signet, he became one of the Principal Secretaries of State to King Henry VIII., who lying on his Death bed, made him one of his Executors, and appointed him one of the Council to his Son and Successor, King Edward VI."

At St. Paul's School Paget had the famous William Lily to be his schoolmaster; and it is little wonder that, with the natural gifts he possessed, he should become a scholar of such parts and accomplishments as enabled him to fill every high office to which he afterwards attained, with grace and distinction.

From St. Paul's School young Paget went to Trinity Hall, Cambridge, presumably during the mastership of Stephen Gardiner, afterwards Bishop of Winchester, and notorious for the active part he took in the Marian persecutions.

William Paget gave such early proof of his great abilities that his support at the university was undertaken by members of the Boleyn family. While at Cambridge he was an earnest Protestant, and distributed Luther's books there; he is said to have read the reformer Melancthon's "Rhetoric" openly in Trinity Hall. But it is not probable that he was really earnest in matters of religion at any time. It is less probable that Gardiner, who had been Wolsey's secretary, and as such had been engaged in persecuting heretics in 1526, would have permitted Protestant lecturing to go on in his college.

Paget does not appear to have taken any degree at Cambridge, but he remained a good friend of the University, of which he was afterwards High Steward. In 1547, when involved in a dispute with the townspeople, the University appealed to him for help. This led to Paget being appointed a Commissioner (1548) to settle the matter in dispute. In November of that year he was appointed one of the Visitors of the University; he was present at the disputation in 1549, when Grindal—then a young and almost unknown man, but afterwards the famous Protestant Archbishop of Canterbury under Elizabeth—argued about transubstantiation.

On leaving the University Paget was taken into the household of Gardiner, who sent him to study in Paris for a time, and received him again when he returned. In 1528 he was ill of the plague. In 1529, obviously through Gardiner's influence, he was sent to France to collect opinions from the Universities on the subject of the divorce of Henry VIII. This was Paget's introduction to political life, and to the notice of the King.

William Paget first won the favour of his royal patron, Henry VIII., by the zeal and discretion he displayed as a confidential agent employed on the Continent in this matter of the divorce of Catherine of Aragon. For his unqualified success in this delicate mission William Paget was knighted.

Gardiner had been trained in the household of Wolsey, and now in his turn Gardiner had become the patron of the lowly-born Paget.

In 1532 William Paget was made Clerk of the Signet, and in the same year was sent out to furnish Cranmer, then ambassador to the Emperor, with instructions as to what the King (Henry VIII.) was prepared to do against the Turks who had recently invaded Hungary.

A few months later he was sent on a mission to the Elector of Saxony; in 1534 he was again sent abroad to confer with the Protestant Princes of Germany—for his instructions see "Letters and Papers, Henry VIII.," vi. 148. He went by way of France to Germany in 1537 with Christopher Mort, a Lutheran agent of King Henry, to induce the Smalcaldic League of Protestant States to reject the Pope's overtures.

William Paget had been Knighted on October 18th, 1537; two years later, when his royal patron married Anne of Cleves, Sir William Paget, who evidently could speak German, was appointed her Secretary (1539.)

On August 10th, 1540, Paget was sworn in as Clerk to the Privy Council, and in the same year his office as Clerk of the Signet was secured to him for life. On June 1st, 1541, he had a grant of arms; on September 24th he was sent as an ambassador to France in order to perform the delicate mission of explaining the sudden fall of Catherine Howard. In this mission he apparently gave complete satisfaction, for on December 13th the Council increased his emoluments by ten shillings a day. On his return he was also made a Privy Councillor and one of the Secretaries of State (April, 1543.) On being made the Clerk of Parliament, 19th May, 1543, he resigned the Clerkship to the Privy Council. From this time Sir William Paget, who had attached himself to the Earl of Hertford, became most intimate with the King, and one of Henry's chief advisers. In 1544 he was commissioned (with Wrottesley and Suffolk) to treat with the Earl of Lennox as to Scottish affairs, and the marriage of Margaret, the King's niece, with Lennox.

Accompanying King Henry VIII. to Boulogne, which was captured, 1544, Paget took part in the subsequent peace negotiations.

In this year he received the office of Master of the Posts, within and without the realm. In the following year (1545) he took part in the new negotiations with the German Protestants. In 1546 he was one of those who visited Anne Askew, the Protestant martyr, in the Tower, for the purpose of trying to persuade her to change her opinions.

Paget's intimacy wtih the royal family may be gauged by recorded incidents. In 1546 he made a present of a sandbox to Edward, the little Prince of Wales. As the King grew older he relied very much on Paget; he consulted him about his will, and left him £300, appointing him one of the governors of the young prince during his minority.

Just before, and immediately after Henry's death, the Earl of Hertford held solemn conferences with Sir William Paget, though he declined to follow the advice which the latter gave. The morning after Henry's death Paget read aloud part of the King's will in Parliament, and then took a leading part in the plot formed to set it aside!

It was the year 1546 that the youthful Edward VI. succeeded to the throne.

Hertford became Protector, and took the title Duke of Somerset.

In the new reign Paget appears as the supporter of Protector Somerset, though himself inclined to courses of greater moderation. He proposed a protectorate in the Council; and expressed to Somerset his opinion that there was really no religion in the country at that unsettled period. There is printed on "Strype's Memorials" (II. i., 87), a State paper, which Paget wrote for the instructions of the Council, and which shows how ably he could explain his views.

Paget's position at once improved. He was made K.G. 17th February, 1546, Comptroller of the King's Household on March 4th, a Commissioner for determining the Boundaries of Boulogne, and in July. 1547, he became Chancellor of the Duchy of Lancaster.

Letters of Paget are extant in which he seriously warns Somerset of the policy he was pursuing; and when in 1549 he visited Oxford University as a Commissioner, he clearly showed that he was not in favour of the rigorous measures then being enforced against the Catholics.

Paget strongly disapproved of the Heresy Commissions, which were then issued, boldly telling Somerset that to alter the religious state of the Kingdom would require ten years' deliberation. Hence he gladly set off in June to Brussels to endeavour to persuade the Emperor to join with England in an attack upon France.

At the Emperor's court he was received with profound respect; but the religious tumults in England, upon which he was unable to place a satisfactory construction, prevented anything being done. He advised a firmer course with the rebels than that which the Protector had taken, notwithstanding that his own brother was a leader in the western rising (Dixon's "History of the Church of England," iii., 63.) His negotiation with the Emperor closed the same year; and in writing to Sir William Petre to explain his failure he said—"Alas, Mr. Secretary, we must not think that heaven is here, but that we live in a world" There is preserved in "Strype's Memorials" a curious conversation in which he took part during the negotiations with the Emperor, respecting the prerogatives of the French crown as compared with that of England or Germany.

Although Paget suffered considerably for the sake of his friend the Protector Somerset, and remained with him during the insurrections of October, 1549, he was actually in secret communication with the lords of the opposite faction, and showed them how they might capture Somerset. Into all this, he was created Baron Paget of Beaudesert, Staffordshire, 23rd January, 1552, the day after Somerset was beheaded. In 1549 he had become President of Wales; he also contrived to secure the London house of the Bishop of Exeter, and lands besides; but he ceased to be Comptroller. In January, 1550 he had a Commission to treat with the King of France.

When he became witness against Gardiner (who had been imprisoned by the Protestant Government) it cannot be said he did not merit the reproach hurled at him by Gardiner, that he had "neglected honour, faith, and honesty"; that he had "shown himself of ingrate malice, desirous to hinder his former teacher and tutor, his former master and benefactor, to whom he owed his first advancement."

During the whole reign of the boy King, the unscrupulous Paget took every advantage of the two factions which were contending for supreme power in the Councils of State. From that zealous reformer, the Protector Somerset, he did not disdain to accept a number of benefices, tithe-rents, and other properties stripped from the church; in return for which he, to all appearance, attached himself warmly to Somerset's party.

The acceptance of these ecclesiastical properties seems strange conduct on the part of one like Paget, who had stedfastly refused to accept the Protestant faith; but he immediately salved his conscience by exchanging this property of the church for some other property which was not less valuable.

Among these valuable properties were Shugborough (or Sowborough), Cannock town and forest, Longdon, Rugeley, and Beaudesert; at the first and last-named were ancient episcopal residences, the latter of which "Lord Paget re-edified," and whereby he procured himself the title "Lord Pagett of Beaudesert."

There were also a great number of hamlets and villages in or adjoining the said forest, which were lands of the Lord Bishop of Coventry and Lichfield, and which were now given in exchange for "certain parsonages impropriate, and other benefices, which the said Lord Pagett had obtained from King Edward VI."

To the court-leet of Longdon, no less than thirty other manors, lordships, and villages owed suit and service; all anciently part of the forest of Cannock, and all now transferred from the bishop to the newly-created baron of Beaudesert.

At the Dissolution of the monasteries in 1539 the richly endowed Abbey of Burton-on-Trent (ante. p. 34.) had almost escaped confiscation of its property by being constituted a collegiate church. But four or five years later it was found impossible for so desirable a property to longer escape the envious grasp of Henry VIII. The dean and chapter were forced to surrender all their lands to the King. These were then granted to Sir William Paget, and included the Manors of Burton, Branston, Bromley, Stretton, Horninglow, Wightmore, and Anslow in co. Stafford; and the manors of Winshall, Stapenhull, Caldwell, Overa Magna, Overa Parva, and Findern in co. Derby.

Bromley had been known as Abbots-Bromley, because it had belonged to the Abbots of Burton. Its name was now changed to Paget's-Bromley. Since 1730 or thereabouts the place has reverted to the use of its more ancient title.

This village was long celebrated for the survival of a very quaint old custom, known as the hobby-horse dance, which, however, is not now practised. The villagers at certain festive seasons danced through the village, one made up as a hobby-horse, and a dozen others with stags' horns on their heads. The masks and other paraphernalia for their performance were stored in the church, and at one time bore the arms of Paget and other great local landowners.

In May, 1551, Paget was appointed one of the Lords Lieutenant for Staffordshire and for Middlesex.

The lords of the faction opposed to Somerset were led by the Earl of Warwick, formerly Sir John Dudley. This wily politician secured the downfall of Somerset, and ultimately his execution (1552.) He made himself Protector to the young King, and conferred upon himself the title Duke of Northumberland.

This ambitious schemer, like Baron Paget, had a local origin. He had secured the barony of Dudley, its castle, and its priory, in 1540. His greedy hands had been laid on numberless lands and properties in this locality (a number of them are named on p. 19 of "Sedgley Researches," and they included the manor and advowson of Wednesbury—p. 62. supra), most of which doubtless found their way back to their original possessors when this interloper came to perish on the scaffold in 1553.

These two notables of local origin now stood facing each other in deadly rivalry. Warwick feared and hated Paget, and had hoped to effect his ruin with that of Somerset.

On a trumped up charge of conspiracy to murder Warwick while in his (Paget's) house,

Paget was arrested and committed to the Fleet Prison, 21st October, 1551, from which he was removed in November to the Tower.

The absurdity of the charge was too palpable, for Paget had openly rebuked Somerset in the Council for courting popularity, and had exhibited the Protector's weaknesses too often to join with him in any such adventure as this.

Action was consequently taken against Paget on other ground. He had resigned his Comptrollership when made a peer, but had kept his other appointments. He was actually degraded from the Order of the Garter, 22nd April, 1552, on the ground of insufficient birth—and also, perhaps, to make room for Lord Guildford Dudley, Northumberland's son.

On June 16th, 1552, Lord Paget was charged before the Court of Star Chamber with offences which he had previously confessed in the Council. His accounts as Chancellor of the Duchy of Lancaster disclosed that he had made large profits at the expense of the Crown. He had sold timber for his own profit, and had taken fines on the granting or renewal of leases. For these offences he was fined £6,000, and all his lands and goods were placed at the King's disposal.

Ponet, the Protestant Bishop of Winchester, afterwards wrote tauntingly—"What at length becometh of our Practising P? He is committed to ward, his Garter with shame pulled from his legge, his Robe from his backe, his Coat Armour pulled downe, spurned out of Windsor Church, trod underfoot."

But "Practising P" was clever enough to extricate himself from all difficulties. Although ordered to go down to his Staffordshire residence, he managed to stay in London, on the plea of his own ill-health and that of his wife, till Michaelmas. In December (1552) he obtained a pardon for all, excepting his debts to the Crown, and was even permitted to compound for his fine. In the following April (1553) a part of the amount still due from him was remitted, and he was once again received in favour.

On the death of Edward VI. Paget joined the Council of "Queen" Jane; but it is charitable to suppose that in this he acted under the compulsion of Northumberland, who was the father-in-law of Lady Jane Grey. Anyway Lord Paget gave his sanction to the proclamation of Queen Mary in London, and with Arundel set off to bring her to the capital. He became one of Queen Mary's Privy Council, and took with his wife, a prominent part in her coronation.

His Garter was restored to him on 27th September, 1553. He was commissioned to treat, with large discretionary powers, as to the Queen's marriage with Philip of Spain (March, 1554.)

Says the old writer, previously quoted—"Before the End of this King's Reign he fell into Disgrace thro' the Power of his Enemies, was depriv'd of his Garter, and fined Six Thousand Pounds, and all because he was a Friend of the Duke of Somerset, who was beheaded about the same Time. He bore these his Sufferings with Patience 'till King Edward's Death, when he join'd with the Earl of Arundel, to set up Queen Mary, in which being successful, he was restored to his former Honours, and obtain'd many more."

Paget set his face sternly against Wyatt's rising to resist the Spanish match; and from this moment he was unswerving in his adhesion to the Catholic Church. However, he would not agree to make it treason to take up arms against the Queen's husband (the King of Spain); nor to the bill directed against heretics. Nor would he fall in with Gardiner's suggestion to exclude Elizabeth from the succession; whereby he gained, for a time, the ill-will of both Gardiner and the Queen, and it was proposed to imprison him.

At times Paget undoubtedly displayed a tolerant disposition, and argued gentler measures for the suppression of heresy; he only inclined occasionally to the persecuting policy which was advocated by Mary's Government.

The High Stewardship of Cambridge University which had been taken from him at Mary's accession, was restored to Paget in August, 1554. In November of that year, he with two other chosen courtiers, went to Brussels to conduct Cardinal Pole to London on his mission of reconciliation between England and the Pope.

Lord Paget was always in high favour with Philip of Spain, who wished on the death of Gardiner, to make him Chancellor. But Mary refused on the ground that he was a layman. Paget, however, was made Lord Privy Seal, January, 1556. Shortly afterwards, being in Brussels with King Philip, he effected—treacherously, it is said—the arrest of Sir John Cheke, a reformer of great learning and high character: a cruel act which led to the humiliation and public recantation of Cheke, who died of shame shortly afterwards.

Lord Paget formed one of an Embassy to France in May, 1556; and when Anne of Cleves died in July, 1557, that ex-Queen bequeathed to him a ring as a token of her esteem.

Queen Mary died in November, 1558, and was succeeded by Elizabeth, her Protestant sister.

At Queen Elizabeth's accession Lord Paget desired to remain in office, although he had retired from the Council in November, 1558, and had ceased to be Lord Privy Seal. He certainly gave Elizabeth the benefit of his advice on two important occasions.

Paget was at least consistent to the trust reposed in him by Henry VIII. That King left the crown to his son Edward; and if no issue to Mary; and if no issue to Elizabeth.

That there was some element of strength in Paget's personality is manifest in the fact that although he remained a strict zealot of the Romish Church, it is recorded that Queen Elizabeth "retained an affection and value for him" to the day of his death. Of all his honours and dignities she allowed him to die fully possessed in 1564, which was the sixth year of her reign. He "was buried at Drayton, in Middlesex, but his monument was set up in Litchfield Cathedral."

The monument was of an imposing character; it was supported by Corinthian columns, over two statues of figures armed and cloaked, with two women kneeling by them; supposed to be emblematical of the two queens he served so faithfully in his life-time. A significant tribute was paid to the man's tact in the carved record that he was "Lord Privy Seal under Queen Mary I., and a faithful Counsellor and friend to Queen Elizabeth to his death." William Paget was a man of very great ability, but of little character. He was exceedingly careful of his estate; and as a Courtier was probably not more rapacious than any of his contemporaries. It must be remembered that he lived in the stormy times of the Reformation, when opinions on matters of religion were often held at the risk of life and honour. Few public men lived through the reigns of Henry VIII., Edward VI., Mary I., Philip and Mary, and Elizabeth, and came out so slightly scathed at the last.

Dugdale's "Baronage" compiled when the incidents were comparatively fresh, in recording the humble origin of the noble house of Paget, states that some of the Paget family were to be found near Wednesbury after the year 1600. This statement is corroborated by Collins' "Peerage," another old work equally trustworthy.

Of that exceptional and dramatic incident in the life of Paget, his public deprivation of the Garter, another old writer (who is also a Staffordshire worthy), gives an interesting account. This was Elias Ashmole, who in his historical work on "The Order of the Garter," says—

"Gentility hath its beginning in the Grandfather, its increase in the Father, and full ripeness in the Son. As to this particular there is a memorable instance in that of the Lord William Paget, divested of the Garter about 5 years ago after his election upon pretence of his not being a gentleman of blood by either Father or Mother."

This degradation was made at a Chapter of the Order on the Eve of St. George's Day, 6 Edward VI., at the instigation of the jealous John Dudley, Duke of Northumberland. Ashmole continues—

"The ensigns of the most noble order were not with more disgrace taken from, than with honour restored to the Lord Paget as soon as Queen Mary came to the throne, and the Garter was forthwith buckled on his leg again by two Knights Companions, the Collar was put about his shoulders," and every circumstance of the pomp and ceremony of a re-installation was observed, while records of the Order were corrected to brand his 'disgrace,' as an injustice perpetrated on one who was both worthy and honourable."

The reproach of his humble origin met William Paget time after time during his remarkable career in the courts of Kings. Here is an anecdote—again almost contemporary, and not improbably concocted by his enemies—which is extracted from "Manningham's Diary," of the date 1602:—

"Lord Paget, a son of one of the Serjeants-at-Mace of the City of London, thinking to have goaded Sir Thomas White, alderman, in a great assembly, asked him what he 'thought of that cloth,' showing him a garment.

"'Truly, my lord,' said he, 'it seems to be a very good cloth; but I remember, when I was a young beginner, I sold your father a far better to make him a gown, when he was sergeant to the Lord Mayor. Truly he was a very honest sergeant!'"

A portrait of this illustrious son of Wednesbury was painted by Holbein, and was recently in the possession of the Duke of Manchester. His Common-place Book was, in 1818, in the possession of Lord Boston.

William Lord Paget married Anne, daughter and heiress of Henry Preston, who came of a Westmoreland family. By her he left four sons.

WILLIAM, LORD PAGET, K.G.   BORN AT WEDNESBURY, 1505.
(From a Painting by Holbein).

XXX.—THE PAGET FAMILY.

Henry, the eldest son of the first Lord Paget, succeeded his father (1563). He had been made a Knight of the Bath at Queen Mary's coronation in 1553.. He only survived his father some four years, dying in 1568 without male issue.

The third Lord Paget was Thomas, the second son of the founder of the family.

He is recorded as having paid one visit to the scene of his father's boyhood. This was in 1572. Lord Paget was a staunch Catholic, and became a bulwark in the county for those of the ancient faith.

In 1572 Queen Elizabeth, fearing a conjunction of Catholic Europe against her, prosecuted searching inquiries throughout the land as to her strength and fighting resources; Lord Paget having gone round the whole county to satisfy himself on the point, wrote authoritatively to the Council declaring Staffordshire to be too poor to bear the expense of supporting large levies of men. Perhaps this report was not regarded as an impartial one.

In 1580 he was imprisoned on account of his adherence to the Roman Catholic faith. The Bishop of Coventry and Lichfield had complained to the Government that on Easter Sunday, Lord Paget being compelled by the conditions of his tenure of Burton-on-Trent to provide the communion bread for the parishioners there, his lordship's " officers would have forced them to use little singing cakes, after the old Popish fashion, varying nothing at all in form from the massing bread, save only somewhat in the print "—communion wafers had generally been stamped with the figure of the Paschal Lamb.

This period is one of great turmoil, caused chiefly by the cross currents of Romanism and Protestantism; 1572 saw the massacre of St. Bartholomew in France; 1586 brought Babington's conspiracy in favour of the Queen of Scots, followed the next year by Mary's execution: and in 1588 came the threatened invasion of the Spanish Armada.

The internal condition of England may easily be imagined; the position of a Catholic of eminence like Lord Paget of Beaudesert was not to be envied. His house was searched again and again for proscribed Papists supposed to be in hiding there.

In 1583 Lord Paget's estates were confiscated on the discovery of his undoubted participation in the Throgmorton conspiracy; whereupon he fled the country.

The connection of the Pagets with the early history of the Staffordshire iron-trade is disclosed by one of the Lansdowne MSS in the British Museum. This relates to the management of Cannock Forest when it fell into the Queen's hands at the "going over" of Lord Paget in 1583.

It appears that his lordship had "left a greate stocke of myne and cole redie caryed and layde at the mylles there," of which the Queen reaped the benefit. Afterwards the management accounts of the Queen show the cost of "digginge," the "myne" or iron-ore, and "lykewise the cutting and coling" of the wood—that is, making the wood into charcoal for the iron furnaces; and it is set down that "3,000 cordes of woode must be imployed to the makinge of 100 toune (tons) of iron."

It was this heavy consumption of wood for iron-smelting which depleted the forests in those times; a very serious consideration for the Government when ships were built of oak, and the national safety therefore depended on a good reserve of growing timber. But in 1588, although the year of the Spanish Armada, it was officially reported of this great Midland forest that—

" Cankewood doth stand in such place as the tymber there cannot be imployed to any of hir ma'ties work [shipbuilding, docks, forts, etc.] by Reason y't standeth farre from the sea, or any part of any navigable Ryver." The report therefore dutifully concluded that Cannock Forest would prove of little value to the Queen " unlesse it be converted to Ironworks to w ch use no doubt L. Paget did mynde to convert it, for all that it is in truth most fitt to be that waye imployed."

About this date was granted a 21 years' lease to Fulk Greville, Esq., at an annual rent of £221 10s. of " Canck Wood, viz., 2 iron-furnaces, 2 iron-forges, all waters thereto belonging, all woods and trees dispersed in the Forest of Cannock, the 5 cottages wherein the workmen lived, and all mines or Ironstone in the Forest of Canck, all which were parcels of the lands and possessions of Thomas, late Lord Paget (except woods in Beudesart Park and Gentle Shaw, and 3,100 trees marked by the Surveyor) and all the hollies in the Forest of Canck and Heywood Park." (Coke MSS).

When Thomas, Lord Paget, on his attainder for favouring the cause of Mary, Queen of Scots, had to fly the country, he went to Paris. On Queen Elizabeth demanding his return, he moved to Rome. Eventually he took up his residence in Spain, and actually accepted a pension from his Most Catholic Majesty, the King of that country.

Here it becomes necessary to introduce Charles Paget, fourth son of that famous William Lord Paget who first saw the light in Wednesbury.

Although his father had left him a fine estate at Weston-Aston, co. Derby, we find him living abroad in exile, and making himself notorious as a Catholic conspirator. Taking up his residence in France, he became secretary to James Beaton, Archbishop of Glasgow, and the ambassador of Mary Queen of Scots at the Court of France. Throughout Mary's imprisonment in England, Charles Paget and one Thomas Morgan were in constant correspondence with the two secretaries of the Royal captive. Paget and Morgan also contrived to secure to themselves the management of Mary's dowry in France, which amounted to no less than thirty million crowns a year.

Into all this, Charles Paget was acting the part of a spy, and supplying political information to Elizabeth's ministers.

In 1583, assuming the name of Mope, Charles Paget paid a secret visit to England, and at Petworth had a private interview with his brother, Lord Thomas. It is believed he was then planning for the invasion of England by the Duke of Guise and the King of Scots.

Continuing his machinations in France after his brother had joined him there, Queen Elizabeth demanded his surrender, along with that of his brother, Lord Paget, Morgan, and two other leading conspirators. The King of France declined to deliver any of them up.

Charles Paget was regarded as being so dangerous that, in 1587, he was formally attainted of treason by the English Parliament. Yet all his plots, which were for the forcible subversion of the Protestant religion in England, failed one by one. It is remarkable that a man so treacherous as was Charles Paget should have been allowed to settle down quietly in England again, as he did when James I. came to the throne.

In the meantime Thomas, Lord Paget, had died in Brussels in 1590.

William, son of Thomas, and grandson of the founder of the family, became the fourth Baron Paget.

James I., who paid some little respect to the memory of his unfortunate mother, Mary Queen of Scots, caused his first Parliament to restore to this Lord Paget all the family estates which had been confiscated in 1583.

By a grant in fee farm dated 22nd July, 1597 William Paget had already become possessed of lands in this county, which included Cannock, with two iron forges, and several manors, woods, and parks, of which Bentley was one. The local influence of the Pagets again become very considerable.

In 1606, William, Lord Pagett (with Robert Stanford, Knt., and others) held an Inquisition at Wolverhampton to determine upon whom rested the liability to keep in repair Tame Bridge, which divides Wednesbury from West Bromwich near Delves. Local knowledge and influence brought about an amicable settlement; certain feoffees of Walsall (the Corporation) seized of a close of land on the West Bromwich side of the Tame, acknowledged their liability in respect of possessing such close, to keep in repair not only Tame Bridge but another wooden bridge, and a way adjoining as far as Fryars Park Corner at a certain tree standing in a lane known as Dead Woman's Buryall.

Ann, the youngest daughter of this (the fourth) Lord Paget, married for her first husband Sir Simon Harcourt, of Stanton Harcourt, Oxon.; and on his death she became the wife of Sir William Waller, the famous Parliamentary General of the Civil Wars.

The restored Lord Paget died in 1628, and was succeeded by his son William, fifth Baron Paget. He died in 1678, and his son William became the sixth Lord Paget. This Lord Paget was ambassador to the Porte for concluding the Peace of Carlowitz, 1698. Dying in 1712, he was succeeded by his son Henry.

Henry, seventh Lord Paget, was created Earl of Uxbridge 1714. This title became extinct on the death of his grandson, unmarried in 1769; but the Paget barony, being in fee, devolved upon a descendant of the fifth baron, one Henry Bayley, Esq., on whom in 1784 was re-conferred the title Earl of Uxbridge.

Field Marshal the Earl of Uxbridge, K.G., served with distinction throughout the Peninsular War; he held an important command at Waterloo, and it was almost the last shot fired on that field which robbed him of a leg. For his valour and ability he was created Marquis of Anglesey. The Bayley-Pagets still hold the family honours.

Besides great estates in Staffordshire and Middlesex the family also have large possessions in Anglesea, the copper mines of which have largely increased the family wealth.

The family seats are Plas-Newydd, Anglesea; Stalbridge Park, Dorsetshire; and the original estate near Lichfield. That quaint old volume of 1730, "Magna Britannia," gives an enumeration of the things memorable then pertaining to this seat of the Pagets. (1). The family arms cut out in coal, dug in the park. (2). The finger-stocks, an instrument of torture to punish those who broke any of the established rules for conducting the usual Christmas merrymakings among the servants and retainers of the estate. (3). A peculiar quality of coal in which "King Charles II. 'head at Lichfield is cut and which edge-ways will burn as bright as a candle." (4). The usual echo, which was always considered noteworthy: and (5) The great elevation of the Castle hill, from which might be seen nine counties, viz., Stafford, Derby, Leicester, Worcester, Warwick, Salop, Chester, Montgomery, and Flint.

XXXI.—THE ANCIENT FAMILY OF PARKES AND ITS CONNECTIONS.

The family of Parkes was of obscure origin; and, although now merged in the noble family possessing the Earldom of Dudley, its ancestors were once nailers in the parish of Wednesbury.

Several bequests to the parish, and some monuments in the Old Church, mark the connection of the Parkes family with the town. The first of the family of whom we have any record was Thomas Parkes, who was born in Wednesbury in 1532, and died here 1602. He was buried in the Old Church, and by his will, dated January 11th, 1602, left a close called "Clay Pit Leasowe" to maintain a Schoolmaster in the town for 80 years; he also left a tenement in the town to be used as an Almshouse, for two persons, for ever. No vestige of these benefactions now remains.

The testator's son, Richard Parkes, was born in this town 1563. The family having by this time attained some position in the county a grant of arms was made to them (by the Norroy King of Arms, February 4th. 1615) in the person of this "Richard Parkes, of Willingsworth, in ye co. of Stafford, to rank him in ye society of men of worth."

This member of the family, by will dated July 4th, 1617, added 40s. per annum to his father's bequest for the maintenance of a Schoolmaster. In Wednesbury Old Church is the tomb of this Richard Parkes; it is an alabaster monument of two recumbent figures; the inscriptions are still plainly legible.

Dorothy Parkes (nee Greaves), wife of the said Richard, gave to the church a silver communion cup, with an inscription dated 1629 (see "Religious Wednesbury," p. 42). She also gave 20s. yearly for four sermons to be preached in the church every year for ever. She, and many other of the female members of this family, found sepulture in Wednesbury Church. A further bequest was made to the poor of the parish by this lady.

The son of these was Thomas Parkes, who exchanged, in 1618, with Richard Jevon, of Sedgley, five-sevenths of the tithes and rectory of Wednesbury (being himself one of the seven co-heirs to William Orme, gent., in the said tithes) for more lands in Sedgley (supra p. 62).

This head of the Parkes family was High Sheriff for the County of Stafford in the first year of the reign of Charles I. (1625). He died in 1660; it was his daughter Anne who married William Ward in 1672.

William Ward was third son of Baron Ward, of Birmingham; he was buried at Wednesbury 22nd December, 1713. This son was the progenitor of the present Lord Dudley; so that Sedgley Manor, which the first Thomas Parkes had purchased from the impecunious Lord Dudley of 1600, was thus carried back to a later bearer of that title. A fuller history of this family of Parkes is given in Chapter XXIII. of "Sedgley Researches."

There was a branch of the Parkes family connected with Smethwick, who, apparently, had some relationship with the Jennins family.

On p. 44 of "Records of Smethwick" it is mentioned that Humphrey Jennins left by will, dated 1689, a bequest to his "cousin Dorothy Parkes," the great benefactress of Smethwick.

Mrs. Esther Booth, who was a sister of the above Humphrey, left by will dated 1696 bequests to her "Cozen Whiteing and Cozen Parkes." Elizabeth Whiteing and Dorothy Parkes were sisters. Elizabeth died before, but only shortly before, the year 1690 (see "Records of Smethwick," p. 51), and presumably before the 14th February, 1689, the date of her brother Humphrey's will, wherein she is not mentioned.

Again, Mrs. Esther Booth bequeaths among other bequests to her servants thirty shillings (one of the largest sums) to "Mary Halfpenny." It is highly probable that the latter was the confidential servant to whom Mrs. Dorothy Parkes left an annuity and certain goods and chattels in trust, besides confiding to her sole care all her private papers.

This Mistress Dorothy Parkes—there was the Dorothy Parkes wife of Richard Parkes, of Willingsworth, just previously mentioned, and whose gift of Communion plate to Wednesbury Church is illustrated in "Religious Wednesbury," p. 42—according to her monumental inscription, lived a single life, and "never thought fit to enter the married state." A probable explanation of her "single life" is now offered.

In Chester's London Marriage Licences is the following entry:—

"Fowke Hope, of Wolverhampton, co. "Stafford, gent., bachelor, about 29, and "Mrs. Dorothy Parks, of Harborne, said "county, spinster, about 25, and at own dis-"posal—at St. Dunstan-in-the-West, Lon-"don, or Harborne, or Woolverton, co. Staf-"ford, 8 June, 1671."

The only other Dorothy of this family then living was Mrs. Dorothy Parkes's niece, daughter of her only brother Thomas, then only 3 years old. But Mrs. Dorothy Parkes was actually 27, so that "about 25" would be a sufficiently accurate statement of age for a woman.

It is conjectured that the above licence was not used owing to the death of Fowke Hope, or to the defection of one or other of the contracting parties. If any such marriage had taken place at Harborne, the entry would have been discovered. No record has yet been found of its having taken place at the other churches named.

In Wednesbury Church were formerly the ancient monuments of Richard Jennyns and Isabel, his wife, 1521 ("Religious Wednesbury," p. 41).

Among the Wednesbury wills in the Prerogative Court of Canterbury are indexed—

1508 Jenyns, John, Weddesbury, Stafford.

1558 Jennyns, Elizabeth, Wednesburye, Stafford.

In the reign of Elizabeth the name of Jennens appears in other Chancery Suits than those already mentioned (p. 62) in connection with the Comberford family.

Isabel Jennings and Agnes Heath were defendants, and John Bardell was the plaintiff, in a suit the object of which was a claim by Deed of Gift, the premises in dispute being lands in Wednesbury, Tipton, and Brierley.

Again, Isabel Jenyns, widow, Agnes Heath, and George Badger were defendants in another Chancery action, the plaintiffs in this being Richard Syddowne and his wife. This time it was a claim by descent according to the custom of the Manor. The premises are described as one-third part of a messuage or dwelling-house held in socage of the Manor of Wednesbury, and of one croft, a parcel of ground in Wednesbury aforesaid, called Sylymore, parcel of the copyhold, and customary lands of the said Manor.

In 1628 another Richard Jennings left a sum of 30s. a year to the poor of Wednesbury.

In the will of John Jennens, of Birmingham (whose second wife was one Joyce Weaman), who died 1653, mention is made of his furnaces at Aston, and his leasehold estates at Wedgeburge [Wednesbury], West Bromwich, and Walsall, in the county of Stafford. This will was proved by the testator's eldest son, Humphrey, 10 March, 1653.

According to some correspondence published in a work on the great Jennings's property law suits (" Jennens Estates"—Pawson and Brailsford, Sheffield, 1879) a letter dated from Birmingham, February, 1799, speaks of "John Jennens, proprietor of Wednesbury Hall, which he sold, as will appear from the writings now in the hands of Lord Viscount Dudley and Ward the present possessor. . . . The above-named John Jennens" seems to have lived also at Duddeston Hall. If there is any truth at all in the writer's statement, "Wednesbury Hall" most probably here means Willingsworth Hall. "New Hall Place," Wednesbury, in which the Jennings family were interested during Elizabeth's reign, has already been mentioned on p. 62.

Of Wednesbury Hall, Shaw, writing in 1799 says: "The old Manor House is situated about a quarter of a mile north-east of the church, but has nothing remarkable about it, being now converted into a common farm."

Among the wills at Prerogative Court of Canterbury are those of

1603, Parkes, Thomas, Wednesbury, Stafford;
and
1598, Pershouse, Humphrey, Wednesbury, Stafford.

Now, the family of Persehouse is supposed to be an offshoot of the Parkes family; the Parkes-a-Parkhouse (Sedgley) getting their name abbreviated to Parkhouse, then to Parshouse, and ultimately to Pershouse. The corrupted forms of this local patronymic are as numerous as the various branches of the family are widespread.

In the reign of Elizabeth John Parshowse was plaintiff, and Francis Mountford, Esq., was defendant, in a Chancery Suit. It was a claim by lease of lands in Walsall and Wednesbury, which the defendant demised to plaintiff, whereas the same had been taken under an "extent" (a kind of execution against lands) against the defendant's lands.

The family of Mountfort formerly resided at Bescot Hall. A certain Symon Mountfort of Coleshill was beheaded in 1495, for complicity in the Perkyn Warbeck plot. A grandson of this unfortunate partisan, also named Simon, obtained a reversal of the attainder, in 1534, and recovered a portion of the ancestral estates. The family settled at Bescot and Walsall. The Walsall registers have been fruitlessly searched for the birth of one Ralph Mountfort (who may have been baptised elsewhere) to complete the pedigree of the surviving branch, now in New Zealand. John, son of William Mountfort, of Walsall, was baptised at Darlaston in 1664. A John Mountford was churchwarden of Wednesbury in 1699.

About 1615 one John Persehouse acquired from the Whorwood family the "Manor" of Tipton, together with "an acre of land covered with water, in Tibbington and Wednesbury." It is quite evident that much of the low-lying land between Broadwaters and Sedgley was little better than marsh and morass in the earlier part of the seventeenth century.

In the will of William Westwood, of Kingswinford, dated 1664, mention is made of his

Grandchild Elizabeth, the daughter of Edward Parkeshouse :
Grandchild Mary, the daughter of Nioho. Parkeshouse,

both then under age. The inventory of his goods was made in 1665 by Jno. Parkeshouse and Samuel Parkeshouse. This was evidently an entirely different branch of the family from that which has been treated so fully in "Sedgley Researches."

The notice here given to these local families may appear somewhat scrappy, but they have all been dealt with at some length in the writer's previous works; for Mountfort consult index of "Olden Wednesbury," and for Parkes, Persehouse, and Jennings the same index, and also that of "Religious Wednesbury."

XXXII.—WEDNESBURY DURING THE CIVIL WARS.

Two State Papers give us a glimpse of the political and religious condition of Wednesbury on the eve of the Civil War.

In the reign of James I., Staffordshire, like many other parts of England, was troubled by recusancy, sedition, and plots of ever- description. On February 22nd, 1623, the justices of the county wrote to the Privy Council from Lichfield that they "have committed Randolph Lacy to Stafford gaol, not knowing how far certain words spoken by him may tend to ill." They "enclose the examination of Richard Frankton, of Wolverhampton, and Francis Onions, of Wednesbury, who state that they heard Randolph Lacy say, that had a certain person been living when King James came to England, he would never have been king. Lacy refused to say who this person was, but that it was a man, and no one of his majesty's progenitors; whereupon the constable was sent for and he was taken up. On his own examination Lacy said that the person whom he meant was the late Earl of Essex, but he never knew nor spoke with him, and will not say by whom he heard this said." The justices reported that Lacy was a tailor from Newington, near London, and a stranger in Staffordshire. He was committed to prison, and nothing more was heard in Wednesbury of him or his treasonable utterances. Essex, the favorite of the late Queen Elizabeth, had been beheaded in 1601. The latter part of Lacy's statement was evidently an afterthought, a piece of treasonable subterfuge, to throw his accusers off the scent from Lady Arabella Stuart, on behalf of whose claims to the Throne, Sir Walter Raleigh had been wrongfully accused of conspiring.

Another State Paper is dated 22 November, 1640, in the reign of Charles I. It is a Certificate of Richard Dolphin, Vicar of Wednesbury, that "Richard Stanton, of Wolverhampton, who was one of the three in the disturbance on Easter Day last in the Parish Church of Wednesbury, had made his submission before the congregation, on 1st November, now instant. The like was done by Henry Grosvenor, and Thomas Nocke, the 22nd instant."

Church discipline was severe in those days. The law sternly regarded and protected the State Church, and all its ecclesiastical rights. Underwritten the foregoing document was an order for the discharge of the three offenders who had thus purged themselves before the congregation in Wednesbury Church: it is signed by Sir John Lambe, 27 Nov. 1640.

In 1642 broke out the great Civil War between Charles I. and his Parliament, the ultimate result of which was that the King lost his head (1649), and the Parliamentary faction became masters of the country.

At the outset Dudley Castle was strongly garrisoned for the King, and placed under the command of Sir Thomas Leveson: while Rushall Hall, on the other side of Wednesbury, was fortified and held by Sir Edward Leigh, member for Stafford town, for the Parliament. Walsall produced two stalwarts in the persons of Captain Henry Stone, and Colonel "Tinker" Fox—the latter was really a saddlers' ironmonger, but was dubbed "Tinker" by his Royalist enemies, who had all too good cause to fear his military prowess.

Colonel Lane, of Bentley, was an out-and-out Royalist. So were George Hawe, of Caldmore, and William Hopkins, of Oakeswell Hall, Wednesbury. On the other side we have Edward Dudley, of the Greenhouse, Tipton, who had married a daughter of Squire Shilton, of Wednesbury Hall, and who, from time to time, lent considerable sums of money to the Parliament during the progress of the wars, and who, later, obtained a commission from Cromwell himself to raise troops in Staffordshire.

At Bescot Hall was Symon Montford, whose estate was sequestered by the Parliament in 1646. His brother, William Montfort, lived at Delves, but took no prominent part in the civil commotions.

At Willingsworth Hall, which was one of the largest mansions in the locality, dwelt Thomas Parkes, Esq., who was not only an ardent, but a most active supporter of the Parliamentary cause, and who also raised a troop of horse at his own proper cost.

There was a Parliamentarian Captain Turton, who is believed to have been the master of Oak House, West Bromwich (see p. 66), notwithstanding that his John Turton's wife was a sister of George Hawe, of Caldmore, who, in 1646, was fined £212 for his loyalty to the King. So many families were divided in these times of great political dissension.

Aston Hall, the residence of Sir Thomas Holte, had received a three days' visit from King Charles soon after the war broke out; immediately Charles had left the excited townsfolk of Birmingham, who hated the surly old baronet who had entertained the King, attacked the Hall, and seized the royal plate from the carriage in which it was being removed.

With all the local gentry around Wednesbury were thus arrayed on one side or the other, the people of this town suffered considerable distress. The wretched toilers at the open "coalworks" and in the nailers' hovels had to be content in their most prosperous days with a daily bread, which was baked of the dark heavy meal of "blend-corn"; with enforced war-taxes to pay there was even too little of that hard fare to be had. Each faction, as it came into power, levied contributions for the support of its own troops. For this purpose the country was parcelled out into districts, the weekly payments from which went towards the support of the military force occupying that district. There was no escape from either Royalist or Roundhead. The reluctance with which these enforced payments were made may be gathered from the fact that on April 8th, 1643, the Wednesbury and Rushall people were five weeks in arrear with their contributions, which had been assigned to the support of the garrison in Rushall Hall. Again, on June 22nd, 1644, an imperative order was made that Wednesbury, Walsall, Bentley, and other places around should "continue" to pay for the support of the Rushall garrison, of which Captain Tuthill was then in command.

Another evil the common people had to bear was that of enforced labour. For instance, in the Hundred around Dudley Castle, the men had to proceed with their own spades, mattooks, and other tools to accomplish the repair of the Castle's fortifications. Under the martial law of those times the men of this district were sometimes impressed for duty in the neighbouring garrisons.

One local incident was very dramatic. Colonel Levison, while in command of Dudley Castle, formed a design to get Captain Tuthill to betray the Rushall garrison. To this end he employed as his spy and go-between one or his own tenants, a yeoman of Wednesfield, whose name was Pitt. After many journeyings backwards and forwards, often passing through Wednesbury on his secret missions, Pitt was suddenly arrested. Captain Tuthill had only pretended acquiescence. The whole plot had been duly reported by him to the authorities in London. Pitt was condemned to death under martial law, and suffered the extreme penalty at Smithfield, 12th October, 1644.

On the 16th and 17th of September of the first year of the war (1642), the loyal gentlemen of Staffordshire journeyed to Aston Hall to present themselves in person to their King. It was on the 23rd of the next month that was fought the first and most memorable battle of the war, at Edgehill, near Stratford-on-Avon.

In the March following Lord Brooke, of Warwick, was killed by a dumb marksman while besieging the Royalists in Lichfield, a citadel which, a few days later, fell into the hands of Sir John Gell.

On the 20th of the same month Wolverhampton was taken by the Parliamentary forces, under Sir William Brereton.

It was about the same time that Rushall Hall was attacked and captured by Prince Rupert himself, notwithstanding the valiant defence made by Mistress Leigh in the temporary absence of her husband. Colonel Leigh's neighbour, Colonel Lane, of Bentley, was then left in command, on behalf of the King.

In April occurred the skirmish which is sometimes called the Battle of Birmingham. Prince Rupert, on his way from Henley to Lichfield, forced an entrance into the town, committed several acts of plunder, and then spitefully set fire to it in several places. It was in this action that the Earl of Denbigh was wounded; he died of his wounds at Cannock on the following Saturday.

The Prince after this display of his "burning" love for Birmingham, pressing on to Lichfield, was joined by 300 or 400 proper fellows from Walsall, and, after a continuous assault of 10 days, forced the city to capitulate. Lichfield then remained faithful to the King till the July of 1646.

Colonel Comberford, of Tamworth, who was then in enjoyment of the income from Wednesbury Manor, sent at the first outbreak cartloads of goods and ammunition, and many head of cattle from his place at Tamworth, towards Dudley Castle, intending the same for the support of the Royalist troops in occupation there. But the men of Birmingham getting scent of the convoy, seized and confiscated the whole of it. This was as early as September 16th, 1642.

In May, 1644, the Stafford Committee ordered the seizure of all the horses and cattle belonging to Squire Lane, of Bentley, and those of all the other Cavalier landowners thereabouts. These seizures were duly made, and realised by sale at Birmingham.

To set against this it must be recounted that at the beginning of the same year Colonel Lane had fallen upon a Parliamentary escort conveying provisions to Stafford. The enemy was routed, and the Colonel took no less than sixty horses and fifty-five of their packs, containing chiefly powder and ammunition.

But to give a better idea of the extent to which this system of pillage was carried on, it must be recorded how Rushall Hall during the period in which it was held by the Cavaliers became notorious as a retreat little better than a bandit's cave. When this Hall fell into the hands of Lord Denbigh (a son of the Earl slain at Birmingham, but of the opposite faction), in May, 1644, he must have been astonished at the vast stores of plunder he found hidden there. There were goods and wares, in bales, boxes, barrels, and horse-packs, all of which had been forcibly taken from the carriers plying between London and Chester, along the great north road, and whose contents were valued at no less than £10,000 even as money stood in those times—substantial testimony to the activity of these "Rob-carrier Cavaliers," as they were called.

The Vandalism of this warfare is well known. Allusion has been made to the destruction of the Comberford monument in Tamworth Church (pp. 60, 69): it was also at this period that the Paget tomb in Lichfield Cathedral was maliciously destroyed (p. 73). In Wednesbury Church a fine organ had stood near the chancel; this was wilfully destroyed by a fanatical soldiery whose Puritanical ideas found fault with such mechanical methods of praising God. Of all the magnificent heraldic and other stained glass, which, according to Wyrley's Church Notes of the year, 1597, adorned the windows of Wednesbury Church, not a vestige was allowed to remain.

The first part of the wars came to an end when Charles I. fell into the hands of the English Parliament, a prisoner, 1647.

An important warrant, dated from "Wednesburri, April ye 20th, 1647," and signed "By mee. John Carter, High Constable," directs the Constables and Churchwardens of certain surrounding Parishes to inquire what cattle, what money, and what goods had been taken, collected, seized or sequestered, upon any pretence for the public service during the troubles of the preceding six years. Thus from Wednesbury emanated, within three months of the

King's capture, one of the first steps towards the restoration of law and order in this much distracted locality.

In 1649 an information was laid against Edward Dudley, of Tipton, that he had " assisted the late King." The accusation was brought by a neighbour, John Caddick, of Sedgley, and in all probability was absolutely false. There was much false swearing of this kind. The Committee for the Advance of Money had, about the same time. to investigate a sworn statement to the effect that " Magdalene Lewne (Leveson) lived with her brother Leveson in Dudley Castle, all the late war. John Perry, of Sardon, and Richard Perry, of Wednesbury, owe her £450 "—which the Parliamentary Committee doubtless confiscated.

The chief Wednesbury actor in this great national drama, had been William Hopkins, Esquire, of Oakeswell Hall. He was a staunch supporter of Church and State, and when he was captured at the fall of Rushall (1644) it seemed likely that he would have to pay dearly for his active adherence to those principles he held so sacred. Accepting his life, however, and taking the fortunes of his family now under his best care, he laid down his arms, and prevailed upon his conqueror, Lord Denbigh, to permit him peaceably to return to his home at Wednesbury, where he had sufficient discretion to live afterwards in obedience to all the orders and ordinances of Parliament.

As Parliament got the upper hand in the great struggle, the Royalist leaders were punished by heavy fines and the confiscation of their property. Some relief, however, was allowed; a composition was often accepted by the Government.

Among the State Papers still preserved in London are these Royalist Composition Papers. These interesting national documents generally contain—

1. A confession of delinquency.

2. A pledge of adherence to the (Parliamentary) Government.

3. A full account, on oath, of the delinquent's possessions, real and personal.

Then follows a Report thereon, showing how the party was admitted to compound, in the proportions according to guilt (?): the exaction for a delinquent Member of Parliament was ⅓ the estate; for one who had taken part in either the former or the later war, ⅕th; for

one who had been active in both wars 2-6ths; and so on.

That William Hopkins, of Oakeswell Hall, made complete submission to Parliament is certified by Captain Tuthill, military governor of this district; it is further vouched for by the Committee of Stafford, under date March 17th, 1646. A few weeks before the surrender of Dudley Castle he had freely and fully subscribed to the National Covenant. Like a wise man, he afterwards petitioned for a favourable composition for his delinquency to free his estate from sequestration. This petition was referred to a sub-committee sitting at Goldsmith's Hall, and the statement filed shows the estate for which he desired to compound:

	£	s.	d.
He was seized in fee to him, and his heirs of land in Wednesbury, of the yearly value of	40	00	00
Similar lands in Tipton	09	00	00
And in West Bromwich	10	00	00
A like estate of 1-10th in Walsall...	02	00	00
A parcel of land in Warwickshire ...	02	00	00
Of copyhold in Wednesbury to him and his heirs	06	00	00

But craves allowances for chief rents paid to the Lord of the Manor of Wednesbury, £3 1s. 6d.

In every case, in this and other Royalist Compositions, the land values are carefully specified as being those current " before these late troubles."

With regard to this expression it may be explained that land had considerably depreciated; so much land had been left out of cultivation : so many other lands had remained unlet ; woods had been cut down during the wars. A Compounder had, therefore, to pay not the then value, which was virtually nil, but on the rental or income as it was prior to the war.

The foregoing figures in this Petitioner's statement are checked by the Constable and Overseers of the respective parishes. For instance. the item of £46 relating to lands in Wednesbury is vouched by " William Hawkes, Constable," and " George Meddewe and Thomas Cooper, Overseers of the Poor," for the Parish of Wednesbury.

William Hopkins escaped lightly with his fine of £200, when compared with the forfeit of £872, shown by the Composition Papers of Brome Whorwood, of Sandwell Hall.

XXXIII.—COLONEL COMBERFORD'S COMPOSITION PAPERS.

Our next extract of local interest from the Royalist Composition Papers relates to a Lichfield yeoman, who was a creditor of Colonel Comberford. It runs:

"Thomas Goodall, of Lichfeild, in the county of Stafford, yeoman. His Delinquency that he was in Armes against the parliamte. • •

"That there is due unto him by bond from Coll. Comberford, of Tamworth, in the County of Stafford, the somme of 500*l*., who is Delinquent.

"19 Aprill, 1646."

The following entry, found in the "Memorials of the English Affairs," under date 26 January, 1645-6, may possibly allude to the above-named: "Divers compositions past—that of Mr. Goodall rejected because he lately killed a man in cold blood."

Of Col. Comberford himself, it is easy to account for Royalist proclivities.

On the 18 August, 1619, it is recorded that "James our noble Kinge, and that worthy "Prince, Charles, came to Tamworth. The "Kinge lodged at the Castell, and the Prince "at the Mothall; and Mr. Thomas Astley and "Mr. John Sharp, the baliesses, gave royal en- "tertainment."—(Alrewas Parish Register.)

Not only had the Colonel's house, Moat Hall, entertained Royalty, but the fact that he was High Sheriff of Staffordshire in the year the war broke out (1642) most likely further involved him in the Royalist cause.

As Colonel Comberford was in the enjoyment of the revenues of Wednesbury Manor at the outbreak of the war, the local information given in his Composition Papers is of considerable interest. As the documents do not appear to have been published before, they are now given in extenso:—

"Wm. Cumbeford, of Tamworth, in the County of Stafford, gent.

"His delinquency that he was in armes agt. ye parliamt in ye first Warr.

"He peticioned here the 10th of Aprill, 1649.

"He Compounds upon a particular deliuered in vnder his hand by wch. he submittes to such ffine, etc., and by wch. it doth appeare—

"That he is seised in ffee to him and his heirs of and in certain Landes and Tenemtes, in Bolehill and Glascott, in the County of Warwick, and in Tamworth, in the Countyes of Warwick and Stafford, on the yearly value before these troubles—188*l*.

"And of a like estate of, and in the Tythes of Hopwas, in the said County of Stafford, of the yearly value of 10*l*.

"That he is seised of a ffrancktenemt. for two lives only by severall Leases made by his ffather, whereupon the ancient Rentes are reserved by the heire at Lawe amounting per annum to 86£ 10s. 2d.

"And are of the yearly value above the said Rentes 71£ 9s. 10d.

"And of a like estate of and in a Wood called Hopwas-hay of ye yerely value over and above the yearly rent of 7£ 13s. 4d. reserved—5£ 13s. 4d.

"Out of which he craves allowance of 30£ per annum graunted by the Compoundr. to Humphry Cumberford gent., for his life out of Bolehill by deed dated 10 Dec. 17 Caroli, in pursuance of a decree in the Court of Wardes in 7 Caroli confirming a former graunt of that Annuity graunted by his father 19 Jacobi, out of other Landes sold by the Compounder, with Arrears thereof for six yeares as he saith, amounting to 180*l*. 29*l*. per annum, payable out of the said Estates for two lives to Christchurch, in Oxford, for ever as by oath of Thomas Rogers, gent., with the Arrerages of the said Rent for 7 years last past amounting to 203*l*. as he saith. 150*l*. per annum granted by the Compounder unto Michaell Noble, Esquire, and John Langham, gent., for 60 years, if Ann, now wife of the Compounder, shall so long live being allotted unto her in way of Allemony.

"1,000*l*. debt to Sr. John Curson, Baronett, for wch. the Compounder made a Lease to Sr. John Curson by deed and ffine Surconcessit in Easter tearme, 12 Caroli, of all his lands in the County of Staffes, for 16 years. And had a Statute of 2,000*l*. for further security, upon examinacion whereof before the Committee of Lords and Commons for Sequestracions, the Sequestracion hereof was discharged by order of the third of Dec., 1647.

"1,246*l*. debt for Arrerages of the rentes of 86£ 10s. 2d. per annum, reserved upon the severall Leases for life of the Lands in Staffordshire being Arreare for 23 yeares past, and a Suite was commenced in the Court of Wardes to compell ye heire at Common Lawe to accept of theire Arrerages of Rent.

"19s. 10d. chiefe rent for ever due to ye Corporacion of Tamworth out of the Compounders lands in the County of Stafford, as by oath of Thomas Rogers, gent.

10 May, 1649.   D. Watkines.
    Jo. Bradinge.
        May 15 fined at a fixt.
            434£ 16s. 10d."

"To the Rt .Honorble. the Commissioners for Compounding with delinquents sitting at Goldsmith's Hall, the humble peton. of William Cumberford of Tamworth in ye County of Warwicke, gent.

Sheweth

That your petitioner haueing binn in armes agt. the parliament in the first warre only for wch. his sayed delinquency, your peters'. estate remayneth under Sequestration.

Yr. petire. humbly prayeth yt. hee may bee admitted into such reasonable Composition as to your honours shall seeme meete etc.

Wm. Cumberford."

(Endorsed) "Reed. the 10 Aprill, 1649, and Referrd to the Suboomity.

S.M.
    Jo. Leeoh."

"The particuler of the estate of William Comberford, of Tamworth, esquire, lying in the severall Counties of Staffs. and Warwicke.

" He is seized in ffee of certaine landes in Bolehall and Glascote in Com' Warr. of the yerelie value before these times, 105£ 0s. 0d.

" He is alsoe seized in fee of certaine landes and howses in the towne of Tamworth in the counties of Staffs' and Warr' of the Yerelie value before these times 53 0 0.

"He is also seized in ffee of the Mothall howse wth. all the landes and groundes thereunto belonging in the Countie of Staffs.   30 0 0

" He is alsoe seized in ffee of the tythes of Hopwas, in the Countie of Staffs' of the yerelie value before these times.   10 0 0

" He is alsoe seized of an estate for two lives in beinge, of Aldermills of the yearly value before these times.   30 0 0

" He is alsoe seized of an estate for two lives only in beinge of Certaine landes and tenemtes. in Wiggington, Comberford. Hopwas, Coton, and Tamworth of the yerelie value before these times.   128£ 0 0

" He is alsoe seized of an estate for two lives in a parcell of Wood called Hoppas-haye, and of a parcell of ground called the Deane, of the yerelie value before these times   li.
xiiij.

" The Compounder humbly craves allowance for the particulers followinge:

"A Lease dated 20 April, Anno 13 Caroli, unto Michaell Noble, esqr., and John Langham, for 60 yeres of divers landes and tenemts. in the counties of Staffs and Warr'. if Anne, the said William Comberforde's wife, shall soe longe live all 1d. per annum rente. which landes are of 150l. per annum value, and have bine ever since held and enjoyed accordinglie, and the profittes still received.

"An annuitie of 30l. per Annum yssuing out of Bolehall farme unto Humphrey Comberford, gen', who is still livinge, and areres thereof for 6 years.   li.
clxxx

" A Lease unto Sr. John Curson, knighte and baronett, of all the Compounder's landes in Com', Staffs., for 16 yeres att 10s. rente per Annum, which landes are still in the said Sir John Curson's tenure, and wilbe for 2 yeres and halfe longer, and the profittes are by him received.

"A statute extended upon all other the said Willm. Comberforde's landes in Com', Warr', att the said Sir John Curson's suite, and the profittes still received by the said Sir John Curson.

"Severall yerelie rentes amounting to 86£ 10s. 2d. yssuing and payable out of divers of the said William Comberforde's landes an Com'. Staffs., unto Willm. Comberford, of Comberford, the Compounder's nephew, by vertue of severall leases for lives made to this compounder by his father in his life time.

"The arrerages of the same rentes still due and payable amountinge to   1246 0 0

"The yerely rente of 29£ per ann. yssuing and payable out of all the landes the Compounder holds for lives in Com', Staffs., unto Christ Church Colledge in Oxford.

"The arrerages of the same rentes for 7 yeres laste paste amounting to   l.
203

" The yerelie rente of 7£ 13s. 4d. due to Coll. Edwad. Stanford for Hoppas Haye, for the two lives the Compounder holds the same.

" The arrerages of the same rentes for 7 yeres woh. amounteth to   53£ 13s. 4d.

" The yerelie chiefe rente of 19s. 10d. due to. the Corporacoin of Tamworth for the Compounder's landes in Com., Staff.

"A statute of 1,000£ entered into before these times to Mr. Gillpen, deceased, the purchaser of the compounder's landes in Wednesburye, in Com', Staffs.

" Severall debtes due and owing by the Compounder by specialtie before these times, wherein divers men are his securitye, vizt., Thomas Goodall 500l., Mr. Jackson 550l., Mr. Tho. Rogers 100l., Mr. Humfrey Davies 100l., Mr. Sucklyn 100l., Mr. Yardley 50l., and much use due uppon all these severall bondes.

"Besides, the Compounder is much otherwaies indebted in 700l. to Dorothye Combford, his sister, deceased, payable to her out of Wednesburye landes.

" And divers other debtes due before toe Warre amountinge to 1,000£.

(Endorsed) "Wm. Comberford, No. 2,116.
    15 May, 1649.
    Rep. 6 Dec., 1649.
    ffyne 434£ 16s."
        " Mr. Comberford's Particular."

The search for the Comberford Composition Papers brought to light the prominence in the Civil War of other local names; not the least puzzling of which was that of Francis Wortley.

In the 5th Regiment of the Royal Army of Charles I. were Colonel Sir Francis Wortley and Captain Shelton. The latter (or a Sergeant-Major of the same name) was mortally wounded at Lansdowne fight, 5 July, 1643, by the blowing up of an ammunition wagon. There was a Sir Francis Wortley, of Wortley, in Yorkshire, educated at Oxford, and mentioned in Wood's "Athenæ Oxon." He was taken prisoner near Wakefield, 3rd June, 1644, but the time and place of his death are uncertain, although he is believed to have died a prisoner in the Tower, 1652. His arms were: Argent, on a bend between six mart'ets, gules, three bezants.

On the west wall of the south transept of Wednesbury Church may still be seen, with a shield of 20 quarterings, a mural tablet inscribed thus:—

"In cujus beneficii memoriam Franciscus Wortleius de Wortley, Ebor, miles et baron, (quondam patronus suus) hanc commemorationem illi servorumque fidelitate dicavit. Hic a cunabilis Marti dictatus nil inhonestum non ausus, ardua gressus, sanguinem sudoremque perpessus. In juventute veteranus in arte militari peritus inter cohortes regi Persarum assignatas centurio electus, jam iter facturus in matrem pietate ardens Ithacam petijt, febri maligna insidiatus, Persarum arma deposuit, Christi induit, solita magnanimitate, insolita alacritate animae aromata cum hisce verbis (euge bone fidelisque serve) suaviter exhalavit —sic invictus cecidit non perijt, 1636."

A translation runs—

"In lasting memory of whose kindness, Francis Wortley de Wortley, of York, knight and baron (formerly his patron), dedicated this memorial to him, and to the fidelity of his character. Dedicated to Mars from his birth, dared nought that was dishonourable, surmounting all hardships, he endured wounds and toil. A veteran in his youth, skilled in military tactics, he was chosen centurian among the cohorts assigned to the King of Persia; and, when glowing with filial affection, and about to proceed on a journey to meet his mother, he reached Athaca, he was attacked by a low fever, he laid aside the arms of Persia and put on the armour of Christ, with his wonted magnanimity, but unwonted eagerness of spirit sweetly tempered with these words, 'Well done, thou good and faithful servant,' he quietly passed away. So unconquered he fell, but perished not, 1636."

Who is meant by the phrase "his patron" is not known; nor can it be stated what connection the Wortley family had with Wednesbury. The date "1636" adds to the difficulty.

The connection probably lay through the Comberford interest in Wednesbury. It will be seen in the following Composition Papers "concerning Walter ffowler's delinquency" that Colonel Comberford mentions Sir Francis Wortley as taking part in the military operations of North Staffordshire, whose moorlands roll away northwards, and merge into those of Derbyshire and Yorkshire.

"Depositions of witnesses taken uppon oath the xxvth. daie of September, 1649 . . . . . by order of the Commissioners. date the 6 of September, Anno Dm. 1649.

"William Comberford, of Tamworth, in the Countie of Staffs., esquire. sworne and examined deposeth and saith that when he was made High Sheriffe of the Countie of Staffs. by his late Matie., he alsoe was made governor of the towne of Stafford by virtue of a Commission from his said Matie., and accordinglie did keep the said towne as a garrison for his said Maite., and further saith that not longe after he first possessed himselfe of the said garrison he did, by virtue of his said office and Commission, send out lers. [letters] to all or most of the gentlemen in the countrye there for their present repaire to the said Garrison for the defence thereof. In obedience wherunto many of the gentl', and in particular Mr. Walter ffowler, repaired to the said garrison, and there continued for some space. And this

depot. further saith that very shortlie after this depot. was possessed of the said garrison for his said Mate's. use, the Moorelanders did ryse and approch the said towne of Staffs, And this depot. not knowing the cause of their approch in soe hostile a manner, commanded all the gentlemen and others to march out wih. him to the said Moorelanders, and also commanded the townes men to be readie in armes, as they would answere the contrarie att their perills. He having power from his Matie, to seize the estates of all such as refused to come in to him uppon command. And this depot. being demanded whether the said Walter ffowler did then take command upon him, or did give any Charge against the said Moorelanders wth. Sir ffrauncis Wortley, He saith the said Walter ffowler had noe Command there, but did onlye ryde out armed amongst other gentlemen wth. the Governor of Stafford and Sr. ffrauncis Wortley as they were commanded.

(Endorsed) "For the Honble. the Committee for compounding wth. delinquents att Goldsmiths Hall."

After the restoration of Charles II. (1660) the name of Walter Fowler appears in the list of the intended Knights of the Royal Oak it was then proposed to found. The annual value of his estate was declared to be £1,500.

A pedigree of Walter Fowler of St. Thomas is given in Salt V., part ii. p. 136. He died in 1684; in his will, proved in London, 9 May, 1684, he describes himself as "a true member of the Roman Catholic Church," and he "renounced from his heart all errors and novelties by her rejected. He and his wife (a daughter of Lord Aston) were buried at Baswick.

Walter Fowler was a very active Royalist, being seen "often with his sword by his side, and his pole-axe in his hand; and when the Moorland men came against Sir Francis Wortley he (the witness who deposeth this) saw Mr. Fowler ride forth of Stafford, having a buff coat and armour upon it, with a head piece, sword and pistol. And, further, this deponent saw the said Mr. Fowler, together with Sir Francis Wortley and others, charge the Moorlanders."

After the Restoration, and when Charles II. was firmly seated on the throne, it was reported to the Government by Colonel Lane, of Bentley, that numbers of Cromwell's old soldiers, now disbanded, resorted to meeting-places in Walsall, Wednesbury, and Wolverhampton. More than 800 lived between Cheadle and Lichfield, and it was complained that their Conventicles were not free from suspicion of sedition. As late as 1703 Wednesbury Registers made mention of an "old Oliverian Cornett," whose house at Tipton was used as a Conventicle.

BEAUDESERT, CANNOCK.   Rebuilt by Lord Paget (p. 72).

From 'Ship' Historical Reader V.]

[By permission of Messrs. Longmans, Green, and Co.

XXXIV.—WEDNESBURY MANOR HELD BY THE SHELTON FAMILY.

Here we resume the manorial history from Chapter XXVIII.

As stated on p. 67 there is not the slightest evidence to support Shaw's statement that "one Gilpin" held the manor of Wednesbury in fee; although it is quite possible he may have held it for some time under mortgage or lease.

The only facts ascertainable respecting this individual, who is alleged by the county historian Shaw to have held Wednesbury Manor, are that his name was Gilpin (christian name and former seat are both unknown), and that he was dead in 1649, when Colonel William Comberford petitioned Parliament in the matter of his delinquencies.

It is not improbable that Colonel Comberford sold his Wednesbury estate soon after the outbreak of the Civil War in 1642, in order to raise money on the King's behalf. The Gilpin tenure of the manor of Wednesbury was but a brief one at best, as it had passed to the Sheltons by 1647.

In searching for this local family of Gilpin an allusion was found in Salt V., ii., p. 171. The will of Mary Haw, widow of George Haw, of Caldmore, proved at Lichfield, 1669, makes mention of numerous relatives and friends of the testator. Among the relatives named are her grandchild, Simon Mountford, and his brother Edward and sister Mary—the Mountfords were seated at Bescot Hall; her cousin, Henry Stone, Esq.—the Stones were an important Walsall family; and among the friends mentioned are the Smallwoods, Joseph Gorwey, and a certain "John Gilpin, gent."

It has been mentioned (pp. 66, 69) that George Haw, son of the above testator, married Elizabeth, daughter of William Comberford, of Tamworth, Esq. This George Haw was admitted to the Inner Temple in 1632, and, dying in 1660, was succeeded by his son George, who married Catherine Persehouse, at Walsall, January, 1674 (Shaw II., p. 74.)

But if the "John Gilpin, gent.," above-named, was not the (alleged) owner of Wednesbury Manor, the "Mr. John Gilpin," who was buried at West Bromwich, 10th October, 1709, may have been some connection of this mysterious individual.

In Wolverhampton Church there was formerly in the middle aisle an ordinary quarry stone with an inscription recording the burial there of the children of one Thomas Gilpin, in 1660. Doubtless these were the Gilpins of Tettenhall and Bushbury.

No other local Gilpins of eminence about that time can be traced.

When, or in what manner, Wednesbury passed from the Comberfords cannot be stated with any exactitude. But the manor is next found in the possession of the important local family of Shelton (or Shilton.)

This family was connected with the Rilands of Sutton Coldfield and is mentioned in the history of the latter family. The Shelton Arms were—"Sable, three Escallop Shells, Argent."

The founder of this family was Henry Shelton, of Birmingham. His son, John Shelton, married Barbara, daughter of Francis Stanley, of West Bromwich, and sister to Walter Stanley, also lord of that manor, who provided so handsomely for the advancement of his nephew (Sir), Richard Shelton—all of which is set forth at some length in the writer's "History of West Bromwich" (pp. 29—31.)

This John Shelton was a Mercer in Birmingham, whom Edward VI. made a trustee of the newly-established Grammar School in that town.

By his wife, Barbara Stanley, of West Bromwich, John Shelton had two sons, Robert and Richard. The latter became Sir Richard Shelton, Knt., for some time Solicitor-General to Charles I., and who died without issue in 1647, having previously purchased the Manor of West Bromwich, from the Stanley family.

Robert Shelton, the elder son, remained in Birmingham. He married Mary Temple, by whom he had issue. The first son was John Shelton, of Birmingham and West Bromwich, who acquired also the Manor of Wednesbury.

(1.) JOHN SHELTON, I., LORD OF WEDNESBURY, 1647 (?)—1663:

This John Shelton, lord of the Manor of Wednesbury, matriculated at Queen's College, 4th November, 1631 aged 16, and became barrister-at-law, Inner Temple, 1637. He married for his first wife Mary Knightley, daughter of Richard Knightley, of Burgh Hall, Staffordshire, and Fawsley Northants, by his wife Anna, daughter of Edward Littleton, of Pillington, Staffordshire.

There is no record of issue by his wife. John Shelton's second wife was Elizabeth Holland, of Windsor, by whom he had a family of six; a son and five daughters.

In 1662 he presented to the Rectory of Sutton Coldfield, the advowson of which had been purchased by his grandfather, the Birmingham mercer, in 1586.

In Shaw's list of the Sheriffs of Staffordshire is the following entry for the 12th Charles II.:—

"Humble, lord Ward of Himley and . . Shilton, of Wednesbury."

Hereby hangs a tale of some little historical interest. The 12th year of the reign of Charles II., reckoned from his father's death on the scaffold, was 1660. Charles II. was restored to the throne on 29th May, 1660. The title of Baron of Birmingham had been bestowed on Humble Ward, whose wife was the lady Frances, Baroness of Dudley (the family details are given at length in "Sedgley Researches," p. 26), by a patent of nobility, dated 23rd March, 1643-4—that is, after the outbreak of the Civil War, and while Charles was making Oxford the headquarters of his Army.

Twamley, in his "History of Dudley Castle," says:—

"The titles conferred at Oxford were looked upon with great distaste by all parties. On the 14th December, 1647, the Parliament in one of those attempts at a peaceful settlement, which were numerous during the struggle, and which the King's utter want of good faith and honesty always rendered abortive, passed four propositions, one of which was—'That all lords who were made after the great seal was carried away (viz., 1642) should be rendered incapable of sitting in the house of peers'; and the House of Lords in the session when Charles II. was re-called (viz., 4th May, 1660—12, Charles II.), excluded from parliament all lords created since 1642.   The King, however, on the 31st May, two days after his arrival in London, acquainted the House that it was his desire that those lords who had been created by Letters Patent by his late Majesty at Oxford, should sit as peers. The House appointed the Earl of Berks to acquaint him that matters of honour belonged to his Majesty, and acquiesced in his pleasure; and moreover resolved 'That the order excluding any lords made at Oxford be cancelled'; and we find Lord Ward attending in the House on the 22nd June following."

This explains the mystery of two names appearing on the list of Sheriffs for the same year. It is clear that Humble, Lord Ward, commenced the year of office in the Shrievalty, but as no peer can be Sheriff, the office would become void when he took his seat in the House of Lords; whereupon ". . . Shilton, of Wednesbury," would be appointed in his place for the remainder of the year.

John Shelton (or Shilton) acquired the Manor of Wednesbury about 1647, the year in which his wealthy uncle, Sir Richard Shilton, of West Bromwich, died childless.   He died 1663; in 1666 his widow, Elizabeth, married again (at West Bromwich), her second husband being Mr. Walter Needham.

(2.) JOHN SHELTON II., LORD OF WEDNESBURY, 1663—1701:

John Shelton followed his father as lord of Wednesbury Manor (and also of the Manor of West Bromwich, in the old Hall of which the Sheltons, or Shiltons, appear to have resided), succeeding, at an early age, having been born in 1659.   He also married very young, his union requiring the consent of his mother, "Mistress Elizabeth Needham."

From the Marriage Allegations in the Registry of the Vicar-General of Canterbury, it transpires that this consent was given to the marriage, on March 21, 1676, at All Hallows in the Wall, London, in which the bridegroom, John Shelton, is described as of West Bromwich, Esq., bachelor, about 17; and the bride, Mistress Mary Prickman, of St. Gabriel Fenchurch, London, spinster, about 20.

John Shilton sold the Manor of Wednesbury about the year 1701, and the Manor of West Bromwich about the same time.

Of John Shilton's five sisters it is necessary only to make passing allusions to two. The eldest, Mary, appears from the aforementioned Marriage Allegations to have been married on October 2, 1671, at St. Dunstan's East. Katherine Shilton, the fourth, married John Riland, clerk, who was presented to the Rectory of Sutton Coldfield, by his father-in-law, John Shilton, the elder and who afterwards purchased the advowson from the same John Shilton on account of his (the latter's) adhesion to Nonconformity.

John Shilton, who sold the two Manors of Wednesbury and West Bromwich, was a spendthrift, and died a ruined man about 1714. His son Joseph entered as a student of the Inner Temple, 1680.

WEDNESBURY PINFOLD.

Formerly at the corner of Pound Road.   Demolished 1899.

XXXV.—WEDNESBURY MANOR HELD BY THE HOO FAMILY.

JOHN HOO I., LORD OF WEDNESBURY, 1701—1720:

John Hoo came of a family which, according to one authority, was anciently of Hertfordshire, but had settled at Bradley, near Bilston, for several centuries.

Lawley's "History of Bilston," pp. 136—140, deals at some length with the family of Hoo. There it is stated that the Hoo family took its name from Hoo Marsh which was situated on the Wednesbury side of Bradley Manor; and that the name of the Marsh was not derived from that of the family. Mr. Lawley points out that in mediæval times we find in Bradley such personal names as "Thomas atte Hoo," and "Walter de la Hoo"; and "Hoo" is asserted to be an Anglo-Norman name for a hollow in which the open-air court leets were anciently wont to be held.

It may be added that earlier than these two there was living (in 1291) one "Philip del Hoo, at Bradele" (Salt VII., p. 177). And also that the term "Hoo!" was the cry with which, in ancient times, the Marshall at a Trial by Battle declared the combat at an end. The origin of surnames is a subject needing much research.

There was a John Hoo, of Bradley, in 1524, who held lands in "Woldebur-" (Oldbury), West Bromwich, and Bradley, and also in "the lordship and manor of Wednesbery," all of which it was his desire to entail.

John Hoo, who purchased the manor of Wednesbury from the Shelton family, was born about the year 1658; he became a member of the Bar, and afterwards a serjeant-at-law. He married Mary Hanbury, of Whorestone, Bewdley, but had no issue. Being a lawyer, and having bought the manor of Wednesbury, John Hoo set about making his purchase as valuable as possible. To this end he converted an ancient prescriptive market into a chartered privilege. This subject was fully discussed in Chapter IV. of "Olden Wednesbury," where are quoted the words of Lord Chief Justice Coleridge, who, in 1890, said that market rights appeared to have existed in Wednesbury long before the date of John Hoo's charter.

The text of the Market Charter which was granted in 1709, by Letters Patent from Queen Anne, is as follows:—

"THE QUEEN. To all whom, etc., greeting. Whereas it appears by a certain Inquisition indented, taken at ye parish of King's Swinford, in our county of Stafford, the 24th day of May, in ye 7th year of our reign, before James Wood, Esq., Sheriff of the county aforesaid, by virtue of our certain writ of 'Ad quod damnum,' to ye said Sheriff directed, and to ye Inquisition aforesaid annexed, by ye oath of good and lawful men of ye county aforesaid, that it would not be to ye damage or injury of us, or of any others, if we should grant to our beloved and faithful John Hoo, of Bradley, in ye county aforesaid, Esq., serjeant-at-law, license that he and his heirs might have and hold, at Wednesbury, otherwise Wedgebury, in ye county aforesaid, two Fairs or Marts yearly, for ever (that is to say), one of ye said Fairs upon ye 25th of April, and ye other on ye 23rd of July, unless either of the aforesaid days should be Sunday, and then upon ye Monday next following such Sunday, for ye buying and selling of all and all manner of Cattle and Beasts, and of all and all manner of Goods, Wares, and Merchandizes commonly bought and sold in Fairs or Marts. And also one Market on Friday in every week, for ever, for buying and selling Corn, Flesh, and Fish, and other Provision, and all and all manner of Goods, Wares. and Merchandizes, commonly bought and sold in Markets. And. further, by the Inquisition aforesaid, it appears that it would not be to ye damage or injury of us, or of others, to ye hurt of neighbouring Markets or Fairs, if we should grant to the aforesaid John Hoo, license that he and his heirs might have and hold ye Fairs, or Marts, and Markets aforesaid at Wednesbury, otherwise Wedgbury, aforesaid, in manner and form aforesaid, as by ye said Writ and Inquisition remaining of record in ye files of our Chancery more fully doth and may appear. Now, know ye, that we, of our special grace, and of our certain knowledge and mere motion, have given and granted, and by these presents for us, our heirs and successors, do give and grant to ye aforesaid John Hoo and his heirs, free and lawful power, license, and authority that he, or they, and every of them, may from henceforth, for ever, have, hold, and keep, at Wednesbury, otherwise Wedgebury, aforesaid, two Fairs, or Marts, yearly, for ever, (that is to say), one of ye said Fairs on ye 25th of April, and ye other on ye 23rd of July, unless either of ye aforesaid days shall be Sunday, and then upon ye Monday next following such Sunday, for ye buying and selling of all and all manner of Cattle and Beasts, and all and all manner of Goods, Wares, and Merchandizes, commony bought and sold in Fairs or Marts; and also one Market on Friday in every week, for ever, for ye buying and selling of Corn, Flesh, and Fish. and other Provisions. and all and all manner of Goods, Wares, and Merchandizes, commonly bought and sold in Markets; together with Courts of Pie Poudre at ye time and times of ye aforesaid Fairs, and with reasonable tolls, tollage, piccage, and stallage for Cattle, Goods, Merchandize and Wares to be sold, or exposed for sale, in the Fair and Markets aforesaid, to have, hold, and enjoy ye aforesaid Fairs, or Marts, and Markets, and Courts of Pie Poudre piccage, and stallage, and premises above, by these presents, granted to ye said John Hoo and his heirs, for ever, to ye only and proper use and behoof of ye said John Hoo, his heirs and assigns, for ever, and this without any account, or any other thing to be therefore rendered, paid, or done to us, our heirs, or successors. Wherefore, we will, and by these presents, for us, our heirs and successors, firmly enjoyning, do order and command that ye aforesaid John Hoo, his heirs, and assigns, and every of them, shall, by virtue of these presents, well, freely, lawfully, and quietly have, hold, and keep. and may and shall be able to have, hold, and keep for ever, ye aforesaid Fairs and Markets and Courts of Pie Poudre, tolls, tollage, piccage. and stallage, and other ye premises aforesaid, according to ye true intent of these, our Letters Patent, without ye molestation, disturbance, hindrance, or contradiction of us, our heirs, or successors, or of any Sheriff, Escheators, Bailiff's officer, or Minister, of us, our heirs, or successors whatsoever, and this without any other Warrant, Writ, or Process to be hereafter procured or obtained in that behalf. And, futher, we will, and by these presents, for us, our heirs, and successors, do grant to the aforesaid John Hoo and his heirs, that these our Letters Patent, on ye enrollment thereof, may and shall be good, firm. valid, and sufficient and effectual in law for the said John Hoo and his heirs according to ye true intent of the same.

In witness whereof, etc.

Witness the Queen, at Westminster, 9th of July, by Writ of Privy Seal, 1709."

John Hoo, Serjeant-at-law, died at the age of 62, and was buried in the south chancel of Wolverhampton Church, 1 March, 1720. For Obituary Notices see Political State of Great Britain, vol. XIX., p. 247, and the Historical Register for 1720, p. 10.

The Sergeant had two brothers, Thomas and Joseph; and a sister, Margaret, who married William Bendy, of Shut End, Kingswinford, in whose posterity the manor of Wednesbury is held at the present day.

The Serjeant's heir was John Hoo, Esq., of Barr, the son of Thomas Hoo. He succeeded to the manor of Wednesbury on the death of his uncle, in 1720. (Shaw's "Staffordshire" is in error in saying that Thomas Hoo succeeded his brother.)

JOHN HOO II., LORD OF WEDNESBURY, 1720—1740:

This John Hoo married Mrs. Frances Vaughton. widow, who, in 1715, had succeeded to the possession of the manor of Great Barr, on the death of her brother, Thomas Lacy the younger.

The manor of Great Barr had been carried to Thomas Lacy the elder, of Aldridge, by his marriage (1677) with Eleanor, daughter and heir of Edward Scott, lord of that Manor. Of the issue of this marriage the said Thomas and Frances were the last to survive. Thomas bequeathed Great Barr to his sister Frances for her life, with remainder to her first and other sons. By her first husband (Vaughton), however, she had no son, and their only daughter had died in 1712.

Frances Vaughton, lady of the manor of Great Barr, married again, her second husband, as previously stated, being John Hoo, lord of the manor of Wednesbury. They, and their eldest son, John, levied a Fine and suffered a Recovery of the Great Barr Estates, and settled them upon their family.

John Hoo died at Barr in 1740: his widow died in 1745.

JOHN HOO III., LORD OF WEDNESBURY, 1740—1749:

This John Hoo was the elder son of the last-named John Hoo, by his wife, Frances; he was baptised at Aldridge in 1718. He took his M.A. at Oxford (Magdalen College), 1740, and died without issue in 1749. An abstract of his Will has been published by the Midland Record Society (Vol. III.).

THOMAS HOO, LORD OF WEDNESBURY, 1749—1791:

Thomas Hoo was a year younger than his brother, whom he succeeded. He lived in great affluence at Barr, as a very singular old-fashioned fox-hunting squire. In 1772 he was High Sheriff of Staffordshire.

The house Thomas Hoo occupied at Barr was a very curious ancient half-timbered mansion. In Plot's "Staffordshire" is a plate of this picturesque old residence, showing amidst other rich foliage (some of the great elm trees in front were afterwards blown down in the great storm of 1795), the large yew-tree in the garden. which Plot describes as being cut conically, "like the spire of a steeple eight or nine yards high."

Shaw's "Staffordshire" contains a long account of the very extensive alterations made to Barr Hall and its grounds in 1777.

John Hoo owned more than 200 acres of land in Bilston. He died at Barr on 25 September, 1791 intestate, and without issue. Obituary notices of him appeared in "The Gentleman's Magazine" (p. 970) and the "European Magazine (p. 319).

Arms of Hoo: Quarterly, Argent and Sable, a border of Ermine.

XXXVI.—THE MANOR IN MOIETIES.

On the death of Thomas Hoo, intestate, September 25, 1791, his heir-at-law had to be discovered. Reference has been made to Margaret, sister of John Hoo, of Bradley, the purchaser of the manor of Wednesbury. This Margaret married William Bendy, of Shut End, Kingswinford (a son of William Bendy, a counsellor of Lincoln's Inn, died 1684), at Willenhall, on May 9, 1686; a record of which marriage appears in the Tipton Registers. The Bendy family had been settled at Kingswinford for many years. In 1643, during the troublous reign of Charles I., we find a Mr. Bendy, of Kingswinford, on the side of the Parliament, acting as one of the Committee for the County of Stafford, and voting for the demolition of Stafford Castle (Shaw, Vol. I., p. 63). The Bendy's seat for many generations was the picturesque house at Shut End; their arms are engraved on Plot's map as then residing there. Holbeach is an old mansion which formerly belonged to the Lytteltons, and is remarkable in history, 3 James I., as being the house in which Stephen Lyttelton (son of Sir John Lyttelton, of Hagley, knighted 8 Elizabeth) and others concerned in the Gunpowder Plot were taken. (Shaw gives a long account of these conspirators and their trial). The Holbeach estate afterwards belonged to the family of Bendy; and the William Bendy referred to above was in his time the owner of it. There was issue of William Bendy and Margaret Hoo, two daughters, Margaret and Mary.

(a) Margaret, the elder, first married a Richard Williamson, at Wednesbury Church, 1 July, 1721; upon his death she married, at Stafford, on February 6 1725, the Rev. John Dolman, afterwards Rector of Aldridge. The issue of this second marriage were two children: William Dolman, born at Stafford; B.A. of Oxford 1747; died 1748; and Mary, who married Edward Whitby, Esq., of Shut End, Kingswinford.

In Aldridge Church is a large marble, inscribed to the memory of the Rev. John Dolman, Rector of the parish, Prebendary and Divinity Lecturer at Lichfield Cathedral, who died 1746; and also to the memory of the son, William, who so quickly followed him to the tomb.

Mary Dolman's husband, Edward Whitby, was buried at Himley 1794. He was a son of Thomas Whitby, of Great Haywood, Staffordshire, whose daughter Mary married William Scott, of the Nether-house, Barr, the father of Joseph Scott, who, in 1806, was created a baronet, and is to be hereafter mentioned.

Mrs. Mary Whitby, on the death of Thomas Hoo, in 1791, was one of his co-heiresses, and, as such, became Lady of a moiety of the Manor of Wednesbury.

(b) Mary Bendy, the younger daughter, married, in 1725, at Kingswinford, John Hodgetts, gent., of Shut End House. He died in 1741, and in Kingswinford Church will be found a marble, which not only records his family alliances, but in the florid language characteristic of eighteenth century monumental inscriptions, sets forth his manifold virtues; concluding thus:—

"He had issue by her [his wife Mary] two "sons and two daughters, viz., John, William, "Mary, and Margaret, the eldest of whom, the "present John Hodgetts, of Prestwood, Esq., "has caused this monument to be erected to "his memory. To give a short eulogium on his "virtues (though they are minutely recorded in "everlasting registers) is a tribute due to Posterity. Let it suffice, then, to say that, "actuated by a principle of faith, it was his "highest ambition to adopt those perfections "and graces which discriminate and adorn a "true Christian. He was a lover of Religion "and its sacred ordinances. He was of an "humble and conciliating deportment; charit-"able without ostentation; meek without "pusillanimity; and it may be truly said of "him that he had his conversation in Heaven. "Reader! Whoever thou art, whom devotion, "or curiosity, has led to this hallowed shrine, "mayst thou strike upon thy breast and say, "Let me die the death of the righteous, and "let my last end be like his."

His widow, Mrs. Mary Hodgetts, was buried at Kingswinford, 1761.

John, their elder son, who was M.A. and D.C.L. of Oxford, married Elizabeth, daughter and heir of William Foley, Esq., of Prestwood. She died in childbed of an only daughter, 1759, and was buried at Kinver. The child was baptised at Kingswinford, as Eliza Mary Foley. Mr. John Hodgetts served as High Sheriff of Staffordshire in 1766, and died in 1783.

His daughter and heir married, in 1790, the Hon. Edward Foley (second son of Thomas, Lord Foley, of Stoke Edith, Herefordshire, and Witley Court, Worcestershire). The Hon. Edward had been previously divorced from a daughter of the Earl of Coventry, 1787; he was M.A. of Oxford; in Parliament he sat for Droitwich, 1768-1784, and for Worcestershire, 1784-1803. He died in 1808.

Upon the death of Thomas Hoo, in 1791, the Hon. Eliza Mary Foley Foley, wife of the Hon. Edward Foley, was the other co-heiress of Thomas Hoo, and became Lady of the remaining moiety of the Manor of Wednesbury.

XXXVII.—THE WHITBY MOIETY PASSES TO THE SCOTTS.

(1) MRS. MARY WHITBY (1791-1809):

There was issue of Edward Whitby by Mary Dolman a son, Edward, who died unmarried in 1788; two daughters, one who died an infant, and Margaret, who married Joseph Scott, then of Shut End. Mrs. Mary Whitby, widow, died 1809, and was buried at Himley.

(2) DAME MARGARET SCOTT (1809-1822):

As just stated, Margaret Whitby sole

heiress of this moiety, married her cousin, Joseph Scott, in 1777.

Joseph Scott was born in the parish of Aldridge, 1752; he matriculated at Oxford, 1770; was High Sheriff of Staffordshire, 1779; M.P. for Worcester, 1802-1806; and was created a baronet 30 April, 1806—to which creation passing reference has already been made.

Dame Margaret Scott died in 1822, and her husband, Sir Joseph, in 1828. Their issue were—Edward Dolman Scott,[*] William Scott, who became Rector of Aldridge, and Mary, who died in 1807.

(3) SIR EDWARD DOLMAN SCOTT.

Sir Edward Dolman Scott was born 1793; matriculated at Oxford, 1812, and sat as M.P. for Lichfield 1831-7.

His first wife was Catherine Juliana, eldest daughter and co-heir of Sir Hugh Bateman, Baronet, of Hartington Hall, Derbyshire, to whom he was married in 1815, and who died in 1848. There was issue of this marriage, Sir Francis Edward Scott, Baronet, Edward Dolman Scott, and William Douglas Scott.

For his second wife Sir Edward Dolman Scott married (1848) Lydia, widow of the Rev. Edmund Robinson, of Thorp Green, Yorkshire.

The baronet died in 1851, and his widow in 1859.

(4) SIR FRANCIS EDWARD SCOTT, BARONET (1851-1863):

In the person of Sir Francis Edward Scott, who succeeded to the moiety of the Manor of Wednesbury, is a somewhat uncommon instance of the holder of a dual baronetcy.

He was born at Bath, Somersetshire, 25th February, 1824, and inherited at his birth the baronetcy conferred upon his maternal grandfather, Sir Hugh Bateman, 15 December, 1806, who had married Temperance, daughter of John Gisborne, Esq., of Yoxall Lodge, and whose eldest daughter was Sir Francis's mother. The baronetcy conferred on Sir Hugh was with remainder, in default of male issue, to the male descendants of his daughters, primogeniturely. Sir Hugh died 28 January, 1824, and therefore on the birth of his posthumous grandson, such grandson became a baronet as well as his own father. In 1851, on the death of Sir Edward Dolman Scott, his father, Sir Francis became a dual baronet. Sir

Hugh's baronetcy, it will be seen, was only in abeyance from the 28th January to the 25th February, 1824.

Sir Francis Edward Scott was M.A. of Oxford (1848); he married, in 1854, Mildred Anne, eldest daughter of Sir William Cradock Hartopp, Baronet. There was issue of this marriage, two sons (each of whom succeeded in turn) and three daughters.

The daughters were Mildred Henrietta—married Adrian Hope, Esq.; Catherine Matilda Anne Georgina—married W. B. Farnham, Esq.; Mabel Augusta—married William, eldest son of Sir John Jaffray.

Sir Francis Edward Scott died in 1863. His widow married again, in 1868, her second husband being Edward Pakenham Alderson, Esq., son of Sir H. E. Alderson, baron of the Exchequer; she thereby became a sister-in-law cf the Marquess of Salisbury, who had married a daughter of Baron Alderson.

(5) SIR EDWARD WILLIAM DOLMAN SCOTT (1863-1871):

This, the fourth baronet, born 1854, succeeded his father, but died unmarried in 1871. His brother followed him in the estates.

(6) SIR ARTHUR DOUGLAS BATEMAN SCOTT (1871-1884):

Sir Arthur, born 1860, succeeded his elder brother, and, like him, died unmarried, in 1884.

The title went to his uncle, Edward Dolman Scott, of Hartington, Derbyshire, who has had no connection with the Manor of Wednesbury. Sir Edward is a brother of Sir Francis, and was born in 1826.

The moiety of Wednesbury belonging to this family is now held by the widow of the third baronet, the aforementioned Dame Mildred Anne Bateman Scott, otherwise Lady Bateman Scott, who resides at Great Barr Hall.

*   *   *   *   *   *

Both baronetcies are now held by Sir Edward Dolman Scott, of Hartington, Derbyshire; in default of direct dual heirs each remainder lies in a different line, so that it is see the two baronetcies again divided. The Bateman baronetcy will go to Sir Alexander Hood, Bart.

---

*Councillor James Davies's grandfather was apprenticed to John Wilkinson, the famous iron-master, at Gospel Oak · his grandmother was a Dolman Scott: in the course of an investigation into the family's claim to the property of Mr. Walter Scott, the following abstract of a Bill in Chancery was taken, which is interesting, as showing the price of mining land at that date:—

"Thomas Hoo, Esq., to John Wilkinson, a lease of Tuptree Farm, dated from July, 1770, to January, 1775, for the purpose of getting

the coal, at 12 shillings per acre per annum,
£10 0s. 10d.

"And 43 acres, being part of House Close, Broadfields: 7 acres at 16 shillings per acre per annum, being more valuable land, and 3 acres where the Furnace stands upon. The Bill being
£109 0s. 0d.

"Thomas Hoo, Esq. .of Bradley Hall,
and
"John Wilkinson, of Bradley Works."

XXXVIII.—THE SCOTTS OF GREAT BARR.

In Burke's Peerage it is sought to show that the Scotts of Great Barr Hall are of Scottish origin; as thus—

"In 1296 the ancestor of the present baronet, who was in the suite of John Baliol, King of Scotland, when that Monarch was detained a prisoner in London; and restrained with the rest of his countrymen from passing to the north of the river Trent, under pain of losing their heads, fixed himself as near that stream as the thick forest of Cannock would allow."

However this may be, according to Mr. W. H. Duignan, who has published a paper on the Scotts of Great Barr, the family is more probably of Saxon than of Scottish origin. The name was originally "Shot," signifying "an archer."

This yeoman family is said to have been settled in the locality for centuries, the first reference to it being in 1332, when William Scott, of Great Barr and Aldridge, paid to the Scottish War Subsidy.

At this period there were apparently two local families of this name, one Scott living at Wood End, and the other at Shustoke (? Scotescote), a moated site near the Bell Inn, on the Birmingham Road.

The Stapletons were lords of the Manors of Great Barr and Aldridge, and lived at Hay Head, Great Barr. They came from Stapleton, near Shrewsbury, and were of Norman extraction. An effigy of an armour-clad Stapleton is still to be seen in Aldridge Church.

The Scotts doubtless held their lands under the Stapletons by the tenure of military service.

In the year 1389 occurred one of those romantic episodes of ancient chivalry in which a Stapleton and a Scott were two of the principal actors. The incident is authenticated by a chronicler no less trustworthy than Froissart himself. This writer is always picturesque and vivid, and the leading points in his narrative in which these local men are introduced are worthy of reproduction here. They breathe the nobler spirit of chivalry, and recall all the pomp and circumstance of its magnificent pageantry.

During the minority of Richard II. the English forces in France were for some years engaged in overrunning the more accessible portions of the kingdom.

Charles VI. of France having concluded a three years' truce with the English, the opportunity was seized by three French gentlemen of high enterprise and great valour to issue a challenge to encounter all comers in the lists.

These three were the King's Chamberlains, namely, Sir Boucicault the younger, Sir Reginald de Roye, and the Lord de Saimpi; and they proposed to do their doughty deeds on the frontiers near Calais, then an English possession, in the plain of St. Inglevere.

The challenge was written in clerkly style, and couched in all knightly courtesy, the time fixed being the 20th May following. They announced that for thirty days, Fridays only

excepted, they would abide all knights, squires, and strangers, to joust with them, either jousts of peace or of war.

They offered five combats with pointed lances, or five with pointless lances (rockets), or with both, whichever the acceptor preferred. Outside their tents would be found their shields of arms, namely their shields of war, and their shields of peace. Everyone who proposed to joust should come, or send one on his behalf, to strike with a rod whichever shield he pleased; if he struck the shield of war, then on the morrow he should have the joust of war with pointed lances from the knight whose shield he had struck, or if he struck the shield of peace he should have the joust of peace with rockets or pointless lances.

And all those who accepted the challenge in the manner aforesaid should give their names to those in charge of the shields; and everyone who wished to joust was to bring with him a gentleman on his behalf, who should receive instruction on all points necessary.

And the challengers further prayed all the knights and esquires of foreign countries not to think that they did this through pride, hatred, or malevolence; for it was done to have their honourable company and acquaintance, which they desired with all their heart, and they engaged that none of their shields should be covered with iron or steel [shields were at this period made of cour-bouilli, a preparation of leather], as they requested should be the case with the shields of those who came against them, and that there should be no advantage or fraud on either part.

This challenge is a good specimen of its kind, illustrating, as it does, the true spirit of gallantry and knightly courtesy which chivalry cultivated in its best days.

Now this challenge, although issued to all comers, was specially promulgated in the realm of England, and the pavilions of the challengers were specially fixed on the plain of St. Inglevere, near Calais, in order to be near the English marches. Little wonder, then, that English champions took up the challenge very freely, and sent over to Calais their horses and harness in great plenty.

On the appointed day, the 21st May, there issued from the gates of Calais some sixty English knights and nobles, clad in the full panoply of war, and all prepared for the jousting.

Of these sixty it seems possible to identify at least four who were in some way or other connected with this immediate locality around Wednesbury.

Among the recorded names of those who freely accepted the Frenchmen's challenge were those of Bernard Stapleton, John Scot, Sir Henry Beaumont, and Sir John Clinton.

By the year 1389 the main stem of the Stapletons of Aldridge was extinct. But Mr. Duignan is probably not far wrong in identifying Bernard Stapleton as a cadet of this house. The christian name of Bernard may have been the chronicler's error for Leonard, which the Stapleton pedigree shows to have been one affected by the family.

The squire John Scot is identified by Mr. Duignan as the military tenant of the Stapletons, which again is a justifiable surmise.

Sir Henry Beaumont was not at that particular time identified with a Staffordshire fief. But reference to p. 45 supra will show that he was the 5th Baron Beaumont (died 1413), and the father of the Sir Henry (his second son), who became lord of Wednesbury on his marriage with Joan Leventhorpe.

Sir John Clinton belonged to that neighbouring baronial family whose holdings lay in Warwickshire—they built Kenilworth Castle, tempo Henry I., and gave their name to Baddesley Clinton. This John Clinton was of Coleshill, and a baron of Parliament; he had married for his second wife a granddaughter of Sir Roger Hillary, of Bescot (Chief Justice, tempo Edward III.).

Froissart's allusion to these local names adds an element of romantic interest to our history. We read that after several of the English knights and nobles had done their devoirs there came forth Sir Henry Beaumont; "he caused to be touched Sir Boucicault's shield of war, who was soon ready to answer. They ran together; the Lord Beaumont crossed, and Boucicault struck him so rudely that he bore him to the earth and passed forth. The knight was raised up by his men, and set again on horseback, and so they ran again together two other courses, without any damage."

This was on the first day. Among the jousts described on the third day we read:—

"Then another English squire, called Scott, ran against the Lord de Saimpi.

"The first course they encountered so rudely that their horses staggered; the spears held, yet they lost their spears. Then they made them ready to run the second course; and they met in such wise that the Lord de Saimpi was unhelmed, and the squire much praised for that course. Again the third course they encountered each other on the shields in such wise that John Scott was stricken down over his horse's croup. Thus the Lord de Saimpi was avenged. The English squire was picked up and brought to his company, and ran no more that day.

"Then another English squire, called Bernard Stapleton, touched the shield of the Lord de Saimpi.

"They came together, and struck each other on their helms that the fire flashed out, and so passed by without any other damage, and still kept their spears. The second course they met in their shields rudely, yet they kept their horses, and so passed forth on their course. The third course they unhelmed each other. The English squire ran no more that day"—he had acquitted himself with honour.

And so, after four days' tilting, these memorable jousts came to a satisfactory conclusion. The French champions seem to have had the best of the courses run, although English honour was fully satisfied, and the English knights took a friendly leave of their courteous and gallant opponents, "thanking them greatly for their pastime," and promising to send other English gentlemen to visit them and do deeds of arms. And so this incident closes.

"William Scotte of Barre" in 1575 presented John Scotte to the rectory of Aldridge.

According to Mr. Duignan, the Scotts were frequent purchasers of land in and around Barr between the years 1500 and 1600, and soon after the latter date they purchased the manor of Barr from Thomas Walstead, of Walstead Hall, on Delves Green, an ancient homestead now occupied by Mr. James Bodley.

In 1625 John Scott, senior, and John Scott, junior, of Great Barr, forfeited £10 each to be excused the honour of knighthood, which a money-grubbing monarch would have forced upon them.

From 1618, when they acquired the manor of Barr, the family history is fully recorded—see Shaw's "Staffordshire."

The lords of Wednesbury Manor being (since 1777) seated at Barr, much of the magisterial business of Wednesbury was, for more than half a century, transacted at Barr (Scott Arms Inn). Sir Edward kept a flag flying on the top of the Hall when he was in residence, so that constables and others all round the countryside, having magisterial business to transact with him, could see from a distance if "the Justice" were at home or not.

* * * *

Some confusion has arisen from the fact that within recent years a second landed family of the name of Scott has been settled at Great Barr.

This family of Scott originated at Chaddesley Corbett, but in the seventeenth century migrated to Stourbridge. In 1683 William Scott, of Stourbridge, married Elizabeth, daughter of the Rev. William Fincher, the dispossessed Puritan Vicar of Wednesbury. In 1771 another William Scott, also head of this family, married the representative of the family of Addyes, of Great Barr. John Charles Addyes Scott, of the Red House, Great Barr, Staffordshire, Ratlinghone and Norbr—Salop, died in 1888, and was succeeded in the estate by his widow.

XXXIX.—THE FOLEY MOIETY OF THE MANOR.

HON. MRS. ELIZA M. FOLEY FOLEY
(1791-1805).

There was issue of this lady: (1) Edward Thomas Foley, born 1791, of whom more hereafter; (2) Elizabeth Maria Foley, baptized at Kingswinford, 1793, married in 1813 the fourth Viscount Gage, and died June, 1857; (3) John Hodgetts Foley, baptized at Kingswinford 1797, of whom more hereafter; (4) Thomas Foley, born 1799; (5) Anne Maria Foley, born 1800, married in 1821 to Henry John, eldest son of Sir Henry Lambert, Bart., and died 1857.

The Hon. Edward Foley died, as previously

stated, in 1808. The Hon. Mrs. Foley died 1805.

EDWARD THOMAS FOLEY (1805-1846).

The Hon. Mrs. Foley was succeeded by her eldest son, Edward Thomas Foley. He was M.A. of Oxford (1812), and also D.C.L. (1834). His seat was Stoke Edith Park, Herefordshire; he was M.P. for Ludgershall, 1826-1832, and for Herefordshire, 1832-1841. He married Lady Emily, fourth daughter of James, 3rd Duke of Montrose, and died without issue in 1846.

LADY EMILY FOLEY (1846-1900).

Lady Emily Foley became Lady of this moiety on the death of her husband. She died 1 January, 1900, in her 95th year. She was patroness of St. John's living (Wednesbury).

In the registers of St. George's, Hanover Square, W., printed to 1837, is the entry Lady Emily's marriage. Its interesting nature, from the remarkable galaxy of aristocratic witnesses present at the ceremony, makes it worthy of reproduction here, as the Notes appended to the names will testify:—

"1832, August 16. Edward Thomas Foley, Esq., bachelor, M.P., and the Right Hon. Lady Emily Graham, spinster, daughter of the Most Noble James, Duke of Montrose. Special License.

"Witnesses—	(Notes).
Montrose	[James, 3rd Duke of Montrose.]
C.M. Montrose	[Caroline Maria, Duchess of Montrose; daughter of Duke of Manchester.]
E. M. Gage	[Elizabeth Maria, Viscountess Gage; daughter of Edward Foley, of Stoke Edith.]
Jane Montagu	[Wife of Baron Montagu daughter of Lord Douglas.]
Clive	[Viscount Clive, eldest son of Earl of Powis—he married a sister of the bride.]
Emily Montagu	[Daughter of George, 4th Duke of Manchester.]
Caroline Montagu	[Daughter of Baron Montagu.]
Charlotte Ashburnham	[Widow of 3rd Earl of Ashburnham; sister of 5th Duke of Northumberland.]
Foley	[Thomas, 3rd Lord Foley—new creation.]
Lucy Clive	[Wife of Viscount Clive; sister of the bride.]
A. M. Lambert	[Anna Maria Lambert, sister of the bridegroom.]
Gage	[Henry Hall, 4th Viscount Gage.]
Winchilsea	[George William, 9th Earl of Winchilsea; he married the eldest sister of the bride.]
Henry John Lambert	[Eldest son of Sir Henry Lambert; married to a sister of the bridegroom.]
Montagu	[Baron Montagu, 3rd son of Duke of Buccleuch—had succeeded to barony of Montagu on death of his grandfather the Duke of Montagu.]
Rd. Foley Onslow."	[Richard Foley Onslow (a cousin) whose father was Rector of Stoke Edith.]

PAUL HENRY FOLEY, ESQ. (1900).

Paul Henry Foley, Esq., J.P., of Prestwood, near Stourbridge, is the present lord of this moiety. His grandfather was the John Hodgetts Foley, already mentioned.

John Hodgetts Foley matriculated at Oxford from Christchurch in 1815. He was of Prestwood, and sat in Parliament for Droitwich, 1822-1835, and for East Worcestershire, 1847-1861. In 1821 he assumed, by royal licence, the additional name of Hodgetts, and thereby became John Hodgetts Hodgetts-Foley. He married, in 1825, Charlotte Margaret, daughter of John Gage, Esq., cousin of Viscount Gage. He died in 1861.

Henry John Wentworth Hodgetts-Foley was his first son, born in London, 1828, and matriculated at Oxford from Christ Church 1846. He was of Prestwood, J.P. and D.L. for the counties of Stafford and Worcester; M.P. for South Staffordshire, 1857-1868; High Sheriff of Staffordshire in 1877. He married Jane Frances Anne, daughter of Richard Hussey, first Lord Vivian. He was Captain of the Worcestershire Militia. He died 1894, his wife having predeceased him in 1860.

Paul Henry Foley was born 19 March, 1857, in London. He matriculated at Oxford from Christ Church, 20 May, 1875; B.A., 1880; M.A., 1882; Barrister-at-law, Inner Temple, 1880; J.P. and D.L., Herefordshire; J.P., Staffordshire; Patron of St. John's, Wednesbury.

XL.—WEDNESBURY COURT LEET.

The Manor of Wednesbury, with all its ancient courts, officers, and liberties, not improbably dates back to a period even anterior to the rule of Ethelfleda.

At the Conquest, Wednesbury contained sixteen Villeins (supra p. 23), and in process of time these villeins, or their descendants, obtained their freedom. This emancipation might have been accomplished through the generosity of the Lord of the Manor; or by the escape of the villein for a year and a day. Anyway, however the villein obtained his freedom, he frequently continued to reside on the lands he had cultivated as a slave, holding them by the "Villein Socage tenure" (plough tenure), and rendering a free and certain service; such as reaping the lord's corn, cleansing his fishpond or stream (and when we consider the number of fast days in the year, the fishing rights on an inland manor like Wednesbury were of considerable importance), harrowing two days in the year, or employing three days in carting the lord's timber (Wednesbury Wood was then two miles long and one mile broad, and included Bloxwich; the royal forest of Cannock also reached to Wednesbury brook boundary).

The lands which he thus occupied he naturally expected to descend to his children if they rendered the same service to the lord: this generally happened, and so the descendants of the same family at length considered they had a legal claim to the land. They had their names and tenures entered on the Court Rolls of the Manor.

Allusion to serfdom in Wednesbury is made on pp. 48 and 52; and to the Customs of the Manor in Chap. XVI.

Each "baron" or lord of a manor held a Court within his manor, at which tenants and vassals assembled to render service and fealt~ and to transact the public business of the manor.

For more than a thousand years a Manorial Court has been held in Wednesbury. The last was held two years ago, just before the death of Lady Emily Foley.

The full text of the Precept whereby the Bailiff of the Manor is authorised to call such will disclose the nature of the Courts held in Wednesbury. Here is a copy of the most recent one:—

Manor of
Wednesbury
In the County
of Stafford

(to wit).   To JAMES CAMPBELL, Bailiff of the said Manor

GREETING

These are to require you to give notice within the said Manor that the Court Leet with the View of Frankpledge, together with the Court Baron of the RIGHT HONOURABLE EMILY FOLEY, commonly called LADY EMILY FOLEY, and of DAME MILDRED ANNE BATEMAN SCOTT, the Ladies of the said Manor, will be held for the said Manor at the Anchor Hotel, at Wednesbury, within the said Manor, on Wednesday, the twenty-ninth day of November, One thousand eight hundred and ninety-nine, at twelve o'clock at noon, and to warn all Resiants Freehold and Copyhold Tenants of the said Manor personally to be and appear at the place and time aforesaid, to do and perform their Suit and Service and pay their Quit Rents, Fines, and other duties, as of right they ought to perform and render at such Courts respectively.

AND ALSO to warn all Constables Tything-men and other Public Officers of the aforesaid Leet and Manor then and there to attend and make

and return their several Presentments. AND you are hereby required to summon twelve or more good and lawful men of the said Manor to be and appear at the aforesaid place and time to enquire as well for our Sovereign Lady the Queen as for the Ladies of the said Manor of all such matters as to the said Courts do appertain. And be you there personally with the names of the persons you shall have so summoned, bringing with you also this precept.

GIVEN under my hand and seal, the sixth day of November. One thousand eight hundred and ninety-nine.

John H. Yonge,   (seal)
Steward of the Manor
for the Lady Emily Foley,
and Deputy-Steward of the
Manor for Dame Mildred
Anne Bateman Scott.

From the wording of this Precept it will be seen that in Wednesbury were held both a Court Leet and a Court Baron.

These are usually two distinct Courts, although the two may sometimes be held together.

A Court Leet is the most ancient Court in the land, and is incident to the Hundred. But there is no direct evidence that the Wednesbury Court Leet was at any time the Court for the Hundred of Offlow South. It is a fact, however, that the chief of the officers who were annually appointed was always known as the High Constable, as in a Hundred Court. On p. 81 it has been recorded that in 1647 John Carter issued from Wednesbury a most important public document, which he signs as "High Constable." Mr. John Yardley, who died about forty years ago, was the last High Constable of Wednesbury; his sword of office was till recently preserved by the late Major Nayler. Formerly the Manor was officially described at the "Constablewick of Wednesbury."

A Court Leet was originally held twice a year, namely, at Easter and at Michaelmas: this corresponds with the two dates of the appearances at Court demanded by the Lord of Wednesbury six hundred years ago, as recorded on p. 38, q. v. In modern times the Court Leet has generally been held a month or so after Michaelmas.

At a Court Leet the Steward of the Manor presided in a judicial capacity: he was assisted by a jury of twelve men. The Court's jurisdiction extended to fine, but not imprisonment. The usual method of punishment was by fine and amercement, the former assessed by the steward and the latter by the jury, for both of which the lord may have an action of debt or take a distress. The particular articles anciently to be enquired into by statute were "if all the suit of court be present," "of customs withdrawn, purprestures of lands, woods, etc.; of houses set up or broke down; of thieves and hues-and-cries not pursued; of bloodshed, escapes, persons outlawed, money coiners, treasure found; assize of bread; of all persons keeping ale-houses without license, false weights and measures, unlawful games, idle persons, etc."

Every male inhabitant of the Manor of 12 years of age and upwards, who had been resident therein for a year and a day, was bound to attend the Court on penalty of a fine varying from fourpence to a shilling. The exemptions were old men over 60, clergymen, peers, and "Kings tenants in ancient demesne"—which last the men of Wednesbury rightfully claimed to be (p. 37).

Then there was its View of Frankpledge, for which Wednesbury anciently paid 3s. per annum to the Sheriff.

By View of Frankpledge, which pertains to the Court Leet, is meant the "viewing," or taking knowledge of, the sureties or "pledges," by which all persons over 12 within the Manor were bound for the preservation of the King's peace. Literally, Franknledge signifies "the peace pledge": anciently, among the Anglo-Saxons, every man within a lordship was mutually responsible to the lord for the good behaviour of his fellows, and bound in case of the committal of an offence, to help in delivering the offender to justice. Hence it was the duty of the Steward of the Manor to certify such pledges on view.

As recorded on p. 38, there were formerly two Views of Frankpledge held in Wednesbury each year.

The "Resiants" of the Manor (whom the Wednesbury precept calls upon) were those who had their "resiance," this is, their "continual abiding-place," within any Tithing.

Now a Tithing in Anglo-Saxon times was the unit of society; it consisted of ten men and their families bound together for the peaceable behaviour of each other—as by the "peace pledge." Originally the Tithing was a division of the Hundred; in many instances it developed into a Township.

The Hundred was the division of a County, first ordained by Alfred the Great. This particular Hundred in which Wednesbury is situated (Offlow South) has been mentioned several times (see Index); perhaps the last great occasion on which the ancient organisation of the Hundreds was called upon by the nation was during the Civil Wars, to which reference has just been made in the case of John Carter, the High Constable. A Hundred as a community could be punished for the offences of the individuals forming part of it.

It has been said that the Hundred was originally the district of a hundred Saxon warriors bonded together for mutual protection.

In the year 1293 a jury of 12 men, representing the Hundred of Offlow made presentment to the satisfaction of the King's Attorney, that John de Heronville, lord of the Manor, did legally possess the right of lordship in Wednesbury, including assize of bread and beer, and other manorial franchises. Edward I. was at this time sharply enquiring into the rights of tenure and abuses of local government, charging those concerned with writs of "Quo Warranto" to answer by what right they did, or left undone, certain things. The Wednesbury

pleadings were quite satisfactory. See Bagnall's "Wednesbury," p. 138. and supra p. 31.

We now have to consider the Court Baron, which belonged peculiarly and more immediately to the Manor.

As a Court Baron, it was bound to be kept within the precincts of the Manor. Such a Court could be held by prescription only, that is, by immemorial usage; it could not be created at the present day. This Court sometimes possessed a double nature: as a Freeholders' Court it could anciently try actions for debt under forty shillings; but it was mainly a Customary Court for the customary tenants and copyholders, in which the "Baron," or Lord of the Manor, took cognisance of his manorial lands. At this Court were made, for instance, the surrenders of copyholders; the admittances of tenants taking up copyholds; the amendment of the Court Rolls to agreement with such changes of tenant; and the enfranchisement of Copyholds into Freeholds; the payment of Fines, Customary Rents, etc.

For the old customs of Wednesbury Manor as to Heriots see pp. 38, 41, and 54; Reliefs, p. 38; the rights of Turbary and Estovers, p. 54.

The Homage Jury, consisting of tenants who anciently did homage to the Lord for their respective holdings, inquired into the Services, Duties, and Customs of the Manor, so that their Lord should not lose them on the one hand, and that they should not be unlawfully extended on the other. The Jury saw that the Tenants made their Suits of Court, and rendered the Services by virtue of which they held their lands from the Lord; that they paid their Quit Rents—which were small rents in token of subjection, and by which the tenant went "quiet" and free; that they rendered Heriots due; that they kept their lands and tenements in repair; that they presented and brought to notice all nuisances and trespasses to the prejudice of the Manor; and so on.

Now as to the Manorial officers. The chief was the Steward, or "Prepositus," as the monkish chroniclers wrote him down. (p. 23.) His powers in ancient times were naturally extensive when he acted as judge of the Court.

He had power to appoint officers, such as Constables and Tithing-men—the latter being the sub-constables. In ancient times he was often the resident representative of the Lord. In modern times the family lawyer frequently filled the office.

The next dignitary was the Bailiff of the Manor, whose duties were more of an executive nature. He collected the rents, and levied the fines and amercements. This once active office in Wednesbury Manor has been filled in recent times by Joseph Dawes, John Griffiths, George Caddick Whitehouse, Edward Ellis, and James Campbell, in succession.

Among the ancient manorial officers annually appointed to the present day are an Ale Taster, a Meat Conner, and two Hedgers and Ditchers. Their quaint old offices are, of course, obsolete, such functions being now performed by more modern officials; the first two being perhaps represented by the Municipal Market Inspectors, and the County Inspectors under the Adulteration Acts; and the other two by the Borough Surveyor's department, in succession to the Highway Board of the last century. Allusion has just been made to the Assize of Bread and Beer (also pp. 31 and 38), for which these Victual Tasters were among the responsible officers in olden times.

Reference has been made to the High Constable at Wednesbury: a Headborough, and a second Petty Constable were also elected, who acted as parish constables, their election being confirmed at Vestry Meeting, as they were used to serve parochial summonses for unpaid rates. Similarly the office of Town Crier seems to have been vested in another parochial officer, the Beadle; and another Beadle (for Wednesbury had two) filled the manorial office of Pinfold-Keeper. Doubtless ...ese were all originally Tithing-men, or deputy constables utilised for parochial work by the Vestry.

If the office were a purely honorary one, the candidate's name was merely presented by the Jury; but if it were a paid office, or one to which any emolument were attached, the candidate had to be formally elected. This is shown by the different forms of Presentment

One form, for instance, ran:—

"We present A.B. and C.D. to serve the office of Hedgers and Ditchers for this Manor for the year ensuing."

The other form was:—

"We present, elect, and choose E.F. to be Common Pinner for this Manor, for the year ensuing."

All Manors were not entitled to hold such Courts; Darlaston, for instance, owed suit and service to Sedgley Court Leet, which, however, seems to have been the Leet of the Hundred of Seisdon.

The jurisdiction of the Manorial Court has been gradually superseded by various modern enactments. The Wednesbury Courts have (till recently) been held regularly every year, and have always terminated with a substantial banquet. This Leet Dinner was provided at the expense of the Ladies of the Manor. In modern times all those invited to participate at the proceedings for the first time were mulcted in a friendly and voluntary fine, the proceeds of which provided a second dinner about Christmas time. This was quaintly dubbed "Shoeing the Colts."

THE OLD SHAMBLES AND PIG MARKET

(Now used for the Storage of the Market Stalls).

XLI.—WEDNESBURY MANOR COURT ROLLS.

In modern times one function of a Manorial Jury has been to assist assess the value of the Lord's interest in a Copyhold when a tenant has died, and admittance was being given to a fresh tenant in place of the deceased.

The proceedings of a Court Baron are recorded in the Rolls of the Court; as also, formerly, were the customs of the Manor and the services to be rendered by the tenants for their several holdings. It has been recorded (see p. 38) that Wednesbury tenants had to render such services as the ploughing of the lord's land, the mowing of his grass, and the making of his hay.

In olden times the Villein, who did not hold his land by investiture or public grant (like the Freeholder) had, therefore, only the Court Rolls to appeal to in support of his claim to his land. As his "Copy" of those entries relating to himself was his only evidence, he in time became a "Tenant by Copy of Court Roll," or, in other words, a "Copyholder."

So long as a Copyholder's heirs could produce this "Copy," and were willing to perform the customary services, the lands were secure in their possession, as if held by freehold tenure.

The Wednesbury Court Roll is now admirably kept, the one in use having been entirely re-written in 1894, while the previous one was dated only as recently as 1889.

Had the Manor of Wednesbury been better managed and more closely supervised during the last three centuries, when the parish was developing into a mining and manufacturing district, it would now have been a very valuable estate.

For three centuries the Lord of the Manor of Wednesbury has been an absentee; and during the same lengthened period there seems to have been no resident Steward; one consequence of which has undoubtedly been the loss of considerable portions of the Manorial Estate.

Not only have freeholders encroached upon the lord's estate, and "squatters" built upon his "wastes," and afterwards claimed their sites; but it would appear that in not a few instances buildings and holdings which were once copyhold are now fully held by the right of undisturbed possession for a long period of years.

In 1878-9 the Bailiff of the Manor seems to have conducted a thorough and careful inquiry into this shrinkage of the Manorial Estate; but the investigation proved altogether too late for the successful recovery of the lost lands and tenements. However, his notes made at that investigation are now carefully appended to the various entries in the Court Roll; they make very interesting reading, throwing, as they do, so many side-lights on the parochial history of the nineteenth century.

One source of the loss has unquestionably arisen through the retention of the ancient place-descriptions (which were naturally vague and indefinite in olden times, when the town had so few street names) and the failure to take advantage of modern street names and the numbering of the houses. Such errors and ambiguities of description are now being avoided, although so recently as 1892 an admittance describes a property in Dudley Street as "situate in the Lane leading from the Pinfold to Monway Gate." How few in Wednesbury could locate either of these two ancient landmarks!

The Copyholders of the Manor are now nearly exhausted. The last enfranchisement was in 1899. One Copyhold property in Upper High Street a few years ago cost as much as £600 to enfranchise.

There is an old proverb to the effect that "the oak scorns to grow except on free land." Wednesbury is almost all freehold; yet it has not a single oak growing within its borders. The reason, however, in this case is that the air is too impure, being so highly charged with pollutions from the iron furnaces and chemical works.

It will be interesting to give some entries from the Court Roll, divesting them first of their legal jargon and all circumlocution. The selection which follows has been made chiefly with a view to recalling some of the old place-names and field-names of Wednesbury: in a form as short and concise as possible is given in most instances (a) the date of admittance to the Roll; (b) the name of the Copyholder admitted; (c) a condensed description and location of the Copyhold; and sometimes (d) the money rent now payable in lieu of services anciently rendered to the lord:—

17 Oct., 1783—William Wood's admittance to—1 acre called the Two Butts, with the land of the Machine called Darby's Gin, bounded by the Mott Piece and the Rudgeway Hedge Hatt: two half-acre pieces near Darlaston Pitts: all lying in Kingshill Field: no rent mentioned.

5 April, 1798—George Bayley—1 acre called Mill Piece, lately enclosed out of Kingshill Field.

23 June, 1800—William Clarkson—Cottage, garden, and close, at Delves Green—rent 1s.

27 Oct., 1803—George Newey—Capital messuage called White's Tenement, otherwise the High House, in Wednesbury—rent 6d.

6 Aug., 1808—Edward Crowther and Stephen Falknor Crowther—dwelling-houses, near Spicers Stock—rent 3s.

27 Oct., 1810—Anthony Robinson—Cottage, shop, and garden at Lee Brook Lane—6d. [Acquired by Great Western Railway, 1853.]

22 Oct., 1811—mentions waste land in High Bullen.

29 June, 1816—Simeon Constable for life, and Mary Constable in remainder—malthouse, stable, yard, void land, water-pit, and appurtenances in Hancox Green; also the Malthouse Well in the Street into which well a Sough is laid from and out of a Cellar of a messuage

(named): also the use of the Entry from the street called High Bullen to the back of said premises— and a cottage in High Bullen.

30 Aug., 1820—Seven Cottages in a place formerly called Hancox Green, but now commonly called High Bullen—rent 4d.

18 Oct., 1823—Robert Spittle—six dwelling-houses near a place called Monway Gate—rent 10d.

8 November, 1823—John Rooth and John G. Thursfield—land at Kingshill field, No. 61 on Parish Plan, in Coal Hall Piece, abutting upon Lodge Pitts—with all mines and minerals.

24 Oct., 1825—Mary Sutton for life, with remainder to her children—cottages in Hancox Green, but commonly known as High Bullen— with liberty to fetch water from a Well in the garden adjoining messuage occupied by Richard Parorck. (This property is now kown as "The Horse and Jockey Inn," and within recent years has been the subject of litigation, in which some interesting manorial customs were mentioned in evidence.)

24 Oct., 1825—a croft of half-an-acre, called Byram's Croft—rent 10d.

27 Oct., 1827—Samuel Lloyd and John Rooth—half-an-acre, being 2 selions of lands, or Hadelands, in Urchin-foot, Kingshill Field; also 1 acre in Liberty Corner; also other lands near the Wednesbury and Darlaston Turnpike Road; with mines and minerals.

5 April, 1828—William Adams—Messuage and barn near Bridge End, fronting Holyhead Turnpike Road, and adjoining Hare and Hounds public-house.

25 Oct., 1828—George Watkins Court—cottage in a lane leading from the Pinfold to Monway Gate—rent 6d. (The Pinfold was then in High Bullen.)

25 Oct., 1828—Philip Harrison—3 cottages near the Pinfold—rent 6d.

25 Oct., 1828—Dwelling-house and garden near Beggars Row—rent 6d. (Was in 2 houses in 1854.)

28 Oct., 1829—Two cottages in a lane called Dudley Street, leading from High Bullen to Monway Gate—rent 3d.

21 April, 1831—William Adams and James Richards—land (marked 37 on Parish Plan) in Kingshill Field, and near a newly-intended street or road—rent 1s. 2d. (Since enfranchised from Fines.)

14 May 1831—Stable in Potters Lane, in occupation of Jonathan Rolinson, potter—rent 6d.

31 March, 1832—Cottages in the Roadway leading from the Pinfold towards Lee Brook—rent 6d.

4 Aug., 1859—Cottage and Malthouse, which have been destroyed by mining operations at Monway Gate, with shop, pigstie, garden, and all other privileges, the premises now in the occupation of the South Staffordshire Railway Company. (Robert Spittle was admitted to the last three holdings, the first and third of which since enfranchised.)

21 Oct. 1841—Dairy, Stable, and Outbuildings in High Bullen: a Messuage heretofore called The Cock: an outbuilding or necessary house in High Bullen. (These are mentioned among four admittances to Henry Pitt, and the premises are described at or near Rotten Row, Hancox Field, and Monway Field.)

26 Oct., 1837—Edward Crowther—Copyholds in Kingshill Field and in Church Field.

1 Feb., 1838—3 Habitations in Oakeswell End.

1842—Cottage "near the bridge"—since enfranchised.

1847—Dwelling-houses at Wood Green.

1848—The Upper End and a Cottage between Campfield Lane and the Pinfold Croft. Rent 6d.—since enfranchised.

4 June, 1849—A Messuage with Garden, near the Cross, in Wednesbury, in the occupation of James Drew, except such parts thereof (if any) as are erected upon the Waste of the Lord and Lady of this Manor. Rent 1s. Enfranchised from fines.

9 April, 1849—Charles Geach and Thomas Walker—3½ roods at the Birchalls in Monway Field, near the Birmingham Canal and the Lea Brook, which divides Wednesbury from Sedgley—rent 6d.

29 Oct., 1851—Isaiah Kendrick—land at the Butcroft (enfranchised): also 29 May, 1862, a moiety of a dwelling-house at a place formerly called Dimock's Green, but now Oakeswell End—rent 3d.

24 Oct., 1855—Harriett Pound—a moiety of a dwelling-house situate at a place formerly called Dimock's Green, but now Oakeswell End—rent 3d.

4 Aug., 1859—William Rolinson—the site of the Ancient round Pot-house and Pot Mill in Potters Lane—rent 2d.

26 Sep., 1859—Samuel Lloyd—land in Churchfield, fronting the road leading from Oakeswell End to the Windmill—another parcel of land in Churchhill Field and the road leading from Oakeswell End to the Mill, formerly of James Southwick—land at Kingshill Field called Urchins Foot—land at Monway Field, with mines and minerals—lands at Monway Field near the newly-made Holyhead Road and the Old Turnpike Road—lands at Monway Field near to Ridgway Style—and other parcels, most of them identified by references to numbers on the Parish Plan.

20 Nov., 1861.—Hannah Stone, for life; Josiah Stone, ⅜ths in remainder; Jane Stone, ⅜ths in remainder.—Certain premises which were surrendered at a Court Baron, holden 20 Oct., 1786 (that is to say), the Inn called The Ancient Briton, with Garden in Potters Lane, also land on the Turnpike Road, all in the occupation of Noah Collins and his undertenant: rent 6d.: A dwelling-house, now converted into three, facing the Cross, and other messuages in the Market Place, comprising shops, buildings and gardens—rent 1s. 4d.

13 Dec., 1882.—Trustee for James Russell and Sons, Limited.—Land and houses in Bedlam and Beggars Row, High Bullen.

26 Nov., 1884.—The Bulls Head Inn, Delves.

1 Dec., 1866.—The Attorney of James Russell and Sons, Ltd.—Several cottages, a malthouse, and parcels of land in Beggars Row, and in High Bullen.

The method of admitting a Copyhold tenant in Wednesbury is seen from the following record of the year 1550:—

"Wednesbray to wit.—At a Court of Humphrey Comberford, Esquire, there holden on Sunday, the 19th day of November, in the fourth year of the reign of Edward VI., by the Grace of God of England, France, and Ireland, King, Defender of the Faith, and on Earth of the Church of England and Ireland Supreme Head, It is thus enrolled:—

"At this Court came Richard Field, and surrendered into the hands of the Lord, according to the custom of the Manor, One croft called Sillimor's Hall near Dymock's Green, to the use and behoof of Edward Nyghtingalle, his heirs and assigns for ever: And whereupon here, at this same Court, came the said Edward Nyghtingalle in his own proper person, and took of the Lord the Croft aforesaid, with the appurtenances, to hold to him and his heirs according to the custom of the Manor, by the services therefor formerly due and accustomed: To whom the Lord by his Steward granted seisin thereof: And the said Edward gives to the Lord, for a Fine, 6s. 8d., and does Fealty to the Lord, and is admitted Tenant thereof.

"In Witness whereof to this present Copy I have put my seal, the Day and year above mentioned,

"Examined by me, RICHARD CATHERALL, Deputy Steward there."

Sillimor's Hall, or Sylymore, evidently situated in Oakeswell End, has already been mentioned (p. 79).

The formal Opening of the Manor Court was made by the Bailiff in the manner following:—

"Oyez! Oyez!! Oyez!!! All manner of "persons that do owe Suit and Service to this "Court Leet and Court Baron of the Right "Honorable Lady Emily Foley and of Dame "Mildred Anne Bateman Scott, now to be "holden in and for this Manor of Wednesbury, "draw near and give your attendance and "answer to your Names."

The Form of Oath administered to the Jury was:—

"You shall inquire and true Presentment "make of all such things as shall be given you "in charge: the Queen's counsel, your own, "and your fellows you shall well and truly "keep: You shall present nothing out of "hatred or malice, nor shall conceal anything "out of love, fear, or affection, but in all "things you shall well and truly present as "the same comes to your knowledge. So "help you God!"

The discharge of the Court by the Bailiff was effected in the form following:—

"All manner of persons that have appeared "this day at this Court Leet and Court Baron "may hence depart: and keep this Day and "Hour again upon a New Summons. God "Save the Queen and the Ladies of this "Manor!"

Drawn by]   [F. C. PROCTOR.

WEDNESBURY MARKET CROSS (Demolished 1824), STOCKS,

AND WHIPPING POST.

XLII.—MANORIAL POWERS AND PUNISHMENTS.

But little can be chronicled under this head; of the later period of manorial history the records have been but poorly preserved; and, further, it is somewhat difficult towards the last to discriminate between the jurisdiction of the Lord of the Manor and that of the Vestry of the Parish.

All traces of the old manorial engines of punishment have now disappeared from Wednesbury.

In remote times the Lord of the Leet had power of Gallows. He had always Pillory and Tumbril; and in want thereof the Lord was liable to fine, or even to the seizure of his "liberty" in the Manor. Also all towns in the Leet had to possess Stocks.

The Pillory (collistrigium or collum stringens) was an instrument of punishment consisting of a wooden post at the top of which was a little door with three round holes, through which the offender, while fastened to the post, put head and hands. In the pillory were exposed to public view bakers and brewers who had been detected in offences by which their customers were defrauded—hence the appointment of Meat Conners and Ale-Tasters; forestallers (those who tried to create a monopoly) and users of false weights in the Markets and Fairs; all perjurers and forgers. Wednesbury doubtless possessed a Pillory up to the eighteenth century.

The Tumbril (Trebucket, Castigatory, or Cucking Stool) was an instrument used in every manor which had View of Frankpledge, for the punishment and correction of scolds and unquiet women. The term Cucking Stool in Saxon signifies the Scold's Stool; and it is also corrupted into Ducking Stool because the residue of the judgment is that when she is so placed therein she shall be plunged into water for her punishment. The remnants of the Wednesbury Ducking Stool are said to have existed up to the beginning of the nineteenth century, when they were to have been detected in the Hall Pond, near the Vineyard Well, by the wayside in Manor House Road.

The Stocks stood near the Market Cross at the time of its demolition; they were then removed to near the Shambles. Afterwards they were fixed near to the Pinfold when it stood at the bottom of High Bullen on that piece of manorial land now occupied by the Public Weighing Machine; and their last location was in Hitchen's Croft. This site was really private land, but it was selected for its convenience, the Parish Constable at that time being one Simeon Constable of the George Hotel, at the corner of Union Street and Upper High Street.

The Charter conferring a formal right to hold fairs and markets in Wednesbury, granted by Queen Anne in 1709, conceded the usual right to hold at such times a Court of "Pie Poudre" to administer justice between buyer and seller, and to redress all disorders and offences committed within the precincts of such fairs and markets. (Supra p. 90.)

The name "Pie Poudre" is the Norman-French for "dusty foot," and is so called because the suitors and offenders at such times were generally brought to the court so expeditiously that the dust of travel, by which they had reached the market town, had not had time to be removed from their feet. The Court, presided over by the Manorial Lord or his Steward (Provost) of the Manor, was held in a room above the old Market Cross, which was then situated in the centre of the Market Place.

This building stood on pillars and arches, and its two upper rooms were approached by a flight of steps on the north side; being dirty and dilapidated it was pulled down in 1824 under the instructions of the High Constable, John Yardley, and the materials were sold to defray expenses of repairing the "parish walls."

Evidently the "churchyard walls" are here meant; this is but one of many evidences in Wednesbury of the Parish assuming rights over Manorial property.

The rough and ready Court of "Pie Poudre," whose jurisdiction was generally exercised over pedlars, tramps, and all wandering vagabonds who frequented marts and fairs, has become obsolete. For market privileges claimed by men of the manor of Wednesbury refer back to pp. 38 and 39.

In the previous chapter allusion has been made to the use of the Court Baron by Freeholders for the recovery of debts (p. 97). In later times debts were recovered in Wednesbury by a Court of Requests.

These courts when first established at the beginning of the 16th century were also known as Courts of Conscience; because the commissioners or judges of these courts were empowered to make such orders between the parties concerned as they should find stand "to equity and good conscience." As we read in Hudibras, ii., 2.

"Why should not Conscience have vacation
As well as other Courts o' the nation?"

As a court for recovery of debts it seems to have succeeded the Court Baron or the Court Leet, where small sums under forty shillings were recoverable. Larger sums were sometimes recoverable in the Hundred Court, or Common Law County Court, by virtue of a special writ granted only by the High Court when it was shown that the facts could be better dealt with on the spot.

From "Lewis' Topographical Dictionary" published in 1831 we learn that "a Court of Requests for the townships of Bilston and Willenhall, and for the parishes of Wednesbury and Darlaston, in the county of Stafford (excepting the manor of Bradley, which is in the jurisdiction of the court held at Hales Owen) is held occasionally at Wednesbury, at the White Horse Inn, Bridge Street, for the recovery of debts not exceeding £5."

In 1846 Lord Brougham passed an Act (9 and 10 Vic. c. 95) which established the modern County Courts; and Wednesbury is now within the jurisdiction of the County Court holden at Walsall, one of the sixty districts into which the whole country was divided.

For the convenience of suitors generally and the legal profession in particular the establishment of a County Court in Wednesbury has been suggested. The distance to Walsall makes the recovery of small debts through the County Court there a disproportionately expensive procedure. The joint population of Wednesbury and Darlaston being over 40,000 seems to warrant the establishment of a periodical County Court in Wednesbury.

XLIII.—THE PRESERVATION OF THE PEACE

The Manor was a military lordship, combining a civil jurisdiction. It is interesting to note how this form of feudal government declined before the advance of popular rights as first expressed through the Parish Meeting, in the Church Vestry assembled.

Having considered Wednesbury as a Manor, we now have to consider it as a Parish.

Originally the Court Leet appointed a Headborough, who was chief of the ten "pledges," and nine other tything-men, or deputy-constables. Similarly, since the time of Edward I. (1285), the Vestry has appointed a like number of Parish Constables; and in later times the acting Constables of the Leet and the Parish Constables have usually been identically the same individuals in Wednesbury.

This is how the law worked:—At the beginning of every February the Justices issued a precept to the Overseers to prepare lists of able-bodied residents in the parish. These lists were returnable by March 24th, and, the Overseers having had a Vestry Meeting for the purpose, presented that list between the date named and April the 9th at a special sessions. The Overseers were there examined as to the lists; a man selected was obliged to serve or find a substitute, but not till every other man liable in the parish had taken his proper turn; certain men were exempt, as peers, justices, clergymen, lawyers, doctors, postmasters, various parochial officers, etc., etc., while licensed victuallers, gamekeepers, and convicted offenders were disqualified.

In actual practice the appointments in Wednesbury gave no difficulty; some eight or ten were nominally appointed, but the active work was done by about two, who were put in the lists year after year, and took the fees with the work, and so relieved all others legally liable to serve.

The names of those who last served in this office have been preserved. Thomas Tibbitts (the elder) was an active Constable for many years prior to 1848. The last Parish Constable was T. A. Ellis, who came into the office with William Fairburn, and served nearly 50 years—till his death, in 1901.

The first summons to "Thomas Anthony Ellis, of the parish of Wednesbury, Tailor,"

specifies that a special Petty Sessions of Justices for the County of Stafford, "acting for the West-bromwich, Wednesbury, and Walsall Division," was held at the Public Office, Westbromwich" for the appointment of Parochial Constables on April 1st, 1854, and that the said T. A. Ellis is to be sworn at the "Public Office, Wednesbury" on the 18th, failing which a penalty not exceeding £10 is incurred. The justices signing are John Williams and A. Kenrick.

To a similar summons in 1856, signed by Augustus Calthorpe, A. Kenrick, and Thomas Bagnall, was attached a second document, which was similarly signed, and dated March 29th, 1856, stating that the said magistrates had chosen and appointed from a list submitted to them by the Overseers of Wednesbury, duly corrected and allowed, the several persons whose names, abodes, and callings were thereunder written to act as Constables during the following year for the said parish, "such number of persons being deemed necessary by the Justices, having regard to the extent and population of the said parish"—that is to say:—

Noah Butler, Darlaston Road, gun-lock filer.
William Croft, Delves, farmer.
Thomas Anthony Ellis, Union Street, tailor.
William Grant, Queen Street, butcher.
John Scholefield, Wood Green, agent.
Elihu Smallman, King's Hill Field, mine agent.
Edward Smith, Bridge Street, gas-fitting manufacturer.
Jno. Fredk. Tarte, Moxley, agent.
William Smith, Delves, farmer.

In 1857 the summons was signed by John N. Bagnall and Thos. Bagnall. The accompanying list was signed in addition by (Sir) Francis E. Scott, and the number of Constables was increased by one—Messrs. T. A. Ellis, W. Grant, John Scholefield, Elihu Smallman, Edward Smith, and William Smith being re-appointed, and the new Constables were:—

Joseph Davies, Meeting Street, engineer.
William Downing, Moxley, millwright.
Thomas Turner, Darlaston Road, gunlock filer.
George Caddick Whitehouse, Oakeswell Terrace, yeoman.

The next summons, for Saturday, April 2nd, 1859, required the attendance for swearing-in at West Bromwich Public Office (and not at Wednesbury), and was signed by Thomas Bagnall and Wm. Sharpe. The list, which was signed also by John N. Bagnall, re-appointed Joseph Davies, William Downing, T. A. Ellis, John Scholefield, William Smith, and Thomas Turner. The new Constables were:—

John Cuxon, Mes⁺ Croft, smith.
Ralph Evans, Cook Street, sinker.
Samuel Hackwood, High Street, cooper.
Joseph Hockley, Bridge Street, higgler.
　Among those newly sworn in 1860 were:—
William Elcock, Holyhead Road, gas-tube manufacturer.
Isaiah Platt, Darlaston Road, pattern-maker.
William Taylor, Bridge Street, smith.
　The only new name in 1861 was:—
Thomas Lowe, Moxley, agent.

So the law worked till the "Parish Constables Act" of 1872. This then declared the establishment of efficient police in the various counties, rendered Parish Constables unnecessary. Still, if a Court of Quarter Sessions so determined by resolution, one Parish Constable (or more) might be appointed for any parish. This was done by the Staffordshire justices for Wednesbury parish; and the document, dated 20th May, 1873, was signed by the magistrates, Henry Williams and Thomas Davis. It set forth that the Overseers of Wednesbury (in the Petty Sessional Division of West Bromwich, Wednesbury, and Walsall) had delivered a resolution of the Wednesbury Parish Vestry, passed on the 16th May, that two Constables should be appointed, at a salary of £5 a year each, and that Thomas Anthony Ellis and Thomas Tibbitts, butcher, of Union Street, had been appointed to serve till dismissed for misconduct or incompetenc·· all of which the magistrates confirmed and allowed, and the oaths were administered accordingly.

Long after Tibbitts, his fellow Constable, had ceased to hold office, Ellis continued, the last of a long line of Parish Constables.

The chief duty was the serving of summonses for Poor Rates—the Parish Authorities saving sixpence on each one served by him—and the distress warrants which sometimes followed upon these; for the latter he was paid an extra fee, with an allowance for mileage, if served at a distance from the parish. Another duty was the fixing of all parochial and similar official notices upon the doors of every church, chapel, and place of worship within the parish.

The Englishman's constitutional respect for the law is a relic of the manorial "peace pledge," and that sense of mutual responsibility engendered by the old Saxon forms of local self-government, which had, for their primary aim, the preservation of the peace in the little community.

This trait in the English character was seen nowhere more conspicuously than among the people of the Black Country. For, although their manners were of the roughest, and their ordinary sports of the most brutalising description, their respect for constituted authority was ever exemplified in their relationships with the Parish Constable. It mattered not how old, decrepit, or under-sized the Constable may have been, it was quite sufficient if he intimated that anyone had fallen within the meshes of the law. If the culprit were even a great brawny fellow, accustomed like the rest of his fellows, to settle all little differences by an appeal to fisticuffs, the Constable had merely to say to him "Come!" or "You must come with me!" and the delinquent went unresistingly under arrest, and very often willingly accompanied his captor from Wednesbury to Bilston, or to Barr, or elsewhere to some Justice residing several miles distant from the parish.

Yet, lamb-like as was their obedience when the individual offender was concerned, in times of tumult and civil commotion, when the community was roused to a resistance of the law, no people could be more violent. An entire chapter of "Religious Wednesbury" has been devoted to the Wednesbury rioting of the 18th century. Here may be enumerated some of those which occurred in the last century.

In 1801 riots occurred here on account of the high price of provisions; hucksters, bakers, and other provision dealers in Wednesbury suffered much damage to their shops and property.

The Colliers' Riots of 1826 were thus referred to in a Wolverhampton paper of that date:—"A strike of Black Country colliers against a reduction of wages is announced. Rioting took place at Wednesbury and West Bromwich, whereupon the Riot Act was read, and the military were marched into the district, who awed the men into quietness. The masters proposed to reduce the wages from 4 shillings to 3 shillings and 6 pence a day, with beer and coal to the value of another 6 pence."

In the November and December of 1831 the Colliers and Miners rioted on account of short work and low wages.

In August, 1842, there were about 30,000 colliers assembled in the Turk's (or Russell's) field; a company of regulars were mounted in the Talbot Yard; the colliers on strike went to the pits at work, and ordered the men up that were working, and as each skip came to the top took hold of them and threw them into the canal or reservoir. This rioting caused the magistrates to call out the Yeomanry: the Riot Act was read somewhere at West Bromwich, and the Yeomanry brought some 40 or 50 of the rioters to Wednesbury fastened to their saddle-straps. The Petty Sessions was held at the Turk's Head then, and the greater part of this number were committed to Stafford. Twelve or fourteen were transported for life.

During the Puddlers' strike of 1883 several Wednesbury men were apprehended, and committed to Stafford for their share in the destruction of puddling furnaces, etc. For some time a large body of the County Police, armed with cutlasses, was always kept in readiness for immediate action at the Police Station in the Holyhead Road.*

During the earlier part of the nineteenth century the detection of crime and the administration of justice were very lax.

For years at a stretch there was not a single magistrate resident in Wednesbury; and when the magisterial business of the parish was not transacted at Barr, as already mentioned (p. 94), offenders were most frequently tried at Bilston. A little later county magistrates held sittings in Wednesbury, among their meeting places being the White Horse Inn, the Red Lion Inn, the Turk's Head Inn, and others enumerated in "Olden Wednesbury."

When property was reported as missing, the Constables made a great parade of searching in "Thief Street," as a part of Dudley Street was then called, owing to the residence there of a number of suspicious characters, some of whom were popularly supposed to gain a livelihood as footpads and highwaymen. Nothing came of such searches, as a rule; and so long as the suspected persons refrained from committing depredations within the parish, their presence was tolerated, and their delinquencies winked at.

The Parish Constables preserved the peace till superseded by the modern Policeman. Sir Robert Peel established the London Police in 1829, and ten years later similar bodies were established in other parts of England by the Counties and District Constabulary Act.

It was soon after 1840 that the first uniformed policeman was seen in Wednesbury. The earliest uniform of the Staffordshire force consisted of a dark-blue swallow-tailed coat, buttoned closely down the front by brass buttons, and drawn in tightly at the waist by a broad black leather belt, fastened at the front by a great metal buckle; white duck trousers; and a tall or "top hat," of glistening oil-skin or black leather. This was the police uniform from about 1840 to 1860.

As to Wednesbury places of imprisonment and detention in olden times, nothing is known —the Stocks and Pillory were penal institutions.

There is an entry in Wednesbury Parish Registers under date 1720 relating to a "christening: Thomas, a bastard child of . . . . . and a foolish, half-witted girl. The rogue choosing to go to Walsall House of Correction rather than marry her." Willmore's

"History of Walsall" (pp. 395-6) describes the gaol of that town, but there is no record of a "clink" at Wednesbury.

On the first appearance of the Wednesbury Police, their earliest Lock-up was in Union Street (Camp Street corner), where it remained till a police station was provided in Russell Street some ten years later.

At the Workhouse, in Meeting Street, was a Crib—a cell with an iron-studded door, which door has been removed within the last ten years. This was used by the Beadle for the reception of prisoners; the Master of the Workhouse himself but rarely used it, preferring to deal with refractory paupers by chaining them to the fire-grate.

The Russell Street Station seems to have been called into requisition by the new Act, which in 1846 constituted the Wolverhampton Stipendiary Justice District, of which Wednesbury forms part. The first Stipendiary magistrate here was John Leigh, Esq. (1846), and the first rate to provide his stipend, staff, offices, etc., was ordered by Quarter Sessions to be ½d. in the £, 26th June, 1848. This levy is made through the county rate.

The next Stipendiary was W. Partridge, Esq., appointed January 1861, succeeded by Isaac Spooner, Esq., April, 1863. In May, 1879, he was followed by W. F. F. Boughey, Esq., and in September, 1885, the latter was replaced by N. C. A. Neville, Esq. The salary is £1,000 a year, and the Stipendiary has somewhat greater powers than the unpaid magistracy.

Wednesbury was formerly said to be situated in the Offlow South Police District, when on April 6th, 1846, the Court of Quarter Sessions made an Order for purchasing the Russell Street buildings, to be used as a Court House and Police Station, at a sum of £552. A further grant of £100 for repairs and fittings was made by Quarter Sessions on April 5th, 1852. Again, on October 17th, 1853, the sum of £200 was granted for altering and enlarging the Russell Street Station to meet the growing needs of an increasing population. This, however, was soon found to be entirely inadequate to the requirements of the town, for on April 5th, 1859, Quarter Sessions voted £3,250 for providing the present Police Office in Holyhead Road, which was opened in 1860.

In the earlier Police Administration, Wednesbury was an inferior command to Bilston, and afterwards to West Bromwich (Wednes-

---

*In recent times the town has not always been free from sedition.

In September, 1880, an arrest was made in the Irish quarter of Wednesbury for an agrarian crime in Ireland—the murder of Lord Montmorres: the prisoner was taken to Ireland, but afterwards discharged.

In May, 1884, William McDonnell, manager of the Royal Oak Inn, King Street, Wednesbury, was arrested on a charge of treason felony, and being concerned with Egan and Daly in the Midland Fenian Dynamite Con-

spiracy. A letter from the suspect to Egan, dated 19 June, 1874, appeared to show that Wednesbury was an important Fenian Centre, and made mention of P. Flinn, who kept the British Queen Inn, Trouse Lane, another public-house much frequented by the Irishry of Wednesbury.

In January, 1892, John Thomas Deakin, formerly a railway clerk in Wednesbury, was arrested, charged with being concerned in an Anarchist Conspiracy at Walsall.

bury belonged to West Bromwich Special Sessional Division till 1889); and for a brief space was once known as the Rushall Police Division.

The present Wednesbury Police Division includes Wednesbury (municipal borough), Darlaston, Tipton, Great Barr and Hill Top, which is manned by about 48 police-constables, of whom 16 employed within the municipal area consist of 1 superintendent, 2 sergeants, and 13 men. Each of the three parishes which constituted the Division when Ellis was first appointed to the office of Parish Constable, viz., Wednesbury, Walsall, and West Bromwich, is now a municipal borough with a separate Commission of the Peace, and one has its own borough police force. Wednesbury is still included in the administration of the Staffordshire County Constabulary.

All Darlaston police business was transacted at Wednesbury till January 1898, when a weekly session was established at Darlaston.

In olden times justices held their Courts in their own houses ("Wednesbury Papers," pp. 142-3), and, in later times, in public-houses. Thus at Wednesbury, besides those just enumerated, the Church Hill Tavern and the Talbot Inn, Market Place, have been magisterial meeting places. It was a clever stroke of policy on the part of the Rev. Isaac Clarkson, J.P., to buy the Russell Street Police Station for the county authorities—the building had been put up about 1845, as a Chartist Hall, by means of capital raised in £1 shares; and, the proprietors being in difficulties, the sale of their assembly-room most effectually broke up the Chartist agitation in Wednesbury.

By the Summary Jurisdiction Act cases must now be decided in open court, at regular and fixed sittings of one or more justices, at the Petty Sessional Court House or the occasional Court House: and, as Conservators of the Peace, magistrates now hold their courts in nearly every parish.

The county justices acted for Wednesbury till the Charter of Incorporation in 1886, which added the Mayor, and ex-Mayor for one year after office, to the magistracy.

In July, 1893, the Borough of Wednesbury was granted a separate Commission of the Peace, with jurisdiction limited to the borough; the powers of the borough magistrates run concurrently with those of the county justices, except that the licensing of public-houses is exclusively in the hands of the borough magistrates. The county justices hold a fortnightly court on alternate Tuesdays with the Stipendiary; the borough magistrates a weekly petty sessions every Friday.

The Wednesbury Town Council should, as a matter of course, appoint a Watch Committee, which is a Statutory Committee with large powers for police control; but no such Committee exists.

Photo by]   [W. FRANCIS.

WEDNESBURY WAKE, 1898, HELD ON PRIVATE LAND IN RIDDING LANE.

XLIV.—NINETEENTH CENTURY PAROCHIALISM.

Let us take a peep at Wednesbury under the sway of Bumbledom, when the Parish Beadle was a power in the land. The briefest of glimpses may perhaps enable us to form some conception of the social and moral atmosphere of the place at the beginning of last century.

Chapter xxxii. of "Religious Wednesbury" deals fully with the decay of the civil power of church: And chapter xli. of "Olden Wednesbury" treats at length of the administration of the Poor Laws; from both of which may be gathered the extent to which Churchwardens and Overseers of the Poor exercised powers and jurisdiction in the centuries just passed. So important were these parochial functionaries, Bagnall's "Wednesbury" includes a list of the Churchwardens and Overseers from the year 1561 to 1717 (pp. 63-66 of that work).

Churchwardens were then recognised officials in civil as well as ecclesiastical administration. Joined with the Overseers of the Poor they made the rates for the relief of the poor, and could set up parish trades for the employment of the poor. In the 18th century the paupers who were able-bodied men were all made parish nail-makers in this and the adjacent parishes. The Churchwardens also placed out the parish apprentices from the Workhouse; and in the early part of 19th century these were nearly all put to the gun-lock and affiliated trades. Part of their obligation to the interests of the ratepayers charged the Churchwardens with the duty of looking after the weekly payments due under bastardy orders. There was a chest in Wednesbury Old Church full of dusty documents, chiefly of two sorts; the first lot were indentures of parish apprentices, and the second were bastardy orders; publication of the latter would have smirched the good names of not a few of the older families of the town.

The dearth of resident magistrates encouraged the Churchwardens to assume many unwarrantable powers and jurisdiction in addition to those which they legally did possess. In the same way the Beadle of the Parish became an executive arm of the law, probably acting as a sworn Constable. It was the Beadle who performed the public flogging of culprits.

Flogging was a mode of punishment applied to both sexes indiscriminately, the whipping of women having been abolished as late as the first year of George IV.

The flogging of vagrants to make them leave the town is almost within living memory; but the more common incidence was the infliction of this punishment upon unruly boys and runaway apprentices, generally administered by the authority of the Churchwardens, the Beadle being the official wielder of the whip.

The Wednesbury Whipping Post stood beside the Stocks near the Market Cross. If there are none living who remember public floggings of offenders, there remain a few who can remember the Beadle gliding round the church to rap sleepy boys and other unruly urchins on the head with a long staff kept for that purpose.

The Churchwardens had the power to chastise disorderly boys by law; they were empowered to take off the caps of those who irreverently kept them on, to prevent noise in church and the contending for places; they might even apprehend anyone who disturbed the minister. By statute they could levy penalties on those who did not attend church, and against profaners of the Sabbath. They had power to search the ale-houses on Sunday for tipplers therein during divine service. This was sometimes done in Wednesbury; but the raid was always conducted in a remarkable manner—the tavern nearest the church was always systematically missed, because the "singers and ringers" made a practice of adjourning there during the intervals in which their services were not required.

The Beadle of the parish was quite an imposing sight when arrayed in all the trappings of his office. At the beginning of the nineteenth century he wore breeches and stockings, shoes with silver buckles, a gold laced coat with cape attached, and a cocked hat. This form of dress may be seen in the illustration p. 16 of "Olden Wednesbury," and how it was afterwards modified is shown in the portraits on pp. 96 and 98 of "Religious Wednesbury." The Beadle always carried a tall staff in his hand when processioning round the boundaries, or proclaiming the fairs; on which occasions the Constable shouldered a halberd.

Under the direction of the Beadle till sixty years ago were the Night Watchmen, who were paid by the Vestry a small weekly wage. They were also provided with lanterns, rattles, staves, and watch-boxes at the public cost. In Wednesbury there were two wards, or "patroles," taking in only the central portion of the parish. These Watchmen called out the hours of the night and the state of the weather in the usual manner; meeting each other at fixed times with the cry "All's well!" near the White Horse Inn.

The last official Watchmen in Wednesbury were Richard Tibbitts, and afterwards Moses and Joseph Palmer. But there were unofficial Watchmen later than these, privately appointed as late as 1857.

Thus in the December of that year a meeting of the inhabitants of the Holyhead Road (then in the hands of the Bilston Turnpike Trustees) was held, at which Mr. Benjamin Stevenson presided. It was resolved "That as there was (sic) no Gas Lights in that important thoroughfare it was desirable for the protection of property that a Watchman be employed, whose beat should extend from Mr. Stevenson's Timber Yard, to the end of the houses towards Bilston." The following committee was appointed to carry out the proposal:—Messrs. B. Stevenson, Simkin, Lowe, Hawkins, W. Elcock, Stringer, and Brevitt; with Mr. J. Goddard as treasurer. A man named Harrod was afterwards appointed as Watchman, and subscriptions were freely paid.

The same committee charged Messrs. Elcock and B. Stevenson with the presentation of a memorial to the Board of Health, praying for the road to be lighted with gas.

The great annual events in which the Beadles and other parish functionaries were to be seen in the full glory of their offices were the Proclaiming of the Fairs—a full account of the old custom of Walking the Fair at Wednesbury is given in Bagnall's "Wednesbury," p. 153—and the Perambulation of the Parish Boundaries.

It is over 70 years since the Wednesbury "bounds were beaten." On the Darlaston side the boundaries are all artificial, and often most arbitrary. This anomalous state of things is said to have originated in the early days of the Poor Rate, when a parish to escape the liability of maintaining its own poor would sacrifice any outlying cottages to the neglected condition of a parochial "No Man's Land." (See "History of Darlaston," p. 167.)

Pinfold Street, for instance, is an artificial boundary line, one side being in Darlaston parish, and the other in Wednesbury.

In the eighteenth century, during a great depression in the gun-lock trade, the Master of Darlaston Workhouse suddenly ceased to collect the Poor Rates from the cottagers on the south (or Wednesbury) side of the street. At that time every one of the said cottages was occupied by a married apprentice; and as the wives and families of the improvident youngsters were likely to come upon the parish for maintenance during the long spell of bad trade, which the authorities saw looming ahead, the non-collection of the rates was a preliminary to the repudiation of all liability in connection therewith. The parochialistic plot succeeded so effectually that this side of Pinfold Street has been excluded from Darlaston parish ever since.

Another anomaly is found near Sparrows Forge Road, where one house is partly in Wednesbury and partly in Darlaston. The occupier of the tenement, in a parochial dispute of many years ago, was made chargeable upon the parish in which his head lay when he was asleep in his bed; the Solons of the two contesting vestries deciding that the parish to which he only relegated his feet must escape all responsibility for the maintenance of his pauper body.

When the Bounds were beaten, one man was always sent scrambling across the roof of this house to mark the exact line of demarcation.

The Perambulatory procession consisted of the Beadle and other parochial officials, and in later times started from the Elephant and Castle Inn, High Bullen, where a feast of roast beef and strong ale terminated the proceedings. Tame Bridge was reached about midday, where boys were thrown into the brook to impress their youthful minds with the location of the boundary line there. Bread and cheese and beer were then served gratuitously at the Bull's Head Tavern.

The Beadle was usually the Pinner and sometimes also the Town Crier.

Whatever the Crier's announcement, whether relating to a lost child, or to a sale by auction, it was invariably introduced by the form " Oyez! Oyez! Oyez! This is to give notice "— and so on; and brought to a conclusion with " God save the King!" and a final peal of the bell.

Now as to the appearance of the old town as it was early in the nineteenth century. From every point of view the streets of Wednesbury were then mean and insignificant. The irregularity of the building line, which still exists in the older parts of the town is a relic of those times.

Not only were all sanitary precautions utterly neglected, but gross negligence prevailed in all other departments which are now brought under the strict surveillance of local government authorities. Had the legally constituted authority of those days even attempted to enforce bye-laws or regulations, its powers would undoubtedly have been set at defiance by the oligarchy which actually governed the public affairs of Wednesbury—an oligarchy consisting of the heads of the principal families, the chief property owners, and those holding official positions in the parish.

The most important building after the church was the Market Cross. Bagnall's "Wednesbury," p. 154, says of the Market Cross :—

" It was built upon pillars and arches and consisted of two upper rooms, to which there was an entrance at the north end by an uncouth flight of steps."

After mentioning the school kept there, supported by the parishioners even to the extent of clothing eight of the boy scholars, and to the use of the Cross for preaching purposes, Bagnall continues :—

" Here, too, Commissioners held their Court of Requests : Magistrates sat to administer justice : and on the top of the steps, tied to the door posts many a culprit has been flogged by the Beadle."

According to Bagnall the Cross had become dilapidated and dangerous, the arches a receptacle for filth, and often the scene of vice —presumably after night-fall.

After many ineffectual appeals to the Steward of the Manor to repair and improve the Market Cross, its demolition was decided upon. It was taken down in 1824 under the direction of Mr. John Yardley, Constable of the Leet, and the materials sold—some of the bricks were seen till recently, part of the old garden-wall in Ridding Lane which once belonged to Mr. Addison. The proceeds of the sale were appropriated by the Churchwardens, as previously stated (p. 102).

Of the Day School which was held in the upper rooms behind the little diamond panes of the Market Cross the last schoolmaster was one Mr. Shore. This pedagogue was also organist at the old parish church; and when his name seemed to be repeated in one of the hymns it was always a source of intense amusement for his scholars to have to sing

" Thy praise shall sound from shore to shore
" Till sun shall rise to set no more."

This school was undoubtedly a most useful institution for the parish at that time, and could scarcely have come under the general designation of a " parochial nuisance," the excuse put forward for pulling down the building. The scholars numbered something like a hundred, were taught on the newly invented monitorial system, and paid a fee of twopence per week.

Under the shadow of that old Cross have been effected sales not only of ordinary marketable commodities, but of a nature so strange as now to be deemed incredible. But they were strange times, and peculiar ideas of the marriage tie prevailed among all the lower orders. The selling of a wife by public auction in Wednesbury Market Place has been witnessed not once, but on several occasions, by the old inhabitant whose authority for the statements is beyond doubt.

In selling a wife the only precaution which was deemed necessary to ensure the legality of the transaction was the formality of bringing the woman to market with a halter round her neck, and with having previously gone through the ceremony of paying a toll for her at some toll-gate, taking the toll-ticket as carefully as if the wife were the man's beast of burden, like his horse or his ass.

Some anxious husbands have been known to take tickets from the three different Trusts round Wednesbury, one at Wood Green gate, one at Holloway Bank gate, and one at Moxley Road gate. This was to make assurance trebly sure. The highest price ever fetched for a wife in this market, of all the transactions witnessed by the deponent, was thirty shillings. Some ale was usually paid for by either the vendor or the purchaser, of which the woman usually partook; so that the three principals concerned always parted good friends, and the woman went away contentedly with her new spouse—perhaps in some cases by previous private arrangement, if the truth could be known.

More legitimate sales of live stock were, of course, effected in Wednesbury market in those times. If there were no cattle at the Walsall Street end, there were nearly always pigs for sale near the Shambles.

The water supply necessary for market purposes was forthcoming from two wells; one was situated in a yard on the south side of the Shambles, now built upon: the other, commonly known as the Tackers' Well because of the proximity in olden times of a number of nailers and tack-makers, stood at the bottom of Church Street. The former was a drawwell, but from the latter the water had to be " laded " in a ladle, the operator descending the well, and striding across its lower arch.

As Alderman Williams has recounted in his reminiscences, the Market was looked upon as a most important institution up to the forties. There every Friday were to be encountered not only buyers and sellers from all the countryside around, but parading up and down for an hour or so before noonday were to be seen all the best men of the town—heads of families, parish officials, and almost every man who was well-to-do and of good standing; not a few of the more old-fashioned of them in their knee-breeches, and sporting their buckled shoes. Not only were there market dinners at the various taverns, but Mr. Williams says that one or two of the richer residents regularly took a party of their friends home to a private midday dinner which was specially prepared every market day. As the market was over by twelve o'clock the afternoon was devoted to social enjoyment, usually accompanied by long pipes, and something else stronger but of a liquid nature.

XLV.—INTER-COMMUNICATION WITH WEDNESBURY—ITS HIGHWAY BOARD.

In olden times Wednesbury, like every other parish, was more self-contained than it is at the present day, because communication with the outer world was then difficult. Travelling was restricted when roads were few, and bad at that.

In those times the parishioners turned out some six days in each year, and with their own personal labour, using their own spades and mattocks, employing their own horses and carts, repaired the roads and the lanes. Owners of ancient ditches had to cleanse them, and sometimes new drains had to be cut. All this was unsatisfactory in its results, even when the Vestry appointed " Waywardens."

The roads were often in deep ruts, and quite impassable for wheeled vehicles. In some parts of the towns " Causeways " were occasionally made with cobble stones—" stoneroads" as they were also called, of which the Wednesbury Portway and probably the Market Place offered examples. Into all this, a " townend," such as John Wesley in his Journals (1745) calls the quagmire on the outskirts of Wednesbury at Hoo Marsh " where the road was in a ruinous condition," made inter-communication difficult, if not dangerous.

For this reason pack-horses were used instead of wheeled vehicles; even coal or raw iron was carried in " dassells " or stronglymade panniers; and only bridle-paths existed across such stretches of waste as West Bromwich Heath—for traffic in which direction towards Aston Furnaces a " Hollow-way " was cut from Wednesbury Bridge to Hill Top.

The first great change brought about by the increase of traffic was the introduction of Turnpikes (1663). The tolls taken on these main roads, running from town to town, kept them in repair. But the original unevenness of the roads took many years to remedy; and a " flying machine," or heavy coach drawn by six stout horses, as yet took a whole week to accomplish the stages between Wolverhampton and London.

The first turnpike road that came through Wednesbury was made in 1727. This Act of George I. was for repairing several roads leading out of Birmingham; one through the town of Wednesbury "to a place called High Bullen"; another to Great Bridge and from thence to Gibbet Lane near "Bilson" on one side, and through Dudley to Kingswinford on the other side.

The ancient road from Birmingham to Wednesbury had passed under the shadows of Handsworth and West Bromwich churches and of West Bromwich Hall. It was in 1766 that the continuation of the road north of Wednesbury, through Bilston, was first turnpiked. The third and last turnpike trust to acquire control of roads through Wednesbury was the Walsall Trust. There are still to be seen a few iron posts which marked out the turnpike Trusts; one is in Trouse Lane at the top of Meeting Street, and another is in the middle of Portway Road. At the formation of the Local Board in 1851 there were the three turnpike Trusts still existing in Wednesbury parish—the Birmingham, the Bilston, and the Walsall; but it was then officially reported "They do not any of them pass through the town (? Market Place), the several Acts of Parliament prohibiting them."

In this midland district the toll gates disappeared between 1872 and 1882. Wood Green toll-gates, which had a side-bar for Blases Lane, which is now called Brunswick Park Road, disappeared soon after November, 1870; the old toll-houses may yet be seen at Helloway Bank and on the Darlaston Road; the gates at Lea Brook and at Moxley Road have left no traces, although there is a more ancient toll house yet standing in Dangerfield Lane which marks the route to the north before the existence of Holyhead Road, first opened for traffic in 1827.

It was not till 1786 that the roads of England had been brought to that pitch of perfection which permitted the introduction of "fast coaches," timed for an average speed of over ten miles an hour. The zenith of coaching was reached about 1837. A great number of coaches passed through Wednesbury (an enumeration is given on p. 118 of "Wednesbury Papers"), besides post-chaises for private travelling. At the Duke of York Inn—an ancient three-storey hostelry in Lower High Street, which formerly stood on the site of the Board School-house—lived a family of the name of Collier, who were horse contractors. For four generations the head of this family drove one of the London through-coaches. There was a duty on post-horses which the Government farmed out to contractors; the last man in Wednesbury to collect this tax was one Felix Webb, afterwards a tube manufacturer.

The time occupied between Birmingham and Wednesbury depended on the class of coach. Towards the close of the coaching period, for instance, the "Wonder" and coaches of the same class averaged about five minutes twenty seconds to the mile. The time, therefore, from Birmingham to the Dartmouth Inn,

Holyhead Road, would be timed for 43 minutes, and the same rate was maintained on to Wolverhampton. Many of the coaches ran from Birmingham to Wolverhampton without a change; some changed at the Red Lion in Bridge Street, some at the Swan Inn, Holyhead Road, and some changed at West Bromwich; these arrangements altered from time to time according to the horse contractors. The Turks Head then had a long range of stabling on the opposite side of the High Street.

The character of coaching changed very substantially from time to time; but the busiest period at Wednesbury was undoubtedly about 1837, just prior to the opening of the Grand Junction Railway.

Going back to the year 1817, here is a list of vehicles which then plied through Wednesbury (for a description of the town's appearance at that date see "Olden Wednesbury," p. 3):—

(1) From the King's Head (now George Hotel, corner of Union Street)—
The Waterloo (day coach) to Birmingham every day, 8.30 a.m., returning 6.30 p.m.

(2) From Talbot Inn, Market Place—
Market coach to Birmingham, four days a week, 8.30 a.m.; to Darlaston, 7 p.m.

(3) From Turk's Head Inn—
Mail to London daily 1.30 (noon) and to Holyhead 12.30 (noon).
Old Mail to London daily 12 (noon) and to Holyhead 2 p.m.
New Prince to London daily at 1 (noon); to Shrewsbury 12.30 (noon).
Old Prince to London daily 4 p.m.; to Shrewsbury 12 noon.
The Bang-up to Liverpool 7 a.m.; to Birmingham 7.30 p.m.
Prince of Orange to Chester daily (except Mondays) 7.30 a.m.; to Birmingham 6 p.m.
The Union to Shrewsbury daily 11 a.m.; to London 11.30 a.m.
The Retaliator to London daily at 12; to Shrewsbury 11 a.m.
Daily Coach to Birmingham every morning at 9, returning 6.30 in the evening.

With the through roads as busy as this there can be little wonder that there was a great necessity to improve these roads; hence the building of Wednesbury Bridge and the cutting of the new (Holyhead) Road, a national work commenced about 1821.

In addition to the passenger traffic there were—in the same year, 1817—two local Carriers for the conveyance of goods:—

(1) John Disturnal, to Birmingham every Tuesday, Thursday, and Saturday: to Wolverhampton every Wednesday and Friday, from [Upper] High Street.

(2) Josiah Forster, to Birmingham every Tuesday, Thursday, and Saturday from High Bullen.

The Post Office was also in High Street, and the Postmaster in 1817 was named Mr. Thomas

Rogers. The mails were despatched as follows:—

To London at 12 and at 1.30 noon.
To Holyhead at 12.30 noon.
To Shrewsbury at 2 p.m.

In 1835 the Postmaster was Mr. Martin Worcester, and then London letters arrived at 8.12 a.m. and were despatched at 5.30 p.m. Birmingham letters arrived 10.30 a.m. and 3.45 p.m., and were despatched at 11 a.m. and 5.30 p.m. Wolverhampton letters arrived at 11 a.m. and 6 p.m., and were despteched at 8 a.m. and 3.30 p.m.

It is easy to understand that when all communication with the outside world lay along the higaways that the highways should occupy the foremost place in the system of local government then in vogue.

By the adoption of the Highway Acts of the early nineteenth century, a Highway Board, or a Board of Surveyors as they called it in Wednesbury, was constituted to take charge of the 13½ miles of road then existing in the parish. (There are some 28 miles of streets now.)

Obviously the first duty of a Highway Board was to look after the " highways and common streets " of the Parish, which they were bound to keep in repair, as well as the ancient bridges, ditches, and watercourses. The Board might erect boundary stones and finger-posts (the last remaining guide-post in Wednesbury is to be seen at the junction of the Walsall and West Bromwich Roads in Oakeswell End); it might level the roads having steep inclines, widen narrow parts, and cut off sharp corners when the turnings were awkward for the fast coach traffic.

All parishioners were eligible to serve on a Board of Surveyors. But in the larger Highway Districts like Wednesbury they were empowered by the Act to appoint " one skilled person " at a salary to do the actual work; and the last man so appointed in Wednesbury to fill the joint office of Rate Collector and Road Surveyor was named Whitehead.

The Election for the members of this Board took place about March 25 in each year, generally by show of hands in the Parish Vestry, although a poll might be taken if demanded.

The number of members might range from 5 to 20. Among the members serving this local authority towards the last might be found the well-known Wednesbury names of the Rev. Isaac Clarkson, Messrs. Joseph Smith, James Negus, E. Elwell, Jesse Whitehouse, Benjamin Round, James Frost, Israel Yardley, and Edward Blakemore.

Between the Highway Board and the Turnpike Trusts there was constant disagreement respecting the maintenance of the main roads —as is usual in all similar cases of dual responsibility. The paving of the footpaths, for instance, was one source of disagreement. A compromise was arrived at in respect of this; the Trust would provide the labour if the frontagers would provide the material. This compromise commended itself to the Vestry, who also adopted it for the other streets; and so some of the principal thoroughfares of Wednesbury had the footpaths paved with pebbles —those " petrified kidneys," to walk upon which was habitual penance for the Wednesbury wayfarer.

The dominating principle which actuated all public governing bodies was that of " keeping down the rates." In Wednesbury there was a determination that the Highway rate should never exceed 5d. How little public work could be accomplished in the parish with a rate of this small amount may be gauged by the amounts realised during the last five years the Highway Board was in existence:—

1846 at 3d. in £ the amount raised was £347 18s. 11d.

1847 at 5d. in £ the amount raised was £547 19s. 8¾d.

1848 at 3d. in £ the amount raised was £336 3s. 9¼d.

1849 at 5d. in £ the amount raised was £544 1s. 4d.

1850 at 4d. in £ the amount raised was £463 17s. 10¼d.

The responsibility for lighting of the through roads was another matter of contention between the two bodies. The Swan Village Gas Works were erected in 1825, and within the next ten years the South Staffordshire Gas Company had laid 90 miles of gas mains, of which some of the local Turnpike Trusts had taken small advantage for the public lighting of some few portions of their main roads.

As late as the coronation of Queen Victoria in 1838 the " illuminations " were effected by means of candles. Every shop and house window then consisted of a number of small panes; and on each pane was stuck a lighted candle. The richer inhabitants used wax candles, but by far the larger portion of the houses were lit up with tallow candles, the product of the numerous chandleries which represented a flourishing industry in Wednesbury at that time.

Street-lighting, what little there was of it, was still effected with oil lamps. Two of these antiquated lanterns had to suffice for the Five Ways; one was suspended from a bracket on Disturnal's shop at the angle of Church Street and Upper High Street; a second dismal lamp hung from the opposite corner between the Market Place and Walsall Street, then occupied by a quaint little butcher's shop with half-doors, and a crow-step gable facing the Market Place; and this was the best lit space in the whole of Wednesbury.

Such was the aspect of the locality when the commencement of the railway era began to put an entirely new face upon the internal intercommunications; and so far as Wednesbury itself was concerned, did so much to develop and change certain forms of industry—the old coach-iron trade of the town, for instance, developing into the manufacture of railway axles, railway wheels, and other railway material.

The Grand Junction Railway, which touched Wednesbury only tangentially at Wood Green, was opened 4th July, 1837. The South Staffordshire Railway, from Dudley to Alrewas, passed through Wednesbury, and planted its station in a fairly central position; it opened 1st May, 1850, and is now the L. and N.W.R. line. The Great Western came into Wednesbury and placed a second railway station within a few yards of the other; and from that time—it was opened 14th November, 1854—to the present, the advantages of making one joint station in place of the two never seems to have occurred to either of the Companies. Such advantage must have been doubly palpable when, in 1863,

two branches were opened from the very intersection of the two rival lines, namely, one branch to Darlaston, and a second to Princes End through Ocker Hill. Had a joint station existed the Darlaston branch need never have been closed, because of the through communication which would have been given to that town. As it is, the Tramways attracted all the traffic between Darlaston and Wednesbury, and a lawsuit which the authorities of the former town undertook in 1892 could not succeed in compelling the London and North-Western Railway Company to re-open the Darlaston branch for passenger traffic—all of which has been previously mentioned on p. 4.

WALSTEAD HALL, DELVES GREEN, WEDNESBURY

(See Index for " Walstead.")

XLVI.—INSANITARY WEDNESBURY—A BOARD OF HEALTH ESTABLISHED.

The cholera visitations of 1832 and 1848 have been fully described in chap. xviii. of "Wednesbury Papers"; and statistics relating thereto for the whole Black Country region have been given in chap. lvi. of "Sedgley Researches." There is, therefore, no need to recapitulate them here.

Between the two cholera epidemics of 1832 and 1848 a Royal Commission inquired into the sanitary condition of all the large towns and populous districts of the country, collecting evidence on the systems of drainage then in use, the means by which towns were supplied with water, and inquiring generally what remedial measures were required to better the conditions of life which then prevailed.

Wednesbury was a "populous place," then in a transitional period between its early era of existence as an agricultural town and its more modern development as a manufacturing centre.

The Commissioner, whose report of the sanitary condition of Wednesbury is officially preserved, was R. A. Slaney, Esq., who acted in this Midland district as his colleagues, Dr. Lyon Playfair and other equally eminent scientists, did in Lancashire and the other great centres of population.

In the FIRST REPORT OF COMMISSIONERS ON THE INQUIRY INTO HEALTH OF TOWNS, published in 1844, there is only an Abstract of "Replies from 5 towns as to sewerage," etc., in which Wednesbury is mentioned. The entries are very brief, but to the point :—

(1) No regulations in the town for draining, etc.

(2) No arrangements for under-drainage; public drains much wanted.

(3) No house drains.

(4) Public streets [are] cleansed.

(5) Courts and alleys are not cleansed; in a filthy condition.

(6) There is no local authority vested with adequate powers to enforce cleansing and prevent nuisances.

(7) Badly supplied with water.

(8) No stand-pipes, etc.; supplied with water from the river.

The SECOND REPORT OF THE COMMISSIONERS, printed in 1845, page 206, says :—

"WEDNESBURY consists of one long street, along the turnpike road, with many lateral ones branching into courts and alleys, inhabited by the working classes. There is no drainage worth the name, no scavengers or system of cleansing, and the supply of water very scarce and indifferent. There are no pipes (though there is, it is said, a good supply near it, at a high level above the town), few pumps, and the wells are often bad. The people complain much, and have to carry water near a mile, or to buy at a halfpenny for three cans.

"The Workhouse of the town has very bad water in the well, and they are obliged to fetch it for washing or drinking several times a day.

"The courts, alleys, and small streets are unpaved or illpaved, full of stagnant puddles, privies with open vaults, pigsties, etc.; there is, in fact, no care taken on these points, and the greatest neglect appears. I find it stated 'There is a dreadful stinking tank or ditch at the back of the Turk's Head, where the magistrates always meet, and the public enter by this filthy place.'"

At this point in the Government report are printed the following entries as footnotes :—

"Whitehouse Square — Filthy choked-up privies, and dirt holes overflowing.

"High Bulleyn—Open drains, full and stinking.

"Ledbury's Buildings—Filthy open privies; stagnant liquid filth and receptacles; bad water generally; opposite Court—bad privies.

"Houses opposite Turk's Head—Open receptacle of liquid filth."

Resuming the body of the Report, we read :—

"The reply of the Local Committee to the queries of the Commissioners states: 'The facilities for drainage are remarkably good'; and continues: 'there are not any public drains—such drains are very desirable in this parish.' In another answer to the question, 16, 'If the courts and alleys inhabited by the poorer classes are cleansed by appointed scavengers,' they reply, 'No; consequently they are in a filthy condition.' There is no place where the working classes are allowed to bathe, nor any public walk or place of exercise."

The "Local Committee," we find on p. 231, consisted of "Rev. — Cartwright and committee." This reverend gentleman was probably a dissenting minister.

Again there are footnotes illustrative of the text. They are "taken on the spot," but some of the street names seem to have disappeared so long that it is now impossible to identify the places named in them :—

"Such notices as these are frequent in our notes on the spot: 'Filthy open privies, no water, no drain.'

"Miss Wehley's Court — 'Green stagnant puddles.'

"Bullock's Fold—'Open terrible drains; no water but by buying.'

"Buck's Buildings—'Open privies, pigsties, filth and ashes; open drain full of filth.'

"Workhouse Fold—'Three had the fever in our house (said a woman), one died; privy full, filth overflows.'"

The body of the report, which says that whatever "the neglected state of the poor in Wednesbury," it was worse in Bilston, which, as is well known, was the cholera centre of the Midland district, resumes with the British Schools in Lower High Street; thus:—

"The British and Foreign School, with 140 children, was badly ventilated, few of the windows open at the top. There is a pretty good playground.

"The mortality of the town is said to be no less than four per cent., and the increase in ten years, from 1831, to be 33 per cent., showing that a high rate of mortality is not inconsistent with a rapid increase of population."

A Table of Mortality on p. 322 of the Report shows Wednesbury to be the third worst parish in the district of those enumerated, Kidderminster being the best with 1 death in 48. Thus, Wednesbury statistics stand at the following:—

"Population in 1831 8,437
in 1841 11,625
Annual increase per cent. 1831—1841...3.3.
Deaths in 5 years (1838-42) ... 1,432
Mortality: Annual rate per cent. 2.538.
One death in 39 of population."

Nemesis overtook this wilful neglect of public sanitation, Asiatic Cholera again breaking out in the town in October, 1848. It was over twelve months ere the disease entirely disappeared, in the course of which it had claimed 218 victims in Wednesbury.

So great was the scare that works were closed, business was brought to a standstill, and all the well-to-do inhabitants fled the town, till desolation reigned supreme and grass began to grow in the streets.

The effete Board of Surveyors erected a number of wooden huts in Monway Field near to Moxley to serve as an Hospital. How they also employed a well-known character known as Bonker Turner to act as general undertaker for the parish is told in "Wednesbury Papers" (p. 127). This worthy sometimes accumulated a stack of the coffined victims on either side of the church porch, awaiting the attention of the clergy for the ceremonial of interment.

The mortality at Darlaston was confined almost to one part of that township, and that was at Catherine's Cross on the borders of Wednesbury parish. In this part the people were more than decimated, some homes being nearly cleared out altogether by the fell disease. The cause of this was undoubtedly the sewer of Wednesbury parish, which ran along the boundary line at the back of Pinfold Street —a mere open ditch which lost itself in the hollows and swamps somewhere in the vicinity of Catherine's Cross.

The establishment of a Local Board was but a means to a much desired end. It took years to accomplish the sanitary reformation of the town. Thus the "Wednesbury Observer" of October 17th, 1857, in a leading article on the "Probable advent of the cholera," said:—"It is well known that there are certain places in Wednesbury where the scourge was most terribly fatal on former occasions, and those places are remarkable for filth and wretchedness. The attention of the Local Board was

directed to these places on Monday last, and we rejoice to see that they intend to do their duty. We hope they will fully carry out their intention, and earn for themselves the gratitude and good feeling of the town by the removal of nuisances and the suppression of those dens of filth and abomination (which also are to be found even in Wednesbury) which hold out invitations to cholera, fever, and other diseases."

Dr. Ballard, a Government Inspector, as late as 1875, commented severely on the insanitary condition of certain parts of Wednesbury. A number of slums have now disappeared, among them being Oatmeal Square, Bolton Square, Beggars Row, and Pitts Square. The properties complained of were mostly courts and alleys contained in an area stretching from Portway Road to the High Bullen and Trouse Lane, all densely inhabited. In many other parts pigstyes were allowed too near the dwelling-houses. There was no compulsory notification of disease; disinfection was attempted by the cheap and primitive process of loaning whitewash brushes; and though the general annual death-rate was not particularly high, infantile mortality was at times excessively heavy.

The establishment of the Local Board of Health in 1851 marked an epoch in the history of Wednesbury, at which great changes were coming over the old town. Just prior to this, the ancient civil parish being deemed sufficiently "populous" by virtue of a new Act, had been partitioned into a number of modern ecclesiastical districts; and its spiritual needs, instead of being ministered to by the one mother-church on the hill, had now to be served by a number of daughter churches, namely, St. John's (1846), St. James' (1848), All Saints', Moxley (1851), and the Delves Chapel of Ease (1850)—a history of all which appears in "Religious Wednesbury."

These were gains. Shortly afterwards the parochial institutions were to suffer a loss. This was the closing of the parish Workhouse (September, 1857) in Meeting Street, and the removal of its 60 or 70 paupers to the new Union at West Bromwich (see "History of West Bromwich," p. 102). The latter parish being thus made the head of the new Poor Law Union, an injustice was inflicted on the more important one, which was an old market town; and inasmuch as the Local Government Office in London focussed all its administrative work on the unions, West Bromwich then received an impetus of which it has never since failed to take the fullest advantage. This injustice to Wednesbury was by no means fully redressed when, twelve years later, it became the head of a Parliamentary Borough, which included the parish of West Bromwich.

When the Local Board of Health was first formed, in 1851, it consisted of nine members only. Some years afterwards a Ratepayers' Protection Society, of which the most active agitators were Messrs. William Perry, T. Hitchen, C. Britten, and S. Loxton, secured a more representative body of twelve members; at the same time, however, the property qualification for membership was raised from £500 to £1,000.

Among those constituting the first Board were the Rev. Isaac Clarkson (chairman), and Messrs. S. Lloyd, Joseph Smith, Jesse Whitehouse, Ed. Elwell, Thomas Walker, John Nock Bagnall, Benjamin Round, and James Frost. The first officials were Francis Woodward, clerk; Henry Williams, senior partner in the local bank, Treasurer; John Griffiths, Collector; Dr. Palm, Medical Officer; W. W. Fereday, Surveyor and Inspector of Nuisances. The last-named officer was assisted by his brother, John White Fereday, who five years later succeeded him in the chief office, which he held for twenty-five years. With regard to another office, it is deeply significant that sixteen years later it was even then difficult for the mind of the local administrator to grasp the fact that the first duty in local government was to act as a sanitary authority. In 1867 the Medical Officership of Wednesbury was actually abolished by a formal resolution of the Board of Health! Needless to say that on the vigorous intervention of Mr. Richard Williams the stultifying resolution was almost immediately rescinded.

The newly-constituted authority of 1851 found itself with a wide field of public work before it, but with no organisation to attack that work.

The streets were as yet unlighted with public gas lamps: they were practically unchannelled, and with footpaths virtually unpaved. Worse than all, the town was without any proper water supply. [The establishment of the South Staffordshire Waterworks as a piece of sanitary reform is fully dealt with in Chap. xxi. of "Olden Wednesbury," q.v.] In certain well-known areas zymotic disease always found a congenial home.

The death-rate of Wednesbury for the year 1851 was 26.5 per thousand of the population—which then stood at 14,278. The rateable value of the parish was £31,855.

When this modern form of local self-government had descended upon Wednesbury in the manner above described, it is curious to notice how absolutely devoid the place was of all public institutions. Its municipal equipment was nil. The neglect of past generations of public men had been complete.

In a succeeding chapter it will be interesting to trace the method, and the stages, by which these public deficiencies were sought to be made good.

XLVII.—PROGRESS UNDER A LOCAL BOARD—THE PARLIAMENTARY BOROUGH OF WEDNESBURY.

One of the first duties of the Local Board of Health was to undertake the responsibilities of a Lighting Board for Wednesbury. Along some of the principal streets gas-lamps were erected in 1853; in the sacred cause of economy the lamps were at first placed at double the usual distance apart; but the public were given assurance that the intermediate lamps would be forthcoming at some prosperous but indefinite future.

As a further measure of economy not a single street lamp was lighted within the parish from the May-day of each year to that date in August which was fixed for Wolverhampton Races—a local race meeting which was wont to crowd the Holyhead Road with an enormous amount of vehicular traffic, especially in the evening when the pleasure-seekers were returning from the races. This parsimonious practice in the public street-lighting of the town was in force for twenty years.

When in 1875 the Corporation of Birmingham obtained Parliamentary powers to acquire the property of the Birmingham and Staffordshire Gas Light Co., Wednesbury was one of those local authorities which did not avail themselves of the opportunity of becoming possessed of the portion of the undertaking lying within their respective boundaries. Wednesbury is still supplied with gas by Birmingham; the gas profits, amounting to several thousands of pounds per annum, are a considerable source of income to that city.

In the paving of the footpaths the "penal pebbles" were superseded by blue bricks. A useful blue paving brick with the surface slightly roughened into a checkerwork of diamonds was introduced by the Town Surveyor, Mr. John W. Fereday. Only the main streets received attention; and in many of these the severe rule of economy then in vogue restricted the new paving to that half of the footpath nearer the kerbstone, leaving the other half—much of it under the dripping eaves of unspouted houses—with its old pebble pavement.

In 1861 the Market rights were purchased by the Local Board, from the ladies of the Manor, for the sum of £1,000. At that time the tolls were let to Mrs. Catharine Tibbets for £60 a year. A very full account of the connection of the Tibbets family with the Market Tolls is given in Bagnall's "Wednesbury," pp. 148-154. "Olden Wednesbury" devotes the whole of chap. iv. to "The Markets and Fairs."

After the lighting and the paving, one of the most pressing questions was the provision of Public Offices—the setting up of a home and a habitation for the new authority—a centre from which to direct its operations. A few of the bolder and more progressive spirits even dared to ask for a Town Hall.

The erection of Public Offices for the town proved to be another of those simple matters of rudimentary civic life which could be made to occupy Wednesbury for an unwarrantable length of time. At first the Board of Health held their meetings in the office of their Clerk, then in Offices in Lower High Street (opposite the Turk's Head Hotel), and next at make-shift premises in Little Russell Street.

When the inclusion of a Town Hall was pressed the old spirit of economy manifested itself in a demand for a combined scheme by which the two institutions might be provided at the price of one. Ultimately the Public Offices in Holyhead Road were erected (1867) at a cost of £2,500, which sum included the purchase of land at the rear upon which to erect the proposed Town Hall at some future time. Wednesbury was to acquire its public buildings on the instalment plan.

According to John Wesley's "Journal" the Market Cross was in 1742 designated the "Town Hall." The second edifice in Wednes-bury to bear this designation was the Public Assembly Room in Russell Street, otherwise the old Police Station.

Tremendous opposition was raised to the proposed erection of a real Town Hall ; such a building was looked upon as a luxury quite unnecessary for the simple-minded folk of Wednesbury. Hitherto this community had been quite content to use for their concerts or other public gatherings such large buildings as the school-rooms ; the Theatre (or Public Hall, as it was called for the purposes of hiring) in Earp's Lane ; the Assembly Rooms (or old Police Station) in Russell Street ; the large Music Hall in the Back Field of the Green Dragon Inn ; or not infrequently on popular occasions, as their primitive Saxon forefathers had done, in the open air.

The site in Holyhead Road had been secured mainly because it was cheap ; it had but re-cently been agricultural land, on which wheat was grown. The consent of the ratepayers to put up a Hall for the public assemblies of the town's people was eventually obtained by a plebescite ; and after the estimates had been cut down to the lowest possible figure (£2,700) the work of building was allowed to proceed. Such were the conditions under which the pre-sent Town Hall of Wednesbury was erected ; and by which the town was put in possession of a factory-like structure which seems to im-plore the stranger : "Please do not look at my back !"

On 26th June, 1874, the new Town Hall was opened with some amount of ceremony, Mr. Richard Williams, Chairman of the Local Board, doing the honours, and representing the town on that occasion. Among those pre-sent were the Bishop of Lichfield (Dr. Selwyn), Lord Wrottesley (Lord Lieutenant of the County), Mr. Arthur M. Bass (now Lord Burton), one of the Members for East Stafford-shire, and Mr. Alexander Brogden, M.P. for Wednesbury. The borough member had pre-sented an organ for the new Town Hall, which was opened at the same time by Mr. Best, organist of St. George's Hall, Liverpool. There was a banquet at which congratulatory speeches were delivered ; but even Mr. Richard Williams could not but feel some amount of re-gret for the extreme plainness with which parochial parsimony had endowed the build-ing. His only satisfaction after years of con-troversy was that it would at least fulfil its main purpose as a blessing to the community, by becoming a centre of social and political in-tercourse, and a means of intellectual and moral recreation.

In March, 1868, the Cemetery was opened. Its area was 12¼ acres—an additional 1¼ acres were added at the n.w. corner in 1885—and its cost was £10,000. The controversy which had raged over the provision of this highly necessary public institution was the longest and perhaps the most bitter which had ever ruffled the social and political surface of Wednesbury—it was a relic of the Church Rates controversy (as is fully set forth in "Religious Wednesbury," p. 113) in which it had been proposed to make a Ceme-tery at The Mounts rather than make a further enlargement of the old Parish Churchyard (1851).

In 1874 Wednesbury Wake was formally abolished in an order signed by the Home Secretary, and issued in response to an appli-cation from the Local Board of Health, incited thereto by the action of its Chairman, Mr. Richard Williams, who looked upon the annual occurrence of this ancient institution as a de-moralising orgie of one week's unbridled licence in every year. Perhaps the only good which can be claimed for it was its incentive to clean-liness by an annual purification of the place, a matter of no small moment in those insani-tary days ; for a month before the Wake the good folk of Wednesbury made it a regular cus-tom to clean their houses from attic to cellar, and to accomplish wonderful transformations by the aid of paint and whitewash. This was in preparation for the thousands of visitors who thronged into the town at every Wake, a local holiday more popular than all the national feast-days in the year's calendar. It was purely a pleasure fair, held by prescriptive right in the public thoroughfares ; and at one time extended from High Bullen, through the Market Place, to Bridge Street. In this re-spect, as an obstruction to the growing traffic of the streets, it was an unmitigated nuisance.*

But though abolished from the public streets it survives still wherever a piece of private land may be hired sufficiently large to accommodate the necessary aggregation of shows, booths, merry-go-rounds, and other delights which appeal to the vulgar mind. A monograph on the subject of Wednesbury Wake constitutes chap. iii. of "The Wednesbury Papers."

The Free Library and Public Baths, opened in 1878, were erected at a total cost amounting to upwards of £6,700. Towards the former institution £1,200 were freely subscribed by the public; and at its opening the library of books belonging to the old Mechanics' Institute was transferred bodily to its shelves. Into all this public generosity the Free Library maintains but a struggling existence, owing to the small amount per annum (about £300) provided by the maximum rate of 1d. in the £ allowed for its support by the Act under which it was provided. It was a permissible piece of economy to combine the two institutions under one roof; but in this case the estimates were cut down by the Board so remorsely that the maintenance of the fabric of the Baths has ever since been disproportionately burdensome. The name of one member, Mr. Joseph Wilkes Marsh. will always be honourably remembered in connection with the promotion of the Free Library scheme.

No doubt the crowning work of the Board of Health as a Sanitary Authority was the deep drainage of the town.

It was in 1883 that at length a formal resolution was passed, after years of controversy, that the town should be sewered; the estimated cost was £35,000.

A few months previously a Government Inquiry had been held at Wednesbury Town Hall respecting a joint scheme for treating the sewage of Wednesbury, Darlaston, Tipton, and Coseley, which had been submitted to the various authorities concerned in October, 1882. The Joint Outfall Works were to be in the Tame valley near Newton Road Station; a Joint Board of fifteen members, called the Wednesbury Union Drainage Board, was to manage the scheme—Tipton having 6, Wednesbury 5, Darlaston 3, and Coseley 1 representatives respectively. The estimated joint population was then 68,151; but provision was made to deal with the sewage of 90,188, at a total cost of £79,500. The other three places were not favourable to a united effort, and so the scheme fell through.

There is extant an official Report of this Inquiry; it gives the evidence in full, as taken down by shorthand writers; it has a number of comparative tables, engineers' reports, and a capital map of the united district; altogether it affords an admirable compendium of a twenty years' controversy.

The system sanctioned in 1883 was not to deal with storm water; the sewage was to be treated in tanks, and then filtered through the land into the Tame. The Wednesbury Sewage Farm at Bescot was opened in 1888. Two years later it was found necessary for the Corporation to borrow another £8,000 with which to make the house connections with the new street sewers—another matter for controversy and wasteful delay in testing the efficacy of a scheme which had been provided at the expenditure of so much time and money.

It was Alderman Richard Williams' boast in 1886 that the Local Board of Health had "found Wednesbury a lazar house, and left it a Black Country sanatorium." The death-rate was 17.7 per thousand of the population (estimated at 25,000), as against 26.5 in 1851, and below the average of the whole country.

The rateable value of Wednesbury was £85,960 in 1886.

* * * * *

Wednesbury was one of the first towns to take advantage of the Elementary Education Act. and elected its first School Board in March, 1871. Chap. vii. of "The Wednesbury Papers" deals with the subject of the town's educational progress. The triennial Reports of the School Board officially record the progress of elementary education in Wednesbury for the past thirty years; the town, however, has never possessed any high school or other equipment for giving secondary education.

* * * * * *

Although constitutionally reluctant to spend money itself upon public improvements, the Local Board was always willing to grant facilities for the provision of public conveniences through the efforts of private enterprise. In this spirit the introduction of Tramways into the town was cordially welcomed.

In 1882 was established the South Staffordshire Tramways Company, on the flotation of which such an excessive amount was spent as "promotion money" that the concern was overloaded with capital beyond the utmost possible capacity of its earning powers. Although not a financial success, it has been a great advantage to the travelling public of Wednesbury, which became the centre of this system of tramways, with the offices and sheds located at King's Hill. The first section was completed in 1883. In 1884 were opened the lines from Wednesbury to Dudley, and from Darlaston to Moxley; then from Wednesbury to Bloxwich, and from Darlaston to Pleck. How far the tramways adversely affected the local railways has already been mentioned as regards the Darlaston Branch Railway (pp. 4 and 112). In 1890 the railway train service from Wednesbury (L. and N.-W.R.) to Ocker Hill and Princess End was also suspended — both branches had been opened in 1863. The whole of this tramway was at first worked by steam traction; but in 1893 all the sections on the Walsall side of Wednesbury had overhead electric traction substituted.

* * * * * *

During the reign of the Local Board of Health Wednesbury secured an accession of dignity by being made a Parliamentary Borough.

Undoubtedly Wednesbury received a great impetus when, by the Reform Bill of 1867, it was selected to be the head of a new Parliamentary Borough, which included the populoue parishes of Wednesbury. West Bromwich, Tipton, and Darlaston. Staffordshire was then (since 1832) in two Parliamentary Divisions, North and South; these four parishes being part of the South Staffordshire Constituency. Not only was Wednesbury erected into a borough, but the county was made into three electoral districts, respectively named North, West, and East; Wednesbury "forty-shilling freeholders" being in East Staffordshire for their county voting.

Wednesbury has always been a working-man's constituency, and in those days there were never lacking good electoral cries to take the popular fancy. Hence there were plenty of Liberal candidates forthcoming, among them being Mr. Robinson, of Wednesbury Oak; Mr. Waddy, Q.C., whose mother was a Wednesbury woman; Commissioner Kerr, a London Judge; and Mr. Alexander Brogden, who was ultimately selected to fight the Liberal cause. The other candidates who went to the poll were Mr. Thomas Eades Walker, of the Patent Shaft Works, Conservative; and Dr. Kenealy, Independent.

The nominations were made on Monday, November 16th, 1868, from a wooden husting erected along the south side of the Market Place, and looking towards Upper High Street. The whole space was thronged, each candidate's supporters marching in with colours flying from the several parishes constituting the Parliamentary borough; every window and house-top in the Market Place was one vast sea of heads. How lively the proceedings were may be gathered from the newspapers of the period; they were worthy of the best traditions of an old-fashioned election. There was some amount of rioting, and special constables had to be sworn in. Next day was the polling, and a force of 300 police was marched into the borough. It was then open voting, and the state of the poll, as gathered by mounted messengers visiting every polling booth in the constituency, was published from hour to hour. Of the 15,000 voters, 10,995 actually went to the poll. The result was declared:—

Brogden (L.)	... ...	6,201
Walker (C.)	... ...	3,809
Kenealy	... ...	985

Thousands of pounds were spent upon this contest; some notice of the remarkable election literature issued is given in "Wednesbury Papers," pp. 88-89.

At the next general election (1874) Mr. Brogden was opposed by Mr. Richard Mills, a Darlaston ironmaster. The result of the election was:—

Brogden (L.)	... ...	7,530
Mills (C.)	... ...	5,813

In 1880, at a general election, Mr. F. W. Isaacson, who afterwards sat for Stepney, opposed Mr. Brogden; but, finding the candidature of a Conservative hopeless, endeavoured to withdraw. His withdrawal was too late, and the result was that the few votes recorded for him cost the remarkable sum of £18 2s. 1d. each, by far the highest average of any candidate in England at that election:—

Brogden (L.)	... ...	6,212
Isaacson (C.)	... ...	207

The next Re-distribution Bill (1884) took West Bromwich out of the Borough of Wednesbury, and erected it into a new separate Parliamentary Borough of itself. At the same time the populous county of Stafford was made into seven electoral divisions, Wednesbury freeholders having to vote in the Handsworth Division, one of the largest one-member constituencies in the kingdom, as the borough of Wednesbury had formerly been.

Mr. Alexander Brogden, who was a mineowner, and member of a large firm of contractors—in 1862 Messrs. Brogden had a disputed claim of £250,000 on contracts executed for the Government of New Zealand—had failed in 1884 with liabilities amounting to £728,830. This being so, Mr. Brogden was not asked by the Liberals to stand again at the general election of November, 1885. Among those brought forward were Mr. William Willis, Q.C., and Mr. C. W. Plowden, who afterwards sat for Wolverhampton; but the candidate selected by the Wednesbury Liberal Federation was the Hon. Philip James Stanhope. When the election was over, it was found that the Conservative cause, when fought by a candidate with strong local connections was by no means hopeless, his opponent being Mr. Wilson Lloyd, a Wednesbury ironmaster, and a native of the town. The poll was:—

Lloyd (C.)	... ...	4,628
Stanhope (L.)	... ...	4,433

Early next year Mr. Gladstone challenged the constituencies on his famous Home Rule Bill; at Wednesbury the same two candidates went to the poll, which was taken 6th July, 1886, and the result declared was:—

Stanhope (Home Ruler)	...	4,888
Lloyd (C.)	... ...	4,221

The same great question of Irish Home Rule was fought out again at the next general election between these same two political antagonists, and the result declared at midnight 6th July, 1892, was:—

Lloyd (C.)	... ...	4,986
Stanhope (H.R.)	... ...	4,926

At the general election of 1895 the candidates were Mr Walford Davis Green, a barrister, and a grandson of the late Mr. Thomas Davis, ironmaster, of Hill Top who stood as a Unionist and Conservative; and Mr. Charles Roberts, University lecturer, who stood as a Gladstonian Home Ruler. The poll declared at midnight, 16th July, 1895, was:—

Green	... ...	4,924
Roberts	... ...	4,733

The next general election was an appeal to the country on the question of vigorously prosecuting the Boer War. On this occasion the Liberals adopted the policy of running a candidate with strong local connections, selecting for their purpose Mr. Enoch Horton, a Darlaston manufacturer. But Home Rule had so shattered the Liberal party in Wednesbury, as elsewhere in Great Britain, that even these tactics availed them little. The poll, taken October 3rd, 1900, resulted as follows:—

Green (C. and U.)	... ...	4,733
Horton (L.)	... ...	4,558

XLVIII.—THE MUNICIPAL BOROUGH.

The inception of the idea to incorporate the town of Wednesbury had its rise among the few progressive spirits on the Local Board of Health. But the Clerk of that body, in response to their request, made a report on the subject which was distinctly adverse to the proposal. Mr. Joseph Smith's report, dated July 8th, 1880, while admitting that the election of representatives by ballot, instead of by voting-papers (as was done in the case of Local Boards), would be "a decided advantage," and that there was "no ground for the current belief that a Municipal Corporation would be more expensive than a Local Board," gave with no uncertain voice his legal and official opinion that the advantages hoped for would prove "of a sentimental rather than of a practical nature"; and that unless Darlaston could be included within the boundaries of the proposed municipality, so as to warrant the setting up of a borough magistracy, and the taking over of the control of the police, the proposal should be abandoned.

The proposal, however, was revived a few years later, the promoters this time being outside the Board. It was sought to quicken the interest in the public life of the town, and to elevate it by an accession of civic dignity.

In the face of much latent opposition, the promoters had to proceed warily. Tactfully all opposing interests were eventually reconciled, and a Town's Meeting was held to consider the question of Incorporation on December 9th, 1884. The Wednesbury and other local newspapers of that date will disclose those particulars of the memorable meeting in the Town Hall, which it will not be necessary to recapitulate here. The proposed inclusion of Darlaston had been entirely dropped previous to the meeting.

A Consultative Committee was appointed, and a Petition for the incorporation of the Town of Wednesbury as a Municipal Borough was presented to the Privy Council.

A Government Commissioner was sent to hold an Inquiry at Wednesbury Town Hall, on Tuesday, 28th July, 1885, when the scheme was practically unopposed. The evidence then given has been printed and officially published. The Charter of Incorporation was duly granted, and reached Wednesbury on 15th July, 1886. Mr. Richard Williams, J.P., or, in default, Mr. Alfred Elwell, J.P., was appointed to perform all the duties of a Mayor in acting as a Returning Officer for the first election of Councillors on the following November 1st. When the Town Council had been elected, Mr. Richard Williams was unanimously chosen as the first Mayor of Wednesbury.

Mr. Joseph Smith became first Town Clerk. On his resignation, in 1889, he was succeeded by Mr. George Rose, M.A. Mr. Rose died in 1897, and was succeeded by the present Town Clerk, Mr. Thomas Jones.

Whether the incorporation of the town realised the expectations of those who promoted the scheme by raising the tone of its municipal life; or whether it still continued its old-world policy, like the close corporations of former centuries, this is neither the time nor the place to determine. But certain it is that the new borough of Wednesbury heartily accepted all the outward forms and ceremonies of municipal life, and eagerly equipped itself with all the trappings of office necessary to maintain the traditional dignity of a borough town.

At once a public subscription provided a very handsome Mayoral chain, while the first Mayor, Alderman R. Williams, J.P. presented the town with a Mayoral Mace. The second Mayor, Alderman Wilson Lloyd, J.P., gave a Loving Cup, with which to grace the board at all civic banquets. The latest addition to the municipal plate chest was made in 1901, when a Mayoress Chain was given by Councillor John Knowles, J.P., to commemorate his third year of office in the Mayoral Chair.

One of the first dignities with which the new borough had to invest itself was the bearing of heraldic arms. A grant of arms was duly made by Heralds' College in full legal form; and Wednesbury is one of the few boroughs whose arms are not bogus.

In heraldic language the Borough Arms are thus described:—

"Sable, upon a Fesse argent between two lions passant of the last, crowned or, the emblem of the planet Mars between two lozenges of the field. And for the Crest, on a wreath of the colours, in front of the rising sun or, a tower with flames of fire proper, and charged with the emblems of Mars, as in the Arms." In more popular language—the black shield has two silver lions crowned with gold (which was anciently the arms of the Heronville family, lords of Wednesbury), one above and the other below the fesse, or band of silver which runs across the middle of it, and on which are two black diamonds (in allusion to the town's wealth of coal), and the symbol of Mars, which has a double meaning. It is the alchemic symbol of Iron, and it also stands for Woden, from whom the name of the town was derived, because Woden was the Mars of the Saxons, being their God of War. The Crest is a Tower in flames, which was formerly the crest of the Hopkins family of Wednesbury; but the Tower on the borough device bears upon it the symbol of iron, which approximates it as nearly to a blast furnace as the science of heraldry will permit. Behind the Tower is a rising sun, emblematical of the rising hopes which animated the promoters of incorporation for the future prosperity of Wednesbury. The Latin motto, "Arte, Marte, Vigore," signifies "By skill, by iron, by energy"; but here the "Marte" has a double meaning, the second signification being "By arms"—a reference to the old staple trade of Wednesbury in gun-locks and gun-barrels.

There will be little need here to do more than summarise the events in the municipal, political, and social history of Wednesbury since the year 1886. All the municipal records are preserved in great detail in the official Reports of the various Committees, issued yearly by order of the Town Council. Complementary to them, RYDER'S ANNUAL will be found to contain in a retrospective form a perfect survey of Wednesbury life from year to year, in its political, social, religious, and every other aspect—to say nothing of the historic value attaching to these publications by virtue of their pictorial record of all the more interesting contemporary local events.

The Mayoralty of Alderman Williams was signalised by the opening of a public park on Queen Victoria's Jubilee Day in 1887. In the earlier years of the century the people of Wednesbury had made The Mounts their recreation ground, though apparently without any legal right to do so. This land had now become a desolate mining waste, while the Manorial Common Lands at Delves Green had been cut off by railways till they were practically inaccessible. The same promoters who had brought the incorporation scheme to fruition had followed up by promoting this acquisition of a public recreation ground. Some 24 acres of land, a third of them constituting an old pit-mound, were purchased and laid out at a total cost of about £6,000. There can be little doubt as to the popularity and success of Brunswick Park—as the first public " lung " of Wednesbury was called. This municipal venture at least has been thought worthy of repetition. Mr. W. Hy. Lloyd during his Mayoralty dedicated a piece of land in Portway Road as a public playground; and in 1898 a sum of £600 was spent on adapting a colliery waste at King's Hill to the purposes of a public park.

Early in 1889 the Town Council recognised the fact that the open markets were getting later, and issued the following notice with regard to the times of holding the Saturday markets :—

" BOROUGH OF WEDNESBURY."

" TAKE NOTICE, that under the Bye-Laws with respect to the MARKETS, the hours of Market on SATURDAY are from 12 o'clock at noon until 11 o'clock at night.

" AND FURTHER TAKE NOTICE that proceedings will be immediately taken against any Occupier of Stalls who shall not have removed his goods before 11.30 p.m. on any Saturday.

" BY ORDER.

" Municipal Offices, Wednesbury,
" January, 1889."

At various times there have been feeble attempts to supersede the open markets by the provision of a Market Hall. But Black Country people have always evinced a decided antipathy to covered markets.

The Friday market was originally held between 8 a.m. and noon, the produce from market gardeners on the Worcestershire side, and from Lichfield in the opposite direction, being brought in by carts and wagons, which travelled all night. Since the era of railways, and the operation of the Factory Act, it has got later and later till it is now practically an evening market.

The following is a copy of another official notice, which was issued ten years ago, and marks an unsuccessful attempt to establish early wholesale markets :—

" BOROUGH OF WEDNESBURY.

" WHOLESALE MARKET.

" NOTICE is hereby given that on and after Friday, the 4th day of November next, it is intended to hold a WHOLESALE MARKET at Wednesbury, on FRIDAY and SATURDAY in each week, the Market on each day to commence at Six o'clock in the morning.

" For further information apply to the Market Lessee, Mr. Robert Yates, Wood Green, Wednesbury, or to the undersigned.

" GEORGE ROSE,
" Town Clerk.

" Town Clerk's Office, Wednesbury,
" 13th October, 1892."

The new Act, which in 1889 created County Councils, did not constitute Wednesbury a County Borough, because its population was too far below the standard figure, which had been fixed at 50,000. A suggestion was made at the time that Wednesbury should be constituted a county borough by the inclusion of Darlaston and Tipton; a similar proposal was also made to group the Pottery towns. Local jealousies prevented both proposals being carried into effect, although the amalgamation of the group of towns in the northern portion of the county is likely to be consummated in the near future.

As Wednesbury was not made independent of the Staffordshire County Council, it was allotted two representatives on that body. The municipal borough was divided for this purpose into two electoral divisions, known as the Central and Suburban Divisions. At the same time Wednesbury became the magisterial licensing centre for Tipton and Darlaston.

Had Wednesbury become a county borough, as proposed, a calculation based on the figures then in use showed that the three parishes would have benefited to the total extent of £2,362 per annum net, from Imperial taxes given to local purposes.

The idea of an Art Gallery for Wednesbury was first mooted on p. 99 of " The Wednesbury Papers," published in 1884. The suggestion made there evidently bore fruit. When Mrs. Edwin Richards, of The Limes, Wood Green, died, in 1885, it was found that she had made testamentary provision for the establishment of an Art Gallery. She bequeathed to the town her collection of pictures, £2,000 towards a public building in which to place them, £1,000 to be invested towards the maintenance of a curator, and £500 for the re-guilding of the picture frames. A further sum of £2,000 was raised by public subscription to provide a suitable Art Gallery. The building was commenced in 1890 on a vacant site next to the Town Hall. It was opened in 1891, advantage having been taken by the Town Council to improve the approaches to the Town Hall, and to harmonise the two buildings, so as to make one a complement of the other when used on the occasion of any great public function. The wretchedness of the accommodation previously provided by the Town Hall may be gauged by the fact that it cost nearly £2,000 of the public moneys to make this very essential improvement. An "Art Gallery Memento," consisting of a letter-press description of the building, accompanied by suitable illustrations, was issued on the occasion from the office of "The Wednesbury Herald."

The municipal event which signalised the year 1893 was the creation of a Borough Bench for Wednesbury. The Town Council had petitioned the Privy Council for this privilege in 1890; but the county justices of the Petty Sessional Division had petitioned the Lord Chancellor in opposition to the prayer of the Town Council. The opposition was, for the time, successful, but with a change of Government the petition of the Town Council was renewed. The new Lord Chancellor, Lord Herschel, and the new Home Secretary, Mr. Asquith, were favourably disposed, and granted a separate Commission of the Peace for the Borough of Wednesbury.

At the Free Library buildings a philanthropic committee, at the head of which was Mr. Richard Williams, had long carried on some very successful Science and Art classes. In 1884 a Chemical Laboratory had been erected and equipped there. All this work was accomplished solely by voluntary subscriptions and the Government grants earned by the students on examination. Few institutions in Wednesbury ever accomplished so large an amount of good by means of so little money.

In 1892 this voluntary management was superseded by paid official control, when a Municipal Technical School was established. Certain sums of the public revenue were devoted to this object by the Town Council and the County Council. The art classes were removed to the Art Gallery, but the science classes remained at the Free Library till 1895, the last year of their existence there being marred by an examination scandal.

In August, 1896, the Science School in Holyhead Road was opened. This building cost about £2,000, half of which was contributed by the Staffordshire County Council and the Government Science and Art Department in London. The science classes were then removed from the Free Library building (which was re-instated to serve more fittingly as a temple of literature) to the new building in Holyhead Road. Under the joint control of the two Councils the Wednesbury science classes have been conspicuously successful, the results obtained in metallurgy in some years eclipsing those obtained in London or any other town.

Having no municipal gasworks the question of Electric Lighting has engaged the attention of the Wednesbury Town Council for several years past. In 1889 an order for Electric Lighting was obtained from the Board of Trade; but the proposal was abandoned and the order lapsed. In 1898 the Council offered strong opposition to a private company which proposed to supply the town; but the fact remains that at the present time there are two "orders" out for supplying Wednesbury, one public held by the Town Council, and a private one in the hands of the Midland Electric Power Corporation. This company has laid down large works at Lea Brook for the supply of a number of Black Country towns, but has not yet commenced operations. It is not finally decided whether Wednesbury will adopt electricity as an illuminant for public street lighting; for private purposes there have long been a considerable number of private installations in the town.

A recently acquired municipal building is the Fire Station in Upper High Street, which was opened in 1899, when a new steam Fire Engine was also provided. The Fire Brigade is a volunteer body whose willing efforts have always been handicapped by the failure of the authorities to properly horse the engines. An account of the Wednesbury Fire Brigade constitutes one of the chapters of "The Wednesbury Papers."

If it may be looked upon as a permanent building, the newest municipal institution in Wednesbury is the Isolation Hospital at Moxley. The erections are mere wooden shells with coverings of corrugated iron; they comprise two wards, 20 feet wide, one 50 feet long and the other 30 feet in length, the two capable of holding 16 beds, or 24 in cases of necessity. There are also a nurses' room, a mortuary, an ambulance shed, a disinfecting stove-room, and the usual out-offices. The total outlay on the undertaking has been about £1,200; and the result has been the provision of an Hospital that is more useful than ornamental. Previous to this there had long been temporary hospital sheds in Crankhall Lane.

In 1901 the population was returned at 26,544; and in the following year the Registrar-General began to include Wednesbury as one of the large towns in the official list for which vital statistics are periodically published. The death-rate of Wednesbury for the year 1901 was as low as 14.5 per thousand; which really seems to prove that a smoky atmosphere is more fatal to disease germs than to human beings.

The rateable value of the town is now about £94,000: a rate of 1d. in the £ produces £360 for Poor Law purposes, but only £305 for a District Rate—the difference being accounted for by the different methods allowed for compounding.

The rates for municipal purposes are this year (1902) 4s. 2d. in the £. The town possesses no remunerative undertakings, so that there is no income from municipal trading. On the other hand the Sewerage Scheme alone has cost the town £59,000, and requires £1,800 a year for its upkeep. The additional expenditure upon it (see p. 117) since the incorporation of the town has been necessitated by payment for wayleaves where main sewers pass under private lands; by the renewal of sewers broken through mining subsidences; and more particularly by changes at the Outfall Works. The original scheme of treatment was by chemical precipitation and intermittent downward filtration through land; this has recently been modified, and costly experiments have been made with the polarite system and again with the still newer bacterial system.

The municipal equipment of Wednesbury has been effected on so modest a scale that the total value of all its estates and buildings does not equal the amount spent on the sewering of the town. A local evening newspaper recently criticising the last municipal budget said that "for some years Wednesbury has been one of the most backward amongst Black Country municipalities for there have been no gigantic enterprises to drain the public exchequer as in most other places."

Among extra-municipal institutions it may be mentioned that the Post Office built by Government in Holyhead Road was opened in March, 1883, and the Volunteer Drill Hall, Bridge Street, in 1898.

But the extra-municipal institution which has been more intimately connected with the municipal life of the place is the Nurses' Institute, Wood Green Road, erected as a memento of Queen Victoria's Diamond Jubilee in 1897. In the January of that year, at a public meeting the Mayor, Alderman I. Oldbury, J.P., offered to give £250 towards a scheme for providing a Cottage Hospital as a fitting memorial of the Queen's long reign; the proposal was received with favour, and at the adjourned meeting a month later was formally confirmed. In the meantime certain influences had been at work so adverse to the proposed establishment of a Cottage Hospital that the Mayor withdrew his generous offer; and the Town's meeting on May 3rd broke up in disorder, the working classes clamouring lustily for the Cottage Hospital as originally proposed, from which, however, the moneyed portion of the meeting held most resolutely aloof, favouring a substituted proposal for a Nursing Institute. This newer scheme was eventually carried into effect.

While the Brunswick Park commemorates Queen Victoria's Jubilee (1887) and the Nurses' Home her Diamond Jubilee (1897), no separate memorial marks the local celebration of Edward VII.'s Coronation (1902). A slight extension of the Nurses' institute, the inception of which had raised a passing storm in the town five years previously, was deemed all-sufficient to satisfy Wednesbury's aspirations on this historic occasion.

XLIX.—RELIGIOUS CHARACTERISTICS.—THE WEDNESBURY CAREER OF "AN ESCAPED MONK."

The religious life of Wednesbury, from the earliest times to the present day, has been fully treated in the volume entitled "Religious Wednesbury." Therein will be found some account of the Woden worship, from which the town derived its name, and the full story of the parish church from its pre-Reformation days, when—

"The Old Church floor was swept
    By many a long dark stole,
As the kneeling priests round him that slept
    Sang mass for the parted soul."

Concerning the fabric of the Town's most interesting building, it is almost possible to fix the year when the first stone edifice replaced the ancient wooden Saxon church. Hales Owen Abbey was completed in 1218; by 1248 the Abbey had become possessed of the great tithes of Wednesbury: this affords the clue.

When the Abbey was finished, its clerical architect and its building staff, probably formed into a gild, were prepared to undertake other similar work in the neighbourhood. Wednesbury parish probably wanted its wooden nave repaired, and the building gild of the religious community offered to do the work and give a permanent stone structure in place thereof for a consideration. The gilds had no capital, and the parish had no funds, but by an equitable arrangement common to the period this difficulty was overcome. The religious building fraternity did the work, and accepted in payment a perpetual annuity —in other words, the great tithes of the parish. The patron did not give the tithes with the intention of injuring the parish, although this result unfortunately ensued; the intention was to get a permanent church and a cheaper clergyman—a vicarius in place of its rector, or parson.

Doubtless it was by some such mediæval contracting as this that Wednesbury was provided with its first stone-built church, and its first Vicar at the same time, between the years 1218 and 1248.

In tracing the decadence of the Protestant Church of England, it is disclosed that Wednesbury was, perhaps, less unfortunate than some of the neighbouring towns in the character of its parish clergy in the dark and degraded days of the cock-fighting and bull-baiting era a century ago.

At Willenhall, for instance, there was Parson Moreton, who occasionally occupied the pulpit of Wednesbury Church. This cleric of the old school was a sportsman, who did not draw the line at cock-fighting. He was a jovial three-bottle man, whose social qualities made him welcome among any set of his contemporaries. He was always supposed to be a scion of royalty; and tradition says that he once successfully intervened to save from the gallows an individual, closely connected with two of the leading families in Darlaston, who had the misfortune to be convicted of sheep-stealing. It is also a subject of tradition that in riding through Darlaston Parson Moreton never refused to comply with a request to baptise a child, willingly performing the cere-mony in primitive style at the pool on The Green.

The steady growth of Nonconformity in the eighteenth century cannot be a matter of marvel when the negligence of the beneficed clergy is borne in mind. Particularly strong was the hold which Wesley's Methodism took upon the minds of the modern Mercian of South Staffordshire. In this connection it is interesting to note that the well-known novelist, Quiller Couch, accepts a Wednes-bury disciple of John Wesley as the type of man to become the founder of a new sect.

The novelist takes the following incidents as a prologue to his pleasing volume of fiction, "Ia":—

"The Second Advent Saints were founded in Cornwall by the Rev. Onesimus Heathcote, who had gone there from Wednesbury in 1761 to preach the Word as a follower of Wesley. In a small fishing village there he had gathered a large flock around him, but afterwards suf-fered the loss of nine-tenths of it, rather than follow Wesley into Arminianism.

"Heathcote then gave up preaching, and kept a small shop, where he sold gingerbread. Soon after this rupture between the Calvinist Methodists and the Arminian Methodists, a strange thing occurred in this quiet village. One Mary Penno, a maiden lady of some small property, who was amongst those who had adhered to Calvinism when the rest of the Wesleyans had declared against Predestina-tion, had a wonderful vision. According to her own sworn depositions, being then 38 years of age, Mary Penno, on the afternoon of Lady Day, 1773, as she was passing an old pilchard-curing store, saw a bright light therein, and on looking through the open win-dow saw the form of a man lying upon the earthen floor, and writing thereon with his finger, 'Surely I come quickly.' There is the further sworn testimony of others, more or less corroborative.

"The Rev. O. Heathcote had known Mary Penno for several years, and always regarded her as a woman of sound judgment, able to take care of herself in all business matters. Great excitement prevailed in the locality over this vision, and many began to expect daily and hourly our Lord's second coming. Within three months Heathcote married Mary Penno, who had an income of £300 a year; and with her he founded the sect of Second Adven-tists. They built a temple on the spot where Mary Penno had seen the apparition: it was a round house, with a conical roof, and four win-dows, one towards each cardinal point of the compass. A circular pulpit occupied the centre of the floor, giving the preacher a clear view on every side—as it were an outlook for the great advent. The only ornament was a frieze bearing the inscription as continuous and devoid of punctuation as any hiero-glyphic, 'He that testifieth these things said surely I come quickly, Amen Even so come Lord Jesus.' The church government con-sisted of five Elders, elected for life, and who might be either male or female. Heathcote and his wife drew up the articles of Faith and Discipline. When, four years later, Mary Heathcote died in child-bed, there were close on eight hundred followers in the neighbour-hood. The Rev. Onesimus, after another five years, removed (1783) to Brixton, and founded the first affiliated branch of the Saints. At the close of the century the faith had spread, mainly through emigrants, to other conti-nents; and everywhere they built their meet-ing-houses on the same pattern as that of the obscure chapel on the sandhills of Revyer."

The name Onesimus savours strongly of old Black Country Methodism. The whole nar-rative is too characteristic to be entirely with-out some substratum of fact.

Another literary example of the use of a Black Country dissenter, as a type of charac-ter distinctive enough for fictional purposes, is that of Charles Dickens. Doubtless the character is caricatured in true Dickensian fashion; but nevertheless it stands out as a distinctive type.

The character occurs in a sketch entitled "George Silverman's Explanation." "Mr. Verity Hawkyard, of West Bromwich," as the great novelist describes him, was a member of some obscure denomination, who pretended to rescue the child hero from a typhus den in Preston. In reality Brother Hawkyard is all the time defrauding his protege of his inheri-tance—"a courtful of houses in Birmingham," bequeathed by the child's grandfather, "a machine-maker at Birmingham." All the swindling of the helpless orphan is done under the guise of disinterested benevolence, and the character of the unctuous hypocrite is limned as only the pen of Dickens could portray it.

Fact is stranger than fiction. There is a half-forgotten chapter in the religious life of Wednesbury which, though it is not fictional, is even more interesting. The story of "an escaped monk," manufactured for ultra-Pro-testant consumption, is well known; this Wed-nesbury episode is probably not a variant of such stories, but the original fact upon which they were all subsequently based.

The fact that Wednesbury was selected as the place wherein to attempt such an imposs-ture, points to the opinion then prevailing as to the overwhelming strength of its dissenting population, and inferentially of its blind pre-judice against the practices of the Church of Rome. The period, too, for such an attempt was propitious; it was just when the accession to the population of Wednesbury of hundreds of Irish labourers had called for the provision of a Catholic place of worship to meet their spiritual needs.

The following true account of "The Escaped Monk" is extracted from "The Concise History of the Cistercian Order: Appendix O"— a standard work, a copy of which is in the Library of St. Bernard's Monastery:—

"On Saturday evening, January 20th, 1849, a young man came to Mt. St. Bernard's Abbey and asked for lodgings, saying that he had walked a very great distance during that day. He was given some refreshments, and then retired to rest. On the following day he told the guest-master that he was Francis Augustus Arkwright, son of the great Mr. Arkwright, of Derby. He, moreover, stated that on account of his recent conversion to Catholicism he had been cruelly persecuted by his parents, and in consequence he had run away from home. The guest-master suspecting that he was dealing with an impostor politely told the man that he could not be received as a guest without references; he was, however, permitted to stay until Monday morning.

"Before leaving the monastery he requested that his hair might be cut short; this was refused, but he contrived to have this done at one of the cottages in the neighbourhood.

"He then made his way to Loughborough, where he wound himself into the good graces of the Primitive Methodists by representing himself to be a monk escaped from Mt. St. Bernard's, telling a pitiful tale of imprisonment and cruel treatment in that place. He repeated these proceedings at Leicester and at other places, everywhere obtaining money from his credulous sympathisers.

"Finally, he settled at Wednesbury, where he was heartily received by the Methodists. He addressed many meetings, and was always able to thrill his audiences with his blood-curdling accounts of monastic life.

"He, in the month of May, gave to the public his tissue of barefaced lies in the form of a pamphlet entitled "A Narrative of six years' Captivity and Suffering among the monks of St. Bernard, at Charnwood Forest, Leicestershire: By William J. Jefferys." In this work he declared that he was taken to the Abbey against his will, and while there was practically a prisoner. He had been twice bled, though there had not been, as far as he was aware, any need for such treatment; and his body on another occasion had been punctured with a sharp instrument; for six weeks he had been confined in a small room upon one meal of bread and water a day; and he had undergone numerous other heart-rending experiences. This catalogue of sufferings was concluded with the account of his wonderful escape.

"In a postscript he added: Land has been purchased in this town (Wednesbury) near to the Parish Church for the purpose of erecting a Roman Catholic Chapel thereupon. The timely exposure of the practical workings of Popery will, I trust, have its intended effect upon the inhabitants by showing them what the Popish system really is, that is to be introduced into this parish.

"In the meanwhile Jefferys' 'revelations' had had the effect of exciting the minds of the inhabitants in the neighbourhood of the Abbey against its monks, and the community were in fear of an attack being made upon their house.

"The guest-master was, through some providential circumstances, enabled to establish the identity of Jefferys with the man calling himself Francis Arkwright who had appeared at the Abbey some few months ago, and the friends of this man were invited to a strict investigation of the matter by bringing him to the monastery and there subjecting him to a calm and impartial examination. 'So just and reasonable a proposal could not be with honour or justice refused.'

"Accordingly on June 26th, 1849, the investigation took place at the Abbey under the presidency of Ambrose Lisle Phillipps, Esq., of Grace Dieu Manor.

"The following is an abstract of the investigation given by the two persons who arranged and printed Jefferys' pamphlet:—

"We, the undersigned, William S. Nayler, of Wednesbury, in the county of Stafford, and Thomas Ragg, of Birmingham, in the county of Warwick, do hereby testify and declare:

"That for the purpose of the said investigation, we, the undersigned, in company of the Rev. Mr. Cole, of Wednesbury, and a gentleman deputed to accompany the undersigned Thomas Ragg, of Birmingham Protestant Association, took William Thomas Jefferys over to Charnwood Forest on Tuesday, June 26th, 1849. That after he had vainly endeavoured to find the house where he said he had left his monk's habit and had obtained a change of clothes, we took him into the monastery where he was fully identified as one who had been entertained in the guest-rooms for a few days, in the month of January last, when he had written his name in the guest-book as Francis Augustus Arkwright. That, on being more closely questioned as to the statements contained in his narrative he showed his entire ignorance of everything beyond what he had previously learned in the guest-room. He did not know the monastic names of any of the brethren, he did not know what they ate or what they drank, nor where nor how they slept. On being asked to point out the room in which he had been placed in solitary confinement, he pointed out one whose door never had a lock upon it or any other outside fastening; and being asked to point out where he slept he wandered to and fro about the place without being able to find his way into the dormitory; and at length returned into the open square, where, after repeated appeals to confess his guilt before God, he tacitly acknowledged it by falling on his knees before the reverend superior, and bursted into tears.

"We, therefore, the undersigned, do hereby declare our deep and solemn conviction that the narrative of the said William Thomas Jefferys is a tissue of the grossest and most unwarrantable falsehoods; and having taken him safely to prison, to suffer such punishments due to his misdeeds, we feel it our bounden duty to publish this statement to the world as some little reparation for the injury we have been the innocent means of inflicting on the community of Mount St. Bernard. And we hereby, in conclusion, express our heart-felt thanks to the reverend abbot, the reverend prior, and all the fathers and brethren in the monastery for the surpassing kindness with which we were received, the readiness with which they lent us every aid during the painful investigation, and the genuine hospitality with which we were entertained after the investigation was over.

Signed,

W. S. Nayler,
Thomas Ragg."

Jefferys was sentenced at the Petty Sessions, held at Handsworth, the 30th of June, 1849, to be committed as a rogue and vagabond to Stafford Gaol for three months with hard labour."

*   *   *   *   *   *   *

Articles on "Wesleyan Methodism in Wednesbury," written by Mr. G. T. Lawley, and accompanied by a wealth of local illustrations, appeared in the "Methodist Recorder" of 25th April, 1901, and of 3rd April, 1902.

Nothing further on this subject which is new can be added to what is already contained in "Religious Wednesbury"; a volume in which will be found the records, so far as they have been preserved, of every church, chapel, and place of worship within the parish.

Photo by]   [DR. DINGLEY.

OLD HOUSES, LOWER HIGH STREET.

L.—COAL-MINING AND IRON-SMELTING.

Notwithstanding the many centuries of coal and iron mining in this parish, but little that is new upon the subject of the town's industries can be added since the publication of "Wednesbury Workshops."

Evidence exists of the South Staffordshire coal having been worked from the most remote times. One witness of this is the fact, as revealed by a scientific examination, that the 13th century church of Wednesbury was paved with "pockstone."

The early miners got the outcrop coal at the surface by means of open-works, or quarries; and even where they got the thick coal by means of underground pits, they drew out only the lump coal, considering the small coal of no value, and using it merely for the miner to stand upon in order to reach up to the thick coal over his head.

Now wherever the virgin mine has been disturbed in this coalfield there has always existed a remarkable tendency of the shattered coal to set up spontaneous combustion—hence "Wednesbury Wildfire," and subterranean fires throughout the Black Country generally.

On the other side of Dudley the local name of "shattery" has been given to the calcined material, where the ruins of the thick coal workings have burnt away in vast areas. The strata over the burnt-out coal are found calcined into a kind of intensely hard porcelain; to sink through this "upper crust" is a most difficult task, and proposed new shafts have had to be abandoned for this reason; or sometimes the sinkers find the strata running as loose as quicksand. In no case is the shattery found more than a few yards thick; but such a huge mass of coal had been burned away that the overlaying strata have slowly subsided some 15ft. or 20ft., causing it to be very loose and shattered—in fact, "shattery." But in those places where the heat, having been more intense, the strata, including the ironstone, have been run together in huge lumps, is found the "pockstone" previously alluded to —which is really calcined shattery.

Underneath the whole of the shattery and pockstones is found the ash of the thick coal, some 3ft. to 4ft. thick, resting on the ironstone measures below, except in a few cases where the bottom seam of the coal was left; and this seam has been worked later. Over the solid coal, naturally no shattery is ever to be found.

Writing of the year 1619, Dud Dudley describes the streams of hot water then issuing from "soughs and adits, as hot as the bath at Bathe." Speaking of the slack, or little-esteemed small coal, the same writer says:—
"'He that liveth longest, let him fetch fire the further.' Next, these colliers must cast these coles and sleck or drosse out of their wayes, which sulphurious small cole and crouded moyst slack heat naturally, and kindle in the middle of these great heaps; often fals the cole-works on fire, and flaming out of the pits and continue burning like Ætna in Cicily or Hecla in the Indies."

While the most famous coal seam in the kingdom crops out and terminates at Wednesbury, the town of Dudley stands in the centre of that famous 10-yard coal, though in the middle of the town there is no coal, as the underlying limestone measures come to the surface, so that all round Dudley the coal crops out and is then lost. These out-crops have been worked for years by just removing the soil and a few yards of superincumbent earth, the coal is laid bare, and the whole of it worked away. As a rule, the coal is not so hard as that of the deeper coal got in pits.

The crude map of the Dudley district given by Dud Dudley in his "Mettallum Martis" shows the locations in which were the fountains of hot water to which he alludes; and it is there the largest areas of shattery are now found.

On the far side of Dudley, towards Himley, are some hundreds of acres in which the coal has been burnt out, and the surface is now found under cultivation. On this near side of Dudley there is a large area of shattery at Moxley, where the old place-name "Fiery Holes" is a significant one.

By the close of the Tudor period (1600) the timber in and around Wednesbury had all been cut down for the purpose of smelting the ironstone, with which the parish abounded. There remained as remnants of Wednesbury's ancient woodlands only the two small areas of Old Park and Friar Park.

It then became necessary to carry the ore further afield to such places as still possessed growing timber in sufficient quantities to yield a cheap fuel. For as yet, and, indeed, for a century afterwards, all iron-smelting was accomplished with the aid of charcoal; the use of a blast furnace which could successfully burn mineral coal had not come within the range of practicability.

Another desideratum was water power capable of turning the machinery. From Wednesbury quantities of iron ore were conveyed to Perry Barr and to Aston, carried in panniers on the backs of long trains of pack-horses, because these places further down the Tame could offer greater facilities in the way of both wood fuel and water power.

To the modern conception of "power," as supplied by steam engines, it would seem hardly creditable that so insignificant a stream as the Hockley Brook, or even the Tame at Perry Barr and Aston, could supply power adequate for the machinery of an ironworks. But those were the days of small things, and so far as iron-making was concerned of very primitive mechanical contrivances.

Nowhere in the vicinity could be found a really rapid stream that—
                    "rushes down,
"Turns the great wheels of the mills,
"Lifts the hammers of the forge"—
such as Longfellow has described.

There were forges on mere brooks at Sheep-wash Lane (West Bromwich), Friar Park (Bescot), Golds Hill (where the Bagnalls succeeded Mr. Aston), at Bustleholme Rod Mill, and West Bromwich Forge, near Sandwell.

Aston furnaces were the property of the litigious Jennings family, who also held considerable mining properties in Wednesbury. John Jennens, " proprietor of Wednesbury Hall," who died in 1653, bequeathed Aston furnaces, with forges, watercourses, " a hundred loades of charcoale, and thirty tunes of roughe pigge-iron," in addition to lands situate in " Wedgeburge" and other contiguous parishes in the county of Stafford.

Hutton, in his " History of Birmingham," erroneously states that Wednesbury iron had been smelted at Aston for centuries, and adduces as evidence the existence at the latter place of an enormous mountain of cinder. This is utter nonsense; the cinder mound is merely a covering of iron-slag and cinder which has been tipped on to a big sand hill there.

It was not till " about 1745 that the iron-masters of Staffordshire began to reap the benefit of Dud Dudley's enterprise; and by a series of renewed experiments, in which Abraham Darby, of Colebrookedale, and John Wilkinson, of Bradley, took a distinguished part, the object upon which so much inventive thought had been expended was at length attained, and the smelting of iron with coal became an accomplished fact."

John Wilkinson was " a native of Cumberland, the son of an ironworker in humble circumstances, who in his twenty-eighth year came on a pilgrimage to Staffordshire in quest of fortune. He traversed the whole distance on foot and, being penniless, he had, moreover, to beg his way from place to place. Hungry and footsore, he tells us, he reached Wolverhampton, but failing to obtain work there, he went on to Bilston, where Mr. Hoo, of Bradley Mines, had compassion on the young adventurer, and took him into his service. Ten years of hard and faithful work raised the servant into a master, and in 1766 he commenced the erection of Bradley Furnace, the first blast furnace in the neighbourhood." After repeated experiments and many re-constructions of the furnace he was able to inform his friend Matthew Boulton in 1772 that he could produce twenty tons weekly of coal-smelted iron. By 1788 charcoal for smelting purposes began to be discarded in South Staffordshire. With the aid of James Watt he next succeeded in making and applying a blast engine. In 1784 Wilkinson put down the first steam forge in this district. The other industrial triumphs connected with the name of John Wilkinson are:—(1) The erection, under the auspices of James Watt, of the first steam engine on French soil; (2) the construction of the first iron canal boat: (3) the invention of a method of smooth-boring cylinders and cannon: (4) supplying Paris with iron water-pipes; and (5) superseding the antiquated tuyers used in blast furnaces by a superior kind of his own invention.

LI.—INDUSTRIAL SMALL WARES AND ART WORK.

Wednesbury undoubtedly owes its industrial development to the prolific mines of coal, iron, and limestone which were once found within its borders. But although the town's productions now mainly consist of heavy iron goods, this was not always the case.

Perhaps the first time Wednesbury appears in a local history is in Dr. Plot's " Natural History of Staffordshire," published in 1686. The worthy chronicler writes of " divers things remarkable in this Place (Wednesbury)."

" A very distinct Eccho, when the Windmill Windows stand open towards the Church, otherwise there is none at all."

" There was seen," says the garrulous Doctor, " on November 22nd, 1672—a very dark night—a wonderful meteor which continued for about one-eighth of an hour's space to give light, in Wednesbury, at half a mile distance; whereupon there immediately followed after a great storm of hail." In another case he opines that of all the accidents that can befall the trunks of trees, there is none more unaccountable than their being " found buried underground, as they are found in Rotten Meadow, under Wednesbury Hall."

But coming to the subject of the place's natural resources, and its industries at that date, Dr. Plot places on record some interesting information respecting Wednesbury, writing of " an excellent Sort of Pit-coal, which some prefer before Cannel itself; being a fat shining Coal, which burns away with a sweet bright Flame, into white Ashes, leaving no such Cinders as that from Newcastle upon Tine. Of this Coal there is so great Plenty in this County, that there are for the most part 12 or 14 Collieries at work, some of which afford from 2,000 to 5,000 Tons yearly; so that an Acre of Ground has been sold for £100.

" That the Coal-pits here do sometimes take Fire of themselves; there is so much Sulphur, which sublimes by the Heat of the Fire from the Pyrites in the Coal, insomuch that there lies great quantities of it upon the burnt Surface of the Earth, in its true Colour. When there is a due Proportion of Nitre mixed with it, a natural Gunpowder is made, which being pent up in the earth, puts it into these Convulsions we call Earthquakes.

" That that Sort of Iron Ore which in this County is call'd Blond-metal, is found here. This Sort of Iron is used to make Nails, from three Shillings to ten Shillings per Thousand, and all Sorts of Heavy Wares, as Hammers, Axes, &c., all in some Countries Horse-shoes."

A century later "England Illustrated," two handsome volumes published in 1764, says—

"Besides plenty of turf and peat for firing, this county (Staffordshire) yields three sorts of coal, which are termed pit-coal, peacock coal, and cannel-coal. The pit-coal is dug chiefly in the south part of the county at Wednesbury, Dudly, and Sedgley, not far from Wolverhampton. The peacock coal, so called from its reflecting various colours, like those of a peacock's tail, is found at Henley Green near Newcastle-under-Lyne, and is better for the forge than for the kitchen. The Cannel-coal which gives a very bright and clear flame derives its name from Canwil, an ancient British word for candle. It is so hard as to bear polishing, and is used in this county for paving churches and other public buildings. It is also manufactured into snuff boxes and other toys."

Then there was a trade in leather. In Albrighton Parish Register is the following entry of a Burial :—

"1619. July 9. John Stokes of Wedgburye, brydle-maker, being in some quarrelling manner killed."

This may be accepted as evidence of the location of the saddlery trade in Wednesbury at that time. It is well known that buckle and chape making was located at Wednesbury nearly two centuries later.

Tanning was one of the trades practised in olden Wednesbury. The names of several tanners of the centuries gone by are on record. The Baptist Chapel, Holyhead Road, was erected on the site known as the Tan-house Close, or Tanhouse Engine Piece in 1761. In 1715 John Addenbrooke was a tanner of some position in the town.

The leather trades of the adjoining market towns of Walsall and Birmingham have continued to the present day, represented chiefly in their modern saddlery trade. The Birmingham Toll-booth was known as the Leather Hall; an official appointed under an Act of 1563 was known as the Leather Sealer.

Allusion is made in Wednesbury Registers to tow-dressers, weavers, besom makers, dyers, and frequently to potters. Till recent times there were a number of malt-houses in the town: Dr. Plot in 1686 speaks of local malting being accomplished by cokes, otherwise the raw or unprepared coal would "give the malt an ill odour" from its "noxious gases."

It is unquestionable that ornamental goods as well as various small wares were produced throughout the Black Country before the era of the steam-engine. Here is a list kindly supplied by the Birmingham Assay Master of gold and silver goods marked for local manufacturers at the Assay Office :—

1773.—Dewson, Benjamin, and William Taylor, Wolverhampton.

Wares entered—Spectacle frames.

1775.—Bissell, Isaac, Gunsmith, Cradley.

Wares entered—Pistol furniture.

1775.—Jesson, John, Silversmith, Wolverhampton.

Wares entered—Buckles, Sugar-tongs.

1776.—Whitehouse, John, Silversmith, Wednesbury.

Wares entered—Buckles, Seals, Tea-tongs.

1783.—Stringer, William, Gunsmith, West Bromwich.

Wares entered—Gun and Pistol furniture.

1802.—Beardsmore, Benjamin, Kettinsall near Bilston.

Wednesbury's art industry in enamels has been treated very fully in "Wednesbury Workshops." The chief seat of the enamel trade in this locality was at Bilston, from whence Wednesbury manufacturers obtained their hinges, rims, and other fittings. The same peculiarities characterise both Bilston and Wednesbury enamels, so that it is almost impossible to distinguish one class from the other; the close proximity of the two towns made it one industrial area.

Some doubt has been thrown on the correctness of the labels attached to some specimens in Wednesbury Art Gallery. Some small oval boxes, with mirrors inserted in the inside of the lid, are labelled "Ladies' snuff-boxes"; it is claimed that they should be called "patch boxes." But this contention is wrong. The fashion of wearing patches began at the commencement of the eighteenth century (1711), and the belles are rallied on it in No. 344 of the "Spectator"; but the custom had long died out at the period when these boxes were known to have been made in Wednesbury—one of those exhibited bears evidence of having been made in, or about, 1797. So that these particular boxes could not have been patch-boxes, although similar ones may have been used as such. The 8th number of "Gray's Inn Journal" (1752) contained an advertisement of the sale by auction of "the whole stock of a coquette leaving off trade, consisting of several valuable curiosities," etc., amongst which are mentioned "an elegant snuff-box with a looking glass within it, being a very good pocket companion for a beauty," etc.

The "snuff-boxes and other toys," said to have been made of cannel-coal, may possibly have been Wednesbury enamel, done in black.

Clever artists were employed to decorate enamels at Wednesbury as they were to ornament Japan-ware at Bilston. John Harper was a celebrated Wednesbury painter, whose pictures are in great esteem among local collectors, especially his dead game pieces, which are spiritedly drawn and beautifully elaborated, and realise from ten to fifty guineas each.

Among the local tea-tray painters, who rose to be artists of repute, was Moses Haughton, examples of whose works may be seen in Wednesbury Art Gallery. Moses Haughton is usually claimed as a Warwickshire worthy, and his monument is in St. Philip's Church, Birmingham. It is stated in Timmins' "Warwickshire" (p. 143), that he also engraved illustrations for a Bible, published in Birmingham. He was born in 1734, and died in 1804; and, not-withstanding that most of his working life belongs to Birmingham, it is not improbable that he was a native of Wednesbury. In "The Genealogist," Vol. II., N.S., p 215, is found the following Worcester Marriage Licence—"1725. April 8. Moses Horton, of Wednesbury, Co. Stafford, about 21, bachelor, and Mary Tibbotts, of Cradley, of about 21, maiden: allegation by him and Thomas Negus, of Wednesbury." Were these the parents of the artist, and his brother Matthew Haughton, an equally clever painter and engraver?

Wednesbury was celebrated both

"In arms, in arts."

It had a great trade in gun - locks and in gun-barrels, from which latter the tube trade had its origin. In "Pearce's History of Walsall" (1813), p. 143, we read:—

"Some of these, the gun and bayonet (manufactured at Wednesbury, about three miles from Walsall) in the hands of brave British soldiers have conquered the 'invincible' legions of Bonaparte; and the cannon and balls made at Bradley Ironworks (the works of the famous iron-master, the late John Wilkinson, Esq., are situate at Bradley, about three miles from Walsall), and directed by a Nelson, have hurled their thunder upon the heads of our inveterate enemies, and contributed to the maintenance of our British Empire upon the main."

Coming to Wednesbury's small wares, at the latest period of their existence, "Lewis' Topographical Dictionary" of 1831 thus speaks of the town's industries at that time.

"The trade consists of the manufacture of articles of iron; screws, nails, hinges, gunlocks, coach-ironmongery, apparatus for gaslight, etc., etc. A species of iron called Blondi is made here which is well suited for the preparation of axes and other sharp instruments: on the rivulet is an extensive manufactory of edge-tools; also corn-mills."

"White's Directory" for 1855 makes us aware that several industries existed half-a-century ago which have since died out. There were six Straw Bonnet Makers in the town. This female industry is now centralised at places like Luton and Dunstable; but no doubt quick changes of fashion prevented its flourishing in this and other scattered places of production. There were four Tallow-chandleries, from which the town and the collieries were supplied with candles before gas had been laid on. There were still twenty Screw and Bolt manufactories, and as many Coach-iron Factories. The last firm of any magnitude in the screw trade were members of the well-known Danks family. The Coach-iron trade, which produces the heavier goods, is the only one which continues to flourish, for it would almost seem that the manufacture of small, light, ornamental, or artistic articles in Wednesbury must always succumb.

LII.—INVENTORS AND PATENTEES.

As a valuable contribution to this work Mr. Richard B. Prosser, sometime Superintendent of Examiners at the Patent Office, has been good enough to supply the following List of Patents granted under the old law, 1617 to 1852, to persons resident in Wednesbury, compiled from official sources:—

LIST OF PATENTS granted to persons residing in WEDNESBURY from the earliest period down to the passing of the Patent Law Amendment Act, October, 1852.

No. 759, 25 Feb., 1761.

John Wood, Wednesbury, Ironmaster.

"Making malleable iron from pig, or sow metal."

[In Dr. Percy's standard work "Iron and Steel" this invention is alluded to as having "an interesting specification" in which "lime, kelp, and 'soaper's waste' are claimed as fluxes for effecting the conversion of granulated pig-iron into malleable Iron."]

No. 794, 29 July, 1763.

John Wood, Wednesbury, Ironmaster, and Charles Wood, of Low Mill, near Whitehaven, Ironmaster.

"Making all kind of fused or cast iron, as also scull or cinder iron malleable with raw or pit coal."

[For this family of Wood see "Olden Wednesbury," pp. 1, 2, and 56: also "Wednesbury Workshops," p. 116.]

No. 4,263, 14th March, 1818.

John Read, of Tipton, gentleman, and William Howell, of Wednesbury, ground bailiff.

"Working or getting the main or thick mine of coals."

[This is explained in "Olden Wednesbury," p. 28.]

No. 4,504, 23rd October, 1820.

William Taylor, late of Gospel Oak, in the parish of Sedgley, but now of Wednesbury.

"Furnace for smelting iron and other ore."

No. 4,836, 20th Aug., 1823.

Edward Elwell, of Wednesbury Forge, spade and edge tool maker.

"Manufacture of spades and shovels."

[The Elwells are an old Staffordshire family.]

No. 4,892, 19 Jany., 1824.

James Russell, of Wednesbury, gas-tube manufacturer.

"Gas and other tubes."

No. 5,109, 26th Feby., 1825.

Cornelius Whitehouse, of Wednesbury, whitesmith.

"Manufacture of gas tubes."

[See "Birmingham Inventors," pp. 99-100. The extension is No. 7,982, but it does not come into this list as the parties were not then resident in Wednesbury. Cornelius Whitehouse died August 7, 1883. See "Engineer," 24 Aug., 1883. A biography of Cornelius Whitehouse, with portrait, appeared in "Ryder's Annual, 1898." A Cornelius Whitehouse appears in the "Birmingham Directory" for 1770.]

No. 5,958, 19 July, 1830.
    William Taylor, of Wednesbury, engineer.
    "Improvements in steam boilers."

No. 6,637, 18 July, 1834.
    James Hardy, of Wednesbury, Gentleman.
    "Iron axles."

No. 6,807, 4th April, 1835.
    James Hardy, of Wednesbury, gentleman.
    "Iron axles and shafts."
    (Extended for four years, see No. 12,535.)

No. 7,666, 2 June, 1838.
    James Hardy, of Wednesbury, Ironmaster.
    "Rolling shafts, rails, tyre-iron etc."

No. 7,688, 14 June, 1838.
    Henry Davies, of Wednesbury, Engineer.
    [This was a rotatory steam engine. Probably identical with the Henry Davies who took out the following patents:—
No. 7,072.—H. D., of Stoke Priors.
  „   7,325.—   „   „
  „   9,124.—   „   Birmingham.
  „   9,143.—   „   „
  „ 10,024.—   „   Norbury, Staffs.
  „ 10,261.—   „   „   „   ]

No. 9,287, 7 March, 1842.
    Henry Russell, of Wednesbury, iron tube maker, and Cornelius Whitehouse, of Wednesbury.
    "Welded iron tubes."

No. 9,723, 9th May, 1843.
    James Roose, of Wednesbury.
    "Welded iron tubes."

No. 10,272, 24 July, 1844.
    John James Russell and Thomas Henry Russell, both of Wednesbury, tube manufacturers.
    "Welded iron tubes."

No. 10,621, 17 April, 1845.
    George Royle, of Church Hill, Wednesbury, whitesmith.
    "Welded iron tubes."

No. 10,816, 14th August, 1845.
    Thomas Henry Russell, of Wednesbury, tube manufacturer.
    "Welded iron tubes."

No. 11,621, 15 March, 1847.
    Sampson Lloyd, of Old Park Iron Works, Wednesbury, engineer.
    "Wheel tyres."

No. 12,526, 19 March, 1849.
    Thomas Henry Russell, of Wednesbury, tube manufacturer, and John Stephen Woolrych, of Birmingham, chemist.
    "Electro-deposition of certain metals."

No. 12,534, 26th March, 1849.
    Alexander Parkes, of Harborne, chemist.
    "Improvements in the deposition and manufacture of certain metals and alloys of metals, and in the application of the same to various useful purposes."
    [There is a notice by R. B. P. of this man in the "Dictionary of National Biography," from which it appears he was a prolific inventor who has been referred to as "the Nestor of Electro Metallurgy." Alexander Parkes was the inventor of Xylonite. He was long with Elkington and Mason, and his business with Wednesbury was about 1858, when he was giving his attention to the manufacture of seamless metal tubes.]

No. 12,555, 2 April, 1849.
    Extension for four years to Charles Geach and Thomas Walker of James Hardy's patent, No. 6,807.
    [See "Wednesbury Workhshops" pp. 58-68. Geach was M.P. for Coventry from 1851 to death on 1 Nov., 1854. He was a Cornishman, having been born at St. Austell in 1808. He was a clerk in the Birmingham Branch of the Bank of England from 1826-1836. Connected with Park Gate Ironworks and Patent Shaft and Axle Co. Mayor of Birmingham, 1847.]

No. 12,970, 21 Feb., 1850.
    John Stephen Woolrich of Wednesbury, chemist, John James Russell, of Handsworth, tube manufacturer, and Thomas Henry Russell, of Wednesbury, tube manufacturer.
    "Separating cadmium from its ores."
    [Woolrich did good work in the introduction of electro-plating. See Shaw's "Electro Metallurgy" and my book. I think he once kept a chemist's shop in New Street, Birmingham. A John Woolrich was Professor of Chemistry at Queen's College in 1836-8.]

No. 13,028, 26 March, 1850.
    Thomas Walker, of Wednesbury, ironmaster.
    "Manufacture of sheet iron."

No. 13,606, 26 April, 1851.
    Jonathan Ragg, of Wednesbury, coach and axle-tree smith.
    "Railway and other carriages."

No. 14,095, 29th April, 1852.
    John Lintorn Arabin Simmons, of 67, Oxford Terrace, Hyde Park, London, captain in the Royal Engineers, and Thomas Walker, of the Brunswick Iron Works, Wednesbury, Esquire.
    "Ordnance and carriages for the same.

No. 14,133, 22 May, 1852.
    James Russell, of Wednesbury, tube manufacturer.
    "Coating metal tubes."

*   *   *   *   *

As Mr. Prosser rightly says, the number of patents applied for in any particular town may be taken as a fair indication of the industrial activity of the place. It also reflects in the subject-matter of the patents the nature of the local industries. Viewed in these two aspects the official lists of old patents must contain a mass of raw material which has hitherto been much neglected by county historians and topographical writers, but which might be made to afford much interesting matter for the tracing of the industrial development of any given locality.

Mr. R. B. Prosser is the author of a work entitled "Birmingham Inventors," in chapters xvii.-xx. of which he gives a succinct account of the Manufacture of Metal Tubes. The technicalities of tube-making, including the processes of wrought-iron tube making as invented and practised in Wednesbury, are fully described and comparatively treated.

For the benefit of Wednesbury engineering students it may further be mentioned that the standard work on "Turning and Mechanical Manipulations" by Holtzapfell, has a section contributed on the Manufacture of Iron Tubes by Richard Prosser, C.E., of Birmingham, the father of the previously mentioned author. Holtzapfell's exhaustive work was published in five volumes between 1852 and 1884. It is at p. 964 in Vol. II. that Wednesbury students will find this interesting contribution which gives particulars of the various patents granted between 1802 and 1842. The first four, 1808-1817, are the patents of Birmingham inventors and concern gun-barrel making. Following these may be found those relating to wrought iron tubes granted to James Russell, 1824; Cornelius Whitehouse, 1825; George Royle, 1831; Thomas Henry Russell, 1836; Richard Prosser, 1840; and to Thomas Henry Russell and Cornelius Whitehouse in 1842. These are accompanied by drawings, specifications, and full details.

A biographical note may be added on that ingenious inventor, Henry Davies. Henry Davies, the patentee of the Rotary Steam Engine, was the third of six sons, all engineers, of William Davies, of Wednesbury, an engineer, who was articled, when young, to the celebrated John Wilkinson, of Bradley Ironworks. The first Rotary Engine Henry Davies made at Wednesbury; and he being sent to Stoke Prior saltworks on business (when a young man), and Mr. Gossage keeping him there some time, accounts for him being described as of that place, in the patent lists. While there, observing the distinctive action of salt on the leather in the pumps used in pumping the brine from the rocks, necessitating constant renewal, he invented the metallic pump for Mr. Gossage. Then he and others formed a company, and manufactured the rotary engines at Birmingham for some time, which were sent to various parts of England; several went to Manchester. There were two at work in the neighbourhood of Dudley some thirty years ago; the Company also made one of the first three locomotives that ran for trial on the Midland line from Camp Hill to Worcester. The Rotary made its journey in much less time than the others, but was not so well calculated for the trial weights as that of Boulton and Watt, which seems to have been chosen, although the railway company bought the rotary also. Henry Davies next commenced to manufacture steam thrashing engines in Staffordshire, where he resided till about 1849. Having relations in the iron trade in Ohio, he turned his attention to America, and leaving good prospects here, he took his wife, seven sons, and a daughter. He said he did not expect to do better himself, but thought he could buy land, which would be better for his children's prospects. While in Birmingham he made a steam horse to run on the canal towpath; it had legs like that of a horse, to tow boats, but it raised so much opposition amongst the boatmen he abandoned it. Isaiah Davies, another inventor, was not related. Possibly when Henry Davies' machinery was sold he bought some of it: he seems to have tried its capabilities at the Lionel Street Foundry in Birmingham. Henry Davies was an improver rather than the actual inventor of the "disc engine.'

THE END.

AN INDEX.

RYDER & SON
PRINTERS & PUBLISHERS

"HERALD" OFFICE
WEDNESBURY

LaVergne, TN USA
24 September 2010
198192LV00005B/97/P